DATE			

The Second Generation

THE SECOND GENERATION

ESTHER McCOY

Introduction by

Cesar Pelli

Gibbs M. Smith, Inc.

Peregrine Smith Books

Salt Lake City

1984

Library of Congress Cataloging in Publication Data

McCoy, Esther.
    The second generation.

    Includes index.
    1. Architects—California—Biography.
2. Architecture, Modern—20th century—California.
I. Title.
NA730.C2M33 1983   720′.92′2 [B]   83-14898
ISBN 0-87905-119-1

Acknowledgements

I am grateful to the Guggenheim Foundation which made the research and writing on this book possible.

I am indebted especially to the four architects who patiently talked to me about their work, submitted to endless questions, and loaned me prints by missing photographers to fill in the visual story.

I thank the many relatives, colleagues, friends, and clients of the four who shared their memories with me. Among them are Greta Davidson, Tom, Barnaby, Carlos, and Erica Davidson; Ruth (Ain) French, Emily Ain, and Augusta Ain Ford; Josef van der Kar, Joseph Johnson, Alfred Day, James Garrott, Ena Dubnoff; Maynard Lyndon, Robert Boyle, Albert Nogasaki, Bernard Judge, and Emiel Beksky; Mr. and Mrs. Joseph Kingsley, Richard Hoffman, David Rabinowitz, Julius Shulman, and Dr. Theodore Lindauer, Marjorie Eaton, Mrs. Magda Jokl, Mrs. Fred Feldman, Saul Bass, John Blanton, and Richard Tufeld.

I also thank David Gebhard, Alson Clark, John Caldwell, Evelyn Hitchcock, Elaine Jones, Kathryn Metz, Allan Temko, Marvin Rand, David Travers, and Robert Winter. Margaret Conrad and Katherine Fetherston gave editorial assistance.

A part of the Ain section was published in Arts & Architecture (Winter 1981), which in its reincarnation is edited by Barbara Goldstein.

Table of Contents

Foreword

"History moves; the still waters are made swift,"
Jose Orgeta y Gasset wrote in the thirties of the
new art. Now late in the century as architecture
moves from the abstract to a narrative style, the
waters are again made swift. As the old style
recedes it is time to reexamine more of the work
of the second quarter of the century in Southern
California.

It has been a privilege to live through two
periods of change. In retrospect, the similarities are
greater among my four subjects than was apparent
thirty years ago. Their designs are based on the
module (from the Japanese), which gives them
unity and also controlled costs. But the economies
never detracted from the architecture. The four
guarded their talents through the period before
modern design was acceptable, and in their small
offices lavished time on their modest number of
clients. All four lived through the Depression and
the Second World War, which instilled the convic-
tion that architecture is a social art.

California has been diligent in reclaiming its
architectural past but there is much left to document, from Thornton Abell to John Lautner, from
Clark and Frey to Quincy Jones, from Maynard
Lyndon to Carl Maston. Before the passion of this
age for research abates I hope all the bodies will
be found while they are warm.

J.R. Davidson does not really belong with the
second generation as he was older than Schindler
and arrived in Los Angeles before Richard Neutra;
he is here because there is no other convenient
place for him. I have put him first because he is

the oldest of the four, the others following according to age. Ain was the first to be written about
and as that section has more digressions into
California lore it may well belong first.

Esther McCoy

Los Angeles Architects

The Images

Most of the architects who left a mark in Southern California went there from somewhere else. We all went there, attracted by opportunity and some images. The images included some physical qualities such as the sky, the light, and the landscape of Southern California, but most of all we were attracted by the great promise to make a new city. All these combined images are important and have had an effect on the architecture of Southern California.

The Sky. The sky is always blue. The endless days of hazy, dirty yellow are readily forgotten. We are painfully aware of the smog, but we always discount it. It is not natural; it is only an aberrant, temporary condition. Any moment now something will be invented that will eliminate the smog somehow and then the skies will be back to their pristine blue condition.

When we design in Southern California, we design for the normal, we may say eternal, condition of clear blue skies. That is how we imagine, see, and photograph our buildings: sharp and clear against a deep blue sky.

The Light. The light, like the skies, is remembered as always bright, casting sharp, deep shadows. In that light, sometimes described as mediterranean, the building detaches itself from the sky. Architecture is always a sharply delineated object and the colors are brighter than we hoped for. White is a positive and strong color against the blue.

The Landscape. There are always hills in Southern California and some of its most famous buildings were built on them, but the dominant image is that of a flat surface, punctuated by palm trees and criss-crossed by freeways with the hills in the background, detached from the immediate reality. The flat surface is a tabula rasa where anything can happen, perhaps a new architecture.

The Great Promise. The promise of Los Angeles is that it is a city in the process of being made. Outsiders have called it The City of Tomorrow, meaning that Los Angeles is today what the other cities will be like in the future. For an Angeleno, it is also The City of Tomorrow but the meaning is that Los Angeles has not yet become itself. What is there now is somehow temporary and replaceable. The real Los Angeles exists only in the future. In the present, it is a huge and loose experiment being built all the time where there is still ample room for new and better ideas to be tried. This image has an almost irresistable attraction for a young architect, one that leads to some successes and many disappointments.

This quality is now disappearing. Los Angeles is becoming solid like other cities. There is still much that will and should be replaced, but the structures that are built to stay are more and more numerous. I believe it has collectively decided now *to be* and to stop becoming.

Those images and the realities behind them were what made Los Angeles such a great place to experiment if one had the commissions. The lack of commissions has always been the bane of all creative architects there. The city has never appreciated and supported what it so obviously needed. It was always growing, and it could have fully used all its good architects, but it repeatedly favored the mediocre. A significant part of the architectural history of the region is the history of good architects demoralized by the disinterest of their nonclients.

The Region

The terms Los Angeles and Southern California tend to be interchangeable. Often when we say Los Angeles we mean Southern California, a distinct geographical and cultural region: a desert with man-made oases. Thanks to the Owens Valley (and other sources of water), the oases appear to extend forever. It is an area of continued and fast growth with advanced and glamorous industries. It is an economic entity. In the background are the Spanish Franciscan Missions. They are the historical, architectural, and cultural background, never in the forefront but always present. They are the roots.

This vision of Los Angeles always includes Santa Barbara, Palm Springs, Newport Beach, and Orange County; all urbanized Southern California. It used to include San Diego. Today it is not always so. San Diego is starting to emancipate itself so it is seen as part of Los Angeles only within certain contexts. For architects the definition is simple: Los Angeles extends as far as the local commissions and clients do.

Sometimes we say Southern California when we mean Los Angeles. This tends to happen when we speak of the cultural and intellectual life of the region. The museums, the concert halls, the publishers, the major universities, and the architects are in Los Angeles, but their influence extends to all of Southern California.

I shall use the term interchangeably, as an Angeleno, would to refer to the perceived area of work of an architect in Los Angeles or Southern California.

Los Angeles-Southern California was the first of the Sun Belt regions to prosper and to challenge the dominance and achievements of the Northeast and Midwest, the cradle and heartland of America. Unlike San Francisco, which was always seen as a gentler and prettier version of the older America, Southern California is very different: there are no winters and no forest. It is a desert with palm trees. It was first settled not by pilgrims or pioneers but by Franciscan monks and their mark is clearly visible. As seen from the East, it was exotic and there is still some of the exotic left in its image and in its self-image.

The climate was always seen as benign and health-giving. I do not know what the actuarial tables indicate but it is an important factor in the perception of Los Angeles and in motivating other Americans to move there to live. It is also an important factor in Los Angeles's self-perception. Health as a goal, or concern, appears often in the history of commissions of architects in Southern California. There the pursuit of health often acquired theistic and religious overtones.

The Architectural Culture

When moving into Southern California as an architect, one had the belief that the architectural ideology had to be brought in one's baggage because Los Angeles would not provide it. There is some truth to this, and Southern California has served as testing ground for many architectural currents that originated in other places, other countries. However, there are ideological currents in Los Angeles that have affected most of the architects working there. Beyond the expected effect of light, climate, and geography is the pervasive Spanish Colonial vernacular tradition of plan types, building forms, garden design, and a well defined palette of colors, plants, and materials well adapted to the region and quite different from the Anglo Saxon vernacular. Simple massing and large, undecorated expanses of white walls predate by many years the arrival of the International style and prefigure it in some cases like in the architecture of Irving Gill.

Even more pervasive because less obvious is a predilection for something that I call creative pragmatism. This is an important component of the architecture of Los Angeles from Gill through the Case Study Houses program to Frank Gehry.

This creative pragmatism requires optimism, a relaxed understanding of technology, and a readiness to use it in inventive ways for artistic purposes. Southern California is the home of some of the most advanced technological industries in the world and the knowledge and appreciation of this technology repeatedly creeps up in the work of its architects, but it has never produced a high-tech architectural tradition. Technology has been seen not as an end in itself but as a means to artistic, social, or ideological ends. If there was a bias, it was for available, simple, economical technology. The challenge was to make something wonderful, something new with these simple means. One only needs to compare the relaxed and slender steel structures of the Case Study houses, with the contemporaneous architecture of Mies van der Rohe and his followers where the steel is heavy and detailed like a watch. In the Case Study Houses, steel was used because it was available, economical, and allowed an open, informal, lightweight architecture. In the work of Mies, steel was the architecture. Similar cases can be made for the tilt-up walls of Gill, the precast panels of Schindler, my own ceramic glass, and the two by fours and chain link fences of Gehry. This attitude also permeates the work of Harris, Davidson, Ain, and Soriano—also the work of the best Spanish Revival architects.

The intention is creative innovation through good understanding of the process of building. It requires knowing where the process can be stretched and where it should be left alone. The guidelines are logic and cost. Making apparent the logic of the process and the economy of the means is a reoccurring architectural goal in Southern California. This purpose is lacking in the work of Frank Lloyd Wright in Los Angeles and perhaps because of this, it has always appeared foreign to me. In his case, and in Los Angeles, it was art at all costs.

If Los Angeles had been more supportive of the experiments of its architects, they could have coalesced into a distinctive architecture with its own ideological structure. This did not happen, but they still managed to produce some great buildings and many fine ones. Through this work they have influenced the development of architecture in this country.

The Historical Period

I write as a fellow Los Angeles architect, but it will be useful to clarify my point of view and some critical differences. I spent twelve years in Los Angeles and they were critical years in my career. After working for Eero Saarinen I started designing on my own in Los Angeles. It was a good place to start. For me it was the best place. Los Angeles (and the firms I was associated with, DMJM and Gruen Associates) gave me the opportunities and provided the right environment. This, for me, best environment was that of the large professional firms in Los Angeles. Schedules, budgets, and programs were severe and unyielding and forced on me a rigorous discipline, but the aesthetical demands were minimal. If I could design a building in the short time allocated that could be built within the tight stipulated budget and that satisfied all of our client's requirements, I was given considerable latitude on the matter of the building's image and plan type. I was left alone to wrestle with issues of architectural ideology and to find my way towards a coherent, aesthetical system.

The architectural culture of Los Angeles was also quite undemanding. I could dedicate all my energies to try to answer to my satisfaction the most basic questions of architecture which are also the most difficult. In practice, it meant that I was free to design and experiment without much worrying about possible adverse criticism. Of course, I wanted my buildings to be liked by my clients, admired by my peers, and noted in the East Coast and perhaps even in Europe and Japan. The incentive to do well was very strong, but the concern with doing poorly was minimal. I felt it was an ideal environment in which to start my career.

My experience in some critical aspects was quite different from that of the architects that Esther McCoy has written about in this book and in previous ones: I was working within the context of large architectural offices where there was a reasonable assurance of continued commissions and where the work was produced by integrated teams of specialists. All of Esther McCoy's architects had small individual practices, sometimes quite precarious, where their decisions were not challenged. But the cultural environment was similar and I can see that they enjoyed similar freedoms as I did. They also missed a more demanding exchange of ideas and more discriminating clients, the lack of which I started feeling in my later years there.

A more important difference to note is that perhaps Esther McCoy's architects practiced in a different Los Angeles than I did.

The city went through a rapid and perceptible change during my twelve years there and the process seems to have accelerated since then. Los Angeles has been always changing, of course. It is one of its characteristics. But the change I am referring to now is change towards a condition like that of the older eastern cities. In architecture at least, Los Angeles is joining and becoming part of the mainstream. It is fast developing a cultural establishment based on large and new schools of architecture and the exchange of people and ideas with other architectural centers is now commonplace. As it becomes more noticeable, it grows less distinct.

I can perceive now a coherent period of Los Angeles architecture that very roughly starts with the railroads and ends with the jet plane. This is the period we all have in mind when we think of the architecture of Los Angeles. That was the period when the city was young and exotic; a special place far away where wonderful things were possible. The railroad made Los Angeles part of America, but left it distant and distinct. The jet plane made it one with America, near and alike.

This Los Angeles that I did not know firsthand is the place that Esther McCoy has written about. She has rescued that world from incipient oblivion and made its contributions known to us. What is particularly important to me is that Esther McCoy has focused not only on the better known, more successful architects, but also on those that didn't quite achieve their goals but tried just as hard and left some beautiful buildings in the area. It is here that her love for the architecture and the architects of Southern California is more noticeable and her contribution more unique and important. By looking at the region and the profession through these good but not canonized architects, Esther McCoy is able to present us with a sharper vision of its reality. The present book is the best description of the life and practice of the architects of the 1930s. In her terse and beautiful writing, their struggles are our struggles and we get to know them as individuals. The collection of her writings is now the most complete source of information on the architects of the period and the region. It is a field that she mapped out and opened up for others to follow.

Cesar Pelli

THE SECOND GENERATION

J.R. Davidson

Julius Ralph
Davidson, 1889-1977.
Photo: Valeska.

"Ten centuries of continuity brings with it the great disadvantage that man believes himself safe, loses the feeling of shipwreck, and his culture burdens itself with parasitic and lymphatic matter. Some discontinuity must intervene in order that man renew his feeling of peril, the substance of his life." Jose Ortega y Gasset

He was a shy man, and his long face in repose was as solemn as a St. Bernard's. He was five-feet-seven, with muscular arms, and hands too broad for the delicate detail in his drawings. In large groups he looked out from behind his mask and said little; with clients his words flowed as he followed their daily life through the floor plan he had drawn; with old friends he was bantering and affectionate. Let the talk turn to his youth in Berlin, and his guard went up. Clearly, he had been an unhappy young man. Even his son knew little about his childhood.

In his eighties, he could not sort out what he knew from photographs or what he had actually seen. But he was sure he had never seen a Loos or a Mackintosh building, for this was one of his regrets. He remembered well Alfred Messel's Wertheimer department store in Berlin, for it was there he first saw modern design applied to the display of merchandise.

He sketched eloquently. Sitting in one of the light-boned caneback chairs he had designed many years before, he sketched Lucien Bernhard's logo for the chain of booteries he had designed in 1922; he sketched the indirect lighting he had devised for the auditorium of Hupfeld (player) Pianos; he sketched a sideboard for a house in Grunewald, lacquered in blue and so cunningly made that no joint was visible; at the same house some of Bruno Paul's students from the Berlin Kunstgewerbeschule executed Davidson's designs for carvings.

Gropius? "Of course, of course," impatiently. "I went to see the Fagus factory, then I met him." Had he wanted to work for Gropius? "He didn't ask me."

That chance remark was a clue to Davidson's character. All of his jobs had come about through letters of introduction; his clients came through an introduction from friends. He said at one of our last talks that to succeed as an architect in America one had to be aggressive, which he was not. Some commissions did not materialize even then because he could only work in a friendly association; one was Bruno Walter: "He talked too much about his success. I left and did not call him back."

Julius Ralph Davidson (the first name given, the second assumed) was born in Berlin February 7, 1889, the best of times for experiencing reforms in the arts: the full flower of the William Morris movement, and its echo in the Deutsche Werkbund; the appearance of Art Nouveau and its German offshoot, Jugendstil. The road divided in the German Arts and Crafts schools, one branch (led by Peter Behrens) allying itself with industry and throwing off decoration to end up as the Bauhaus; the Berlin branch (led by Bruno Paul) flattening and refining the ornament.

Davidson was an introspective boy who grew up among doers. He sat alone over a sketchbook while at this age his forebears were seeking their fortunes in far countries. His father, David Davidson, born in England, was spurred to travel by the tales of Captain Thomas Cook's adventures. In 1865, some 85 years after Cook in his barque *Endeavor* mapped North and South Islands of New Zealand, the sixteen-year-old David Davidson set out from England with his older brother, Joseph, for the gold fields. They settled in Hokitika, a seaport on the west shore of South Island,

Greta Davidson on their penthouse terrace, Berlin, 1922. With a scarcity of housing at the end of World War I, Davidson remodeled the servants quarters on the roof of a four-story building.

Living room of the Davidson house on Barrington Ave., West Los Angeles, 1947. At the end of a cul-de-sac, it seemed their search for a perfect place to live was at an end. But thirteen years later, large apartments were built on both sides, and they were on the move again. Photo: Julius Shulman.

Bodega, Wilshire Blvd., Los Angeles, 1931. The Depression closed the Hi-Hat Restaurant which Davidson designed in 1929, and when it was taken over by Perino's, Davidson cut off one end to fit in a shop. The Bodega, "shop" in Italian, had its own signage in copper, and a long copper panel separated the restaurant from the shop. Photo: Julius Shulman.

at the foot of the Southern Alps range. Surface mining, still practiced, produced sufficient gold for English boats to pick it up, and to unload comforts from home. The social life in Hokitika kept pace with the expanding wealth. Late in the 1880s, surface mining was exhausted and a long depression began. The brothers decided it was time to leave.

Another branch of the family had also gone fortune hunting. Their cousin Frieda Kauffman, half a generation older than the Davidson brothers, accompanied her husband to South Africa where they lived in a covered wagon. After they amassed a fortune in the rich DeBeers diamond field, Kauffman, who had business relations in Germany in the diamond business, moved his family to Berlin.

It was to Berlin that the Davidson brothers sailed. Kauffman, an excessively cautious man, had two unmarried daughters in their twenties, both born in South Africa; the idea of joining family fortunes was worth exploring. The Kauffman sisters, Frieda and Emelie, apparently did not consider their cousins too mature, for soon their hands and the family fortunes were joined.

Joseph Davidson took Frieda to London, and David Davidson settled in Berlin with Emelie in December 1886; in 1888 their son Ralf was born, Julius a year later, then Friedel. None of the children was given a middle name. (Julius appropriated the name of his brother Ralf after he died as a youth.) The children missed a middle name less, however, than a citizenship. Their births had not been registered. This might have been corrected later, but for tragic events.

The Davidsons spent their summers on the island of Helgoland in the North Sea. The drifting white sands of the beach, reaching all the way to red cliffs, eroded into strange formations of arches and caves, making the shelves of the ocean floor treacherous. The summer that Julius was six, his mother was drowned while swimming there. Julius felt the loss all the more because his father was a silent man. (He was certainly no teller of tall tales about New Zealand, for the boy recalled only that his father was the head of the Masonic Lodge of New Zealand, and that his collection of fern specimens went to the Horticultural Museum in Berlin.)

Julius found his solace in drawing. He saved all his pocket-sized, linen-covered sketchbooks, which do much to record his moods, his growing talent, and his travels. They recorded also his emotions at the time of his father's death when he was fourteen. The skies became grayer in his watercolors, waves dashed over a causeway to the lighthouse on the island of Helgoland. A dark carriage waited in the rain in front of an empty street in Berlin. There were pages of figures dressed in dark colors, all with their backs turned, except for one stylish lady in a fur capelet, carrying a fur muff, and looking with a sad smile directly at the sketcher.

The two children were made wards of their uncle, Solomon Kauffman, a man stingy with money and affection. He sent Friedel to London to her Aunt Frieda and Uncle Joseph, and he packed Julius off to a boarding school in Posen—an unlikely place for a sensitive lad. The city, the center of trade between Germany and Russia, offered none of the cultural advantages of Berlin. Posen was in the section of Poland annexed by Germany, and the repressive measures used by the 6000 soldiers garrisoned in the city to Germanize the Poles led to tensions and open hostilities. The Polish language was banished, children who prayed in Polish were punished.

Julius's superior education in Berlin schools placed him always at the head of his class, but little stimulation was offered an active mind. He spent many hours drawing alone. It was this that brought a confrontation with the garrison. One day as he sketched an officer in the park, the officer ordered him to turn over the sketchbook. Julius was no longer a child, he was a young man of eighteen, in his last year at the gymnasium. He refused. When taken to headquarters, it was discovered that his father was born in England, his mother in South Africa, and that he was stateless. He was not permitted to finish the term and receive his certificate. He was sent home immediately. That was the end of his schooling. Thereafter he reported his place of residence to the police once a month.

Left with a talent for drawing and not much to do with it, he went on walking trips along the Baltic Sea. In a seaside resort he met Peter Behrens and his wife. Behrens, then working on the AEG turbine plant in Berlin, treated the young man's talent seriously; he called him a fine architectural delineator. Davidson began to dream of going to England when he came into his inheritance and studying art or architecture. But his guardian, provoked by his idleness, said it was time for him to find work—perhaps in the office of an attorney where he could read law. Alarmed at this prospect, Davidson grasped at the first straw; he said he would rather be an architectural delineator. His guardian found him a job in the small office of a Hungarian architect, Moritz Hirschler.

At nineteen, he entered a new world. His apprenticeship in architecture brought him into contact with his father's country. The ideal of the simple, natural house, as well as the modernism rooted in a new attitude toward historicism, had already spread from England to Germany through Ruskin and Morris. Hermann Muthesius's 1904 book, *Das englische Haus*, introduced Davidson to most of the important moderns of both the vernacular-based and historical-based schools, and although his interest wavered, he veered toward history revised.

During his two years in the Hirschler office his sketches ran more to architectural details and parts of buildings; there was the rotunda of Schinkel's Altes Museum, a Lutyens chandelier from the Marshcourt billiard room, a fireplace by Mackintosh (the latter two copied from the English architecture and decoration magazine *Studio*). The lists of titles, authors, publishers, and prices of books in German, English, and French in his notebooks indicated his broad interest. (He was bilingual and also had a good knowledge of French.)

He formed a friendship with Greta Wollstein, a designer of some talent who smarted under the limited role women of her day were permitted to play in design. The only field of design open to her in Berlin was fashion; she designed models for Kürter's, a smart shop which sold them to provincial buyers who reproduced them in quantity.

When Davidson came into part of his inheritance at age 21, he set out at once for London. He went first with Greta and their friends for a walking trip in Sweden, staying in villages. There, he was immensely impressed by the village houses. The naturalness of the floor plans, the charm-

ing use of color he called "harmonious and joyous."

Leaving his companions, he continued to Belgium to see Victor Horta's work—his favorite was the Maison du Peuple; in Holland he saw the beginning of rationalism. In London he presented a letter of introduction to an architect, Frank Stuart Murray, who gave him a job as a draftsman.

It was a small office on Tottenham Court Road, near the British Museum, and Davidson found a room nearby on Russel Square. Murray was a short, enthusiastic man in his sixties, with white hair and beard and only one eye (he wore neither a patch nor a glass eye); he was a member of the Royal Water Color Society, and amused his four young draftsmen by using his fingers, handkerchief, and string to produce unusual effects in his watercolors. His roots were in the William Morris school—he was also connected by marriage to the Morris family. The work in the office was interiors for a Cunard and a White Star ocean liner, and yachts for the Sultan of Turkey and the Emperor of Germany.

Davidson spoke glowingly of the camaraderie in the office. He had all at once joined a friendly family. This made

up for his disappointment of not studying architecture; his uncle, opposed to his leaving a job to study, would not advance him funds. He got no further than auditing lectures for a year. His education was in the office and the Sunday treks with other young draftsmen to luncheons at Murray's house in Hampstead Heath, or pilgrimages with a draftsman, Adam Acton, to the work of Norman Shaw, Voysey, Ashbee, Baillie-Scott, and other new buildings around London. He was impressed with the restricted palette of materials, the organization of windows into banks, and the simplification of interiors.

He wrote later of this period: "As a young designer I had the good fortune to work for an architectural firm in London which designed the interiors of ocean liners. This was before the First World War when modern design was shy, but the most provocative of it was the interiors of liners, usually in the smaller boats, and never in first cabin. The best design was always in second or third cabin, very simplified solutions. The experience was invaluable for learning space economy and coordination."

Davidson's meticulous planning of storage spaces, his knowledge of the dimensions of things to be stored, and the circulation within a small space, were present

Entrance hall to the Maitland house, Los Angeles, 1937. Photo: Maynard Parker.

in all his work. Among his papers were pages of dimensioned drawings of objects commonly stored: typical length of men's shoes and women's shoes, height of white and red wine bottles, sizes of kitchen utensils, typical dimensions of cosmetic bottles and jars.

After 2½ years in London, Davidson moved to Paris. Adam Acton and other draftsmen joined him for a holiday; they entered a watercolor competition — Davidson's entry always hung on his wall — Place Vendome in soft blues and golds, with a glimpse of Rumplemeyer's, his favorite *conditerie.* Through Murray, Davidson found part-time work with an English designer of elegant interiors, Fred Osborn.

Davidson's reason for going to Paris was Greta Wollstein. She was coming to the House of Lanvin as an apprentice designer, "from the bottom up," she called it. She had expected the same shy young Davidson, but he had bloomed in London. At 23, he talked happily about his work and his ambitions; however, when he spoke of his reluctance to return to Berlin she saw again "the shadow of the orphan." There was also, she said, "the unpleasantness about the delay in settling his father's estate": under the circumstances he was unwilling to ask for money from his uncle to marry. At the back of Greta's mind, she said, was always the invitation from a childhood friend to come to New York — an invitation which they would accept some ten years later.

Their year and a half together in Paris was idyllic. Her sensuous appreciation of fabrics and color — and an educated sensibility to line and form — found play in all his work. He seemed to have found in her the essence of the Swedish village house with its harmony and joy. From that time forward her high spirits and ease in making friends were the face they jointly presented to the world.

Early in 1913, Davidson went into the office of Paul and Alfred Dumas as a designer for two Norman-style houses in the south of France for the Rothschild families. He had little to say of these except that he kept them unpretentious.

What he remembered best about the

Dumas office was the special workroom devoted entirely to the projects for Paul Poiret, the reigning fashion designer in Paris. Many of the projects were for settings and costumes for Poiret's fabled masked balls.

The prewar years in Paris were noted for the interaction among all the arts, crafts, fashion, ballet, stage design, and costume design. Greta Wollstein described the Paris of 1913 as "saturated with design. . . the vibrations were everywhere. It was the center—all else was less."

Giulia Veronesi in *Style and Design* attributed "the swift rise of decorative arts into a sphere of taste [to] the exceptional cultural climate of the times and the extraordinary refinement of the middle classes."

In the prewar years the color palette in Paris abandoned the Art Nouveau washed-out blues and lilacs and straw yellows for the saturated colors of the *fauve* artists, and colors Leon Bakst used in stage sets and costume designs for Paris productions of the *Ballet Russe*. Poiret led the way in borrowing the strong reds and greens and purples from both sources for his fashion fabrics, and soon these colors were found in shops and drawing rooms. (Poiret had visited the Stockelet house, which he called the most remarkable integration of architecture and decoration.)

In 1948, at a Los Angeles County Museum show of fashions and artifacts of Paris of the teens, the Davidsons relived the period. They exclaimed over the colors, the weaves, gowns by Poiret and Lanvin, the Lalique perfume bottles, the spats and peignoirs and hobble skirts. Davidson said the major influence of Paris was "the colors and fabrics. I always select the fabrics for my houses—or Greta does—and the selection of colors begins with the design."

While Paul Poiret was taking women out of whalebone stays and putting them in gowns that flowed with the body, the cubist movement was rising—Mallet-Stevens had a whole street of houses; Auguste Perret was adapting a new material, reinforced concrete, to historical styles; Le Corbusier was beginning his project for prefabricated Domino houses. And a world war was gathering. At first there were a few scrawled insults to foreigners

A hot cart designed by Davidson for restaurants has a brass frame and fittings, an elegant design which could move in any company. Photo: Willard D. Morgan.

in the metro stations, but by early 1914, the hostility was open. Davidson and Greta returned to Berlin two months before war broke out.

Paris, like London, had left its mark on his design—the free use of color, the essays into montage and cubism.

The Davidsons were married in December 1914, just after he volunteered for military service. He was not called up for duty in the Engineer's Corps until the middle of 1915; then because of his knowledge of French, he was stationed for two years at the border of France. After that he spent 2½ years at the Russian border, where fighting was heavy.

He returned in 1919 to a defeated country, bankrupt by war, with little food or goods of any kind, and a scarcity of places to live. The disastrous Versailles Treaty signed that summer led to an inflation that by 1923 made all money useless, returning Germany to a barter society.

Greta wrote later: "This was the Berlin in which I had grown up, an intellectual center, a city of concert halls and opera houses, of theaters and museums and universities, of race tracks and parades. Now the lights had gone out, all mechanical functions arrested, with bar-ricades in the street and soldiers in bivouacs preparing for the shortlived revolution."

Postwar Berlin became an international city, with many languages heard in the galleries and theaters and cafes. Foreigners lived lavishly on $10 a month. The Romanische Cafe, favorite of the intellectuals, was multilingual. The war had eclipsed the old values in the arts. Kandinsky and Klee were shown in staid galleries; Schönberg and Alban Berg were played at concerts. Experimentation flourished; in the proletarian theater Bertolt Brecht and Erwin Piscator introduced film, the treadmill stage, and other innovations. In the more traditional theater Frederick Kiesler designed sets for *Emperor Jones*, and George Grosz turned *The Merchant of Venice* into a modernistic fete.

The Davidsons remembered the wonderful shock of the experimental films, *The Cabinet of Dr. Caligari* and the Fritz Lang films. But it was in architecture that change was most apparent. In England and France, modernism crept along deviously; now it swept through Germany like a welcome wind. Simplicity was imposed by scarcity; a scarcity of materials and workmen, combined with the need for housing, quickly changed the goals and

Lighting for Sardi's Restaurant designed by Davidson, 1936. Shown here is one of the three lighting fixtures in the main dining room of coral lacquered metal parts and clear crystal balls. Photo: Julius Shulman.

sideboard. The chandelier of enameled copper was reminicent of Lutyens's which Davidson had sketched ten years before. The fee was not paid in the unsteady mark but in a bar of silver.

Other jobs followed with similar clients and tastes; new interiors for the Dupont apartment in Charlottenburg-Berlin, and for a Dupont partner a house in Saxony. The fees were paid in bolts of French silk confiscated by the government during the war. (One of the silks, Davidson recalled, was a pattern of interlocking stripes in several colors, which he used later for upholstering chairs for himself.) For Hans Fiegen, a state's attorney, he designed a house on the Rhine in Bonn, drawing upon Norman Shaw's style for inspiration.

His most exacting job in 1920-21 was remodeling living space for themselves. With housing unavailable, he bought a penthouse on top of an apartment building facing Schöneberg Park; the six small rooms and entry hall, used formerly to house servants, was surrounded by a graveled roof. No room was rectangular, and the walls followed the slope of the mansard roof. He made use of the alcoves formed by the dormers for closets, as a recess for a bed, a bathtub, and kitchen cabinets; the alcove off their new library became a drafting room. Above the dainty fireplace in the living room the Davidsons hung two polychrome angels holding candlesticks—the angels followed them wherever they went, ending up fifty years later in their house in Ojai. Between all rooms he installed double or folding doors so the light could spread. On the roof he arranged a 60-foot-long terrace facing the park; in a corner was a dining bower of metal lath, in summer covered with vines growing from large pots. Along the parapet wall a hedge was planted in a deep metal trough. The 40-foot-wide terrace was built around a cupola lighting the apartment below—occupied by Ernst Wasmuth, publisher of the Frank Lloyd Wright 1910-11 portfolios.

When the apartment was published in December 1924 in *Kunst und Dekoration*, the writer called it "the way the refined middle class build their bungalow in the city. . . . The royal styles have played out, and the people who formerly could not do without a Louis XVI salon with gilt

the means of reaching them. With this went a new excitement and sense of purpose. There were exhibitions of the new architecture in several cities. The optimism was electric, although clients were few.

There were clients, however, for restoration work. In 1919, at age 30, Davidson set up his first office with a commission from a client whose money was in semiprecious metals, a commodity little affected by the money market. Nor was the client interested in new styles; for the Pfeifferling house in Grunewald he designed a new facade in "a cleaned-up baroque" and new dining room furniture. It was here he designed the blue lacquered

decoration now demand greater simplicity in creating comfort."

By 1922, weary of the exercises in classic baroque, he was glad when a type of work opened up which gave greater scope for his talent in modern design—shops and shop interiors. Two of the commissions arose out of an American custom which had just caught hold in Germany—installment buying. Hand in hand with this came branch shops. He did two branch shops for Stiller's shoes. One of Bruno Paul's collaborators, Lucien Bernhard, designed the logo—a stylized pump used serially in sixes. At a time when merchandise was always hidden from sight, Davidson displayed it in glass cases in a forecourt. The brass fittings of the case were so thin that the shoes seemed to float on air, much as the cakes and Napoleons did in the glass dessert carts he designed later for restaurants.

No standard lighting fixtures existed then for indirect lighting, so he designed his own. The glass cases were evenly illuminated by incandescent bulbs concealed in a pocket in the top, with frosted glass spreading the light so there were no shadows.

In the display room and a 200-seat auditorium for a manufacturer of player pianos, the Hupfeld company, he bathed walls in reflected light by aiming hidden incandescent bulbs at the coving around the ceiling. Each method of lighting he used required different kinds of structural pockets.

Except for lighting, his principles of design came from boat interiors. The flush surfaces which were a protection to passengers in rough seas were useful in the restricted areas of small shops. The exquisitely finished hardwoods, which were resistant to salt air, were his decorative features in shops. But it was the lighting that worked the magic. Light masked the smallness of spaces; coming from hidden sources always above or below eye level, it could discreetly spotlight an object on display, or direct the circulation in a small space. His other ally was color; he used it in lines, in various width stripes, and in chevrons, often working from deep purple browns toward a single fine line of vermillion, or from browns to tans and beige, the strongest patterns in the floor covering.

Inflation grew steadily between 1919 and 1922, but the worst was in store. At the end of 1922, a dollar would buy 10,000 marks, and by June 1923, it rose to 110,000 marks. By August the economy was in shambles: the mark stood at 4.6 million to the dollar. Herbert Bayer of the Bauhaus (now retired in Santa Barbara) was commissioned by the government to design the one and two million mark notes.

Greta Davidson recalled: "The price of a dinner in a restaurant rose between courses. We carried our money first in stachels, finally in baskets. When I wrote to my school friend in New York, the envelope wasn't big enough for all the stamps, and I attached a paper to hold the rest. J.R. had been paid an architectural fee of 5000 marks in fur pelts. When we decided to leave Berlin, I took them to a furrier and ordered a coat. The cost for making it was 10,000 marks. When I went for a fitting, just the tram fare was 50,000 marks."

The Davidsons found a buyer for their apartment who agreed to deposit the payment of $8500 in a New York bank. The papers were signed the 12th of December 1923. The bar of silver received as an architectural fee went to the steamship line to pay for tickets on the S.S. *Albert Ball* sailing three days later to New York. When the silver bar was presented in payment, out came the scales and delicate saw; the precise amount of silver was sawed off.

They said goodbye to their neighbor, Ernst Wasmuth, as he was getting into his car. He always drove, his liveried chauffeur sitting beside him.

Their first meetings had not been friendly because he objected to the Davidsons taking the elevator to his top floor, and from there the public stair to their penthouse. Davidson's interest in the Wright portfolio had somewhat softened Wasmuth. "Wright's work of the early period always seemed to me to be 'created,'" Davidson said.

They arrived in New York on New Year's Eve, 1923, and stayed three weeks with Greta's classmate and her husband, Kate and Dan Goldberg. He introduced Davidson to architects with the hope that

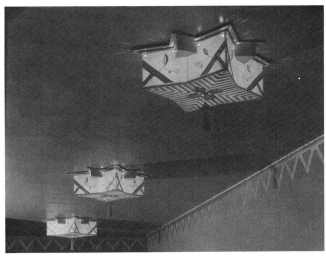

Ceiling lights at the Cocoanut Grove nightclub, Ambassador Hotel, Los Angeles, 1926. Photo: Julius Shulman.

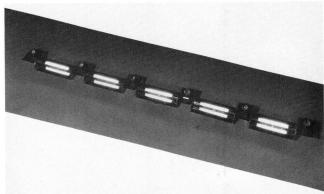

Office lighting designed by Davidson, 1927. Photo: Luckhaus Studios.

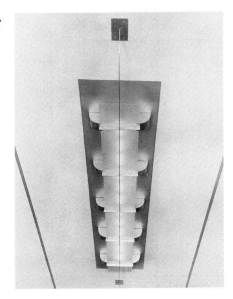

Restaurant lighting, 1927. Photo: Willard D. Morgan.

Lanterns at the Cocoanut Grove nightclub. Photo: Mott Studios.

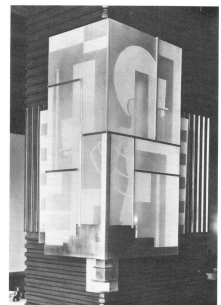

Light post at the Hi-Hat Restaurant, Los Angeles, 1929. In 1930, the Hi-Hat Restaurant became Perino's. Photo: Willard D. Morgan.

they would stay in New York.

Davidson said later that he picked their destination, Los Angeles, out of a hat. This was not quite true. He knew Kem Weber, a former Bruno Paul student who had been domiciled in California during the war as an enemy alien; through Paul, Weber heard of Davidson's plan. Davidson remembered Paul as a generous, witty man, whose work as a teacher and designer began as a cartoonist for the magazine *Simplissimus*; "everything he touched, from a piece of furniture to large houses, had a clarity and refinement."

Davidson celebrated his thirty-sixth birthday in Los Angeles, his adopted city, one where he would spend almost 50 years in practice.

The office of Robert D. Farquhar in Los Angeles was small, the work mainly large residences or small institutional buildings in eclectic styles. In 1924, when Davidson entered the office, the plans were underway for a private library in the West Adams district—now UCLA's William Andrews Clark Memorial Library. The exterior and the ceremonial interiors were designed by Farquhar himself, but the design of the stack areas situated below the garden was left to Davidson. He treated it with the same directness he had the second and third cabin interiors of Cunard and White Star liners in the Murray office. "He gave me a free hand," said Davidson, who applied his knowledge of shop lighting to the stack area. He used bare bulbs painted with concentric blue lines to cut the glare without reducing the illumination. According to Robert Winter, similar bulbs are still in use, and the carefully detailed paneling and cabinet work is unchanged.

The work lasted for nine months, and before Farquhar sailed for a vacation in Europe, he telephoned Cecil B. DeMille to ask him to give Davidson a job designing sets for *The Golden Bed*, a film starring Rod LaRoque.

That was 1925, the year of the Exposition of Decorative Arts in Paris, the event from which came the immensely popular Art Deco style. Called "modernistic" in Los Angeles, it was quickly sanctioned, while the modern style based on industrial usages languished. This was also true in Europe. Giulia Veronesi attributed the rise of this "ornamental syntax made up of the zigzag, the triangle and fawn-like curves" to "an era of prosperity without precedent."

"I spent two years in the studios—sets for Cedric Gibbons's production of Clara Bow in *It*, and so on, but during that time I worked on designs for two Farquhar houses. I wanted to learn the difference between the European and American office. Essentially they were the same, although here they would cover a wall with plywood, with a stile around the molding. Quick and easy."

In 1926, he redesigned the Cocoanut Grove at the Ambassador Hotel, and interiors for the Nickabob Cafe, combining some of the design features of Art Deco with very innovative lighting.

In the studios he met a young man interested in architecture who introduced Davidson to the developers Bilike and Hite who had a block to develop on West Seventh Street across from Westlake (MacArthur) Park. In 1927, he designed a small office building for their activities, with an office on the mezzanine for himself. When the interiors were published in *California Arts & Architecture* he was asked to give a course on interiors at the Chouinard School, where Kem Weber also taught. Through Weber, Davidson had met the Schindlers. Pauline Schindler included Davidson in her 1930 show on modern architecture at UCLA. They also met the Neutras, and Greta and Dione Neutra became lifelong friends.

After Pauline Schindler left Kings Road for Carmel, and the Neutras had left for Europe, Greta often visited Galka Scheyer in the guest studio. "I went in to help her with typing letters," Greta wrote. "Each time work was finished, she took out some records and asked me, 'Bach, Beethoven, or Bali?' We chose Bali, and sitting in the patio of the Schindler house we found true delight in this rare music."

In 1929, Davidson designed facades and interiors for four shops and a restaurant on Wilshire Boulevard for Hite and Bilike. (The shops were a one-story block in front of the Bilike Building designed by Morgan, Walls, and Clements.)

The strict moderns would have made

the shops a single composition, but the only continuous lines are the fascia and signs. Each shop was set within its own frame, given different fenestration, colors, signage. Vertical lines were stressed in all except the restaurant; there, a band of low windows stretched the width of the front, even followed the curved wall of the entrance.

Davidson, unlike Kem Weber, did not welcome in the "zigzag, triangle, and fawn-like curve" of Art Deco. The exceptions were for lighting fixtures, sometimes signage. Manufacturers had begun to copy some of Davidson's lighting devices and put them on the market; but he was always finding new solutions to achieve new effects. Lighting to him was a form of play.

Photographs of his shops and restaurant interiors began to appear regularly in ads, and as his name was mentioned his reputation grew. He was also a reason for rejoicing among the manufacturers of semiprecious metal for architectural trim. For the Hite-Bilike shops he had used cadmium-plated steel and copper; he combined copper and redwood in the Satyr Bookshop, and in the Hi-Hat Restaurant the entire ceiling was of leaf copper which spread a warm glow over tables and diners. The architectural journals as well as the trade magazines published his shops and praised the "richness and refinement." (Hosannahs also came for the sellers of fine woods!)

Davidson's favorite was the Bachelors Shop. Paneling and wall cases of Makassar ebony set in brushed aluminum channels, combined with red lacquered screens, with carpeting of brown and tans, laid in stripes

of various widths; square stools on chrome bases were covered with pigskin.

The market crash came as the shops were opening. Most of them closed or changed hands in 1930; the Hi-Hat sign came down and Perino's went up. (Later Perino's acquired a nostalgic New Orleans decor.)

Before the Depression brought building almost to a halt, Davidson had designed new facades and interiors for two dress shops on Hollywood Boulevard. The Jay Bari was a handsome, scaleless collage of stripes and solid and transparent rectangles, more cubistic that Art Deco. The Lora Lee at the corner of Vine had a deeply recessed entrance, staggered showcases, and canopy and forecourt lighted by neon tubes pointed like an arrow toward the door. The shop set the style for very garish ones during the 1930s, even to the chrome and brass and absinthe yellow.

Then commissions stopped. After some months without work, he had a call from the art director Hans Dreier, who Ernst Lubitsch had brought to Hollywood — would Davidson design sets of the Parliament building for a film on the Reichstag fire? Before the work at the studio was finished, a call came from Dan Goldberg.

Goldberg was in Chicago to take over the management of three hotels that were in receivership. He wanted an architect familiar with the best cafes in Paris and Berlin. In a few months Franklin D. Roosevelt would be inaugurated, and the predictions were that the Volstead Act would be repealed. Goldberg wanted to introduce Chicago to elegant cafe life.

In 1933, the Davidsons left their six-year-old son Tom with the Kem Webers and went to Chicago. For three years they would commute between Chicago and Los Angeles while he remodeled three hotels in Chicago and one in Gary, Indiana.

The dining rooms in all the hotels were expansive and little used, so his plan was to cut the dining rooms in two and turn half the space into a bar with separate street entrances. But it was not the pre-Prohibition barroom that Davidson planned. Nor were they reminders of the "speakeasys" of Prohibition days. He combined discreetness with gaiety, openness and intimacy, elegance and "respectability"

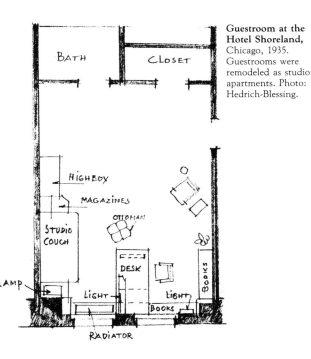

Guestroom at the Hotel Shoreland, Chicago, 1935. Guestrooms were remodeled as studio apartments. Photo: Hedrich-Blessing.

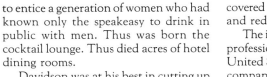

to entice a generation of women who had known only the speakeasy to drink in public with men. Thus was born the cocktail lounge. Thus died acres of hotel dining rooms.

Davidson was at his best in cutting up a small plan into a variety of open and intimate spaces; he used different levels of lighting at the long bar at the end and the tables for three to six around deep corner seats. He avoided booths or any regimented arrangement of tables in the Red Lion Inn at the Sheridan Plaza, the Tavern at the Hotel Knickerbocker, and the Bar and Cocktail Room at the Hotel Shoreland. In the Shoreland, the space was smallest, the most cut up, but was the most popular—although there was seating for no more than 35 persons in 700 square feet. The deep comfortable seating, the lightweight chrome and blue chairs, the small glossy black tables were set in an atmosphere of gold walls and coral ceilings, which gave way to zebra wood paneling by the long bar; it was a fine sequence of happenings. There were four levels of lights at the bar: near the floor, in the barman's work space below the counter, and indirect lighting in the lowered ceiling above the bar. The bar mirror and the columns were covered with sheet chrome, striped in blue and red.

The interiors were published in a dozen professional and trade magazines in the United States, England, and Europe; accompanying the stories were often full details of the lighting. (*Licht und Beleuchtung,* published in Berlin in 1938, which Davidson ordered in Chicago, showed Germany by that time far ahead of America in lighting fixtures and illuminated signs, but there was little about indirect lighting, in which he was a specialist.)

For the Shoreland, which was partially converted to a residential hotel, he cut the size of some rooms and furnished them as bed/sitting rooms. It was probably the first hotel to bring down the horizon line to the new modern level—certainly the first hotel to hang pictures five feet above the floor.

When Davidson returned to Los Angeles in 1936, he received a commission to enlarge and redesign Sardi's Restaurant, which had been gutted by fire. The original design by R.M. Schindler in 1932 used several kinds of indirect lighting; most effective was that below eye level, which kept illumination low while lighting

the floor, the seats, and reflecting some on the table surfaces. Schindler's design had a greater vitality, but by the time of the fire, the restaurant had become so popular that the decision to enlarge the space created two levels, making the entire area more public. Even with the additional space, Davidson had to squeeze in more tables than he wished, a last sacrifice of intimacy.

I think that Davidson depended much more than Schindler on the correctness of his solutions to win a client over – also relying on the client's faith in his judgment and on good manners. Many of his clients were Europeans, who were more apt to defer to the judgment of a professional; many were physiscians who accepted advice in another field as they expected their own to be taken.

Davidson gave longer, more concentrated, study to a plan in the early stages than Schindler, who inclined to let a number of things float; Schindler gave clients a variety of choices, but never on matters central to the success of the design. All his wiles and ingenuity went into the protection of the kernel of the plan.

Davidson fought as hard. He wrote of one case, "I was victorious, to the full satisfaction of the owner."

When Schindler was not permitted to select the colors for the Gisela Benatti cabin, it made him ill. He took to his bed, the owner told me.

In 1936 Davidson received his first two commissions for houses. The first was a complete remodel of the Bel Air house for the Dr. Leslie Maitlands. The commission came first as a request to do working drawings and supervise construction for the architect, George Howe of Philadelphia. Davidson was taken to meet Ruth McCormick Maitland by his friend Galka Scheyer, who had sold Mrs. Maitland a Klee, Miró, Braque, Modigliani, and Chirico. A year or so earlier the Maitlands had gone through a disappointing experience with an architect, the result being that they had a new house they never moved into – one objectionable feature was insufficient wall space for paintings. Mrs. Maitland then asked her friend George Howe to remodel their Georgian style house in Bel Air.

Howe's name is on the early drawings,

but his former partner, William Lescaze, also consulted with the Maitlands on his trips to Los Angeles while planning the CBS building on Sunset Boulevard. But it was difficult to remodel for an exacting client from a distance, doubly so because of Mrs. Maitland's efforts to avoid a second disappointment. Davidson, who had the full confidence of Howe, was given great latitude; finally Howe withdrew, assuring Mrs. Maitland that she was better served by someone who could give the job his personal attention.

The facade and interiors of the Maitland house were stripped of the eclectic details; windows and doors were removed, the arches squared up and cornices taken down, the Georgian mantelpiece ripped off, the hearth made level with the floor, the wall plastered to the opening, and a black Belgian marble hearth installed.[1] Wallpaper and carved wood panels were removed and the stairwell in the entry hall opened up; troughs were built for indirect lighting; new hardware from Davidson's design appeared on the new steel sash and flush-type doors. The details covered thirteen pages.

The original stone was retained, and there was a lengthy search for matching stone from the same quarry. The openings between the social rooms were widened so the library flowed into the new covered terrace and on out to the open terrace. The dining room, with a large Chirico dominating one wall, was given a glass wall facing trees and lawn.

Davidson said, "The location of the openings, formerly based on an axial layout, was changed according to the interrelationship of the rooms and the view. Materials and colors throughout were selected with regard to the pictures, in an effort to secure a neutral background."

In comparing the design of houses with shops, Davidson said that shops must achieve both order and elan, the order real, the elan of a hothouse variety which would stimulate the shopper for an hour. The response to a restaurant must also be immediate but of less intensity.

"For a house I want to achieve serenity and cheerfulness. Most people value these in a house but few clients understand the plan features which produce them.

Stothart house, Santa Monica, 1937. North side. From the left: shade garden off living room, adults' terrace, swimming pool, dining terrace; at far right: children's area. Photo: Ernst Ludwick.

Serenity is achieved through order. The continuous line is the restful one. I line up the cabinets and storage spaces in the living room. I make it a design habit that nothing hangs free of the continuous line except for an accent. The success of the living room does not depend upon size. It is more important that they have both a major and minor axis. They must have both light and shadow—that is why I use light on two sides of a room only."

In his second house, for Herbert Stothart, music director of MGM Studios, the front promised little of the life behind it. The fenestration, the flat roof, and white walls are out of the International style, less true on the garden side. There his use of glass was conservative. He framed his glass with wall, as Eileen Gray did in her two 1920s houses in the south of France. The result was interior wall space which lent itself well to large modern paintings; when the house was sold after Stothart's death its appeal to the new owner, Gifford Phillips, was the rare combination of a classic modern with large wall space for paintings.

1. The marble may well have been in the early Howe plan; in Howe and Lescaze's PSFS Building in Philadelphia, black Belgian marble is used extensively.

15

Stothart house. Glass rolls into pockets to open the north end of the living room to the terrace and a view of the mountains. Photo: Ernst Ludwick.

Stothart house. The unpolished glass screen separates the entry hall from the living room. Photo: Ernst Ludwick.

a more articulated facade than on the street side, where the long driveway passes two tennis courts to reach a recessed entrance between the three-car garage and the curved wall of the service court. Aside from the kitchen and the second floor children's bedrooms, all other rooms face north. The living room does have south light from the high glass in the entry stairwell; the only separation between entry hall and living room is a large screen of unpolished glass.

The living room circulation makes a half circle around the conversation area facing the fireplace, with a lane to double doors to a shade court on the east. The steel and glass doors to the court have the fragile look of International style doors in Italy and Mexico, and one expects the same tinny sound. No; the steel is heavy gauge and the glass is plate.

Gifford Phillips made few changes in the house. Still in place are the cork tile floors, the built-in desks in the master bedroom, the study and the children's rooms, the built-ins in dressing room and bath—even the swing-out seat for the telephone in the hall to the kitchen. The seat was based on ones swinging out from counters in shops, where the customer sat with elbow on a velvet cushion to have gloves fitted. The only out-of-date thing in the house is the space for local telephone books—these have quadrupled in size since 1937. Davidson was pleased that the house was kept intact, but felt that the paintings had usurped the architecture.

Stothart's music studio (later Phillips's office) facing the quiet east court, was soundproofed, and the built-ins were dimensioned to the needs of the composer; one storage space was built to the dimensions of the *London Music Gazette*. The south end of the living room was a music wall, with space for radio, recordings, loud speaker, recording machine, and a projector which was operated from the closet for guests' wraps.

Greta Davidson once said that when they came to Los Angeles there was not a decently detailed wastebasket sold commercially; in the music studio the wastebasket was a bin built into the desk.

The garden side of the house has lost none of its freshness. Forms step down from

His strip windows rarely extend from wall to wall. Only in the living room does glass turn a corner, in the ten-foot floor-to-ceiling glass facing the terrace. The glass slid into wall pockets on both sides to make the whole corner of the living room a part of the terrace. Although many features of the International style are present, structure was never revealed. He used standard framing of two-by-four studs. By 1937, the climate of California had already modified the International style, and by 1940, its major exponent, Richard Neutra, abandoned it. Schindler had developed his own idiom before the International style gained popularity.

Davidson followed Neutra's practice of the five-foot window module (two operable sash or fixed glass panels fitted into the five-foot opening). Neutra's windows, however, were in continuous bands; Davidson usually broke the composition into solid and transparent rectangles. Davidson also interrupted the shear wall plane with overhangs to protect glass from rain and sun.

The Stothart site slopes gradually to the north, and the house is pushed back toward the long view to Santa Monica Canyon, the ocean, and the mountains,

Mrs. Stothart's sitting room on the north. Photo: Ernst Ludwick.

A desk and lamp for Herbert Stothart, composer, designed by Davidson. Photo: Ernst Ludwick.

The child's room on the south has a built-in desk and lamp by Davidson. Photo: Ernst Ludwick.

roof level to bedroom deck to overhang, from living room terrace level to the swimming pool level, to garden, to bath house. The low wall around the curved pool bounds the terrace, takes care of level change, and separates activities.

In 1939, Davidson received a first award from Pittsburgh Glass Institute for the Stothart house, and a mention for Sardi's Restaurant. (One of the jurors was William Lescaze.)

More typical of Davidson's later houses were the two for the Berksons on a six-acre site in the San Fernando Valley. The houses, for parents and daughter, are identical in plan, an **L** shape, with the lower horizontal bar hinged at two points to angle in, thus sheltering the walls from the prevailing wind and creating a protected terrace off living room and bedrooms. In a time before mechanical cooling systems, when design carried the load in reducing heat, the gentle hipped roof was extended with overhangs, and interiors were cooled by a current of air entering from the overhangs and carrying off collected warm air through louvres in the roof. One house is blue, the other light green, and the slab floors a deep plum which is waxed to a high gloss.

In the Gretna Green Apartments of 1940—three apartments with private gardens, and an apartment with trellised deck over the garages—he returned to flat roofs, but the stucco was terra cotta color and the wood trim blue. A good detail is the fascia continuing as trellis member in the garage apartment.

A built-in Davidson began to use at this time was a shoe rack, in which twenty pairs of shoes can be stored in a wall space six inches deep and half the size of a door. Another that appeared soon was a line of small bins on a wardrobe door for holding women's purses. One version of this was the shallow cupboard with bins on the door alternating with pullout trays (for sweaters) on wall shelves. Davidson was the darling of *Sunset* magazine which pulled a house apart and featured good details. Some details, which have gone the way of the large drying yard, were narrow shallow drawers for gloves and handkerchiefs.

From the time Davidson designed his first interiors he kept alive the image of women as not only deserving but requiring a private retreat, one still best described as boudoir—if it suggests a limited role for women it nevertheless provides space of their own. The major bedroom was often labeled as the woman's bedroom, not master bedroom as was the custom. Allurement was suggested in the elegant dressing table; relaxation suggested by a chaise near a window with a view, with table and reading light at hand. The mood was one of reverie rather than a serious activity.

In the various places the Davidsons lived he had a room of his own, monklike compared to Greta's large one; but in hers was a built-in desk (with slide-out typewriter) where she did some of his typing. It was a reversal of the nineteenth-century English house in which the shared bedroom had an adjacent master's dressing room. (When in an English novel a man "slept in his dressing room" you could be sure the marriage was in trouble; there was nothing in the plan to indicate a woman's retreat.)

The prevalance of flexible interiors over impressive facades did not change. In the vacation house in a ten-acre citrus grove in Ojai for the Vigevenos, the entry is along a side porch interrupted by a louvred screen. The tight entry hall funnels into the living room and the kitchen—the lane to the latter skirting a lavatory and laundry. But once inside the living room the reason for the blocked porch is clear. It screens out a sitting porch on the northeast with a view of the mountains. On the opposite side of the living room is a second

Gretna Green Apartments. Patio off an apartment. The upper-floor apartments all had decks.

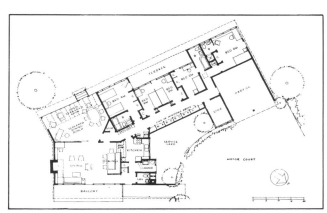

Vigeveno house plan.

Vigeveno vacation house, Ojai, 1941. The living and dining porch on the south looks out on the Ojai Valley. Photo: Julius Shulman.

Vigeveno living room. Door to a narrow porch with a view of the mountains to the north. Photo: Julius Shulman.

Vigeveno house. A walk along the side of the house to the front door. Photo: Julius Shulman.

and larger porch, for dining and recreation, which faces a sweeping view of the Ojai Valley.

The plan is a long rectangle with a smaller block set at an angle of fifteen degrees, the latter containing living room, entry, and kitchen. The angle widens the porch to take care of a table seating eight, used when the family gathered on weekends.

The redundancy of a second dining table a dozen feet away at the end of the living room gives an idea of Davidson's willingness to pinch space to offer a magnanimous option. The option of the two view porches is as welcome. There are three bedrooms in the small house, and a fourth that can be divided by sliding wall. Much of the storage space is congregated in continuous cupboards under strip windows in the wide bedroom hall. Space is also pinched in two bedrooms to cut in a six-foot-wide view porch, and again to find room for three small baths and a lavatory.

Vigeveno, an art dealer, later closed his gallery in Los Angeles and carried on his business from the Ojai house. Davidson designed a house on the property for another member of the family in 1953, and two for Krishnamurtie on the property.

Thomas Mann house, Pacific Palisades, 1941. A view from the lemon grove toward the raised terrace. Mann's walled garden off of his study is behind the terrace. Photo: Gottlieb.

The commission for the Thomas Mann house came to Davidson in 1940 through a mutual friend at a film studio (probably Ernst Lubitsch). The design was discussed in general terms with Mann and the particulars with his wife Katia. Mann was more interested in talking with Davidson about his native city of Lübeck, and the German colony in Hollywood.

Typical of Katia Mann's witty and sometimes sharp tongue was her reply to Greta's comment that she had read *The Magic Mountain* twice. "So," responded Mrs. Mann, "one hears a Beethoven symphony dozens of times."

The site was on one of the winding streets in the Italian Riviera section of Pacific Palisades, high above Sunset Boulevard. The house forms an open angle at a curve in the road, the motor court and planting screening it from sight, and

the service areas and entrance hall at the front baffling the sound of the occasional car. Davidson lost the decision to turn the living and dining terraces to the southeast, and was not altogether satisfied with placing Mann's study so close to the social rooms. However, by angling Mann's study off from the major rectangular block he gave it a southeast orientation. A solid wall toward the terrace, and a high-walled court off the study closed out the activities on the terrace and in the garden. The enclosed court leads to a retreat in a windfree space on the east. The entrance to Mann's study was off a hall with a lavatory and a private stair to his bedroom. This was the only direct entrance to Mann's bedroom. From the second floor, the entrance was only through his wife's bedroom. The five bedrooms opened onto a wide, partially covered, view porch.

The roof is hipped (required by the tract code), although the design is in the idiom of Davidson's flat-roofed houses with white stucco walls. Almost the entire wall is continuous windows and sliding glass on the garden side, more openings than Davidson liked on the south. The large glass areas in Mann's studio, however, are single, symmetrically placed sheets of glass, framed on four sides by wall.

Mann thanked Davidson often for his foresight in giving him his own private bath off his study, and stairs to his bedroom by which he could escape unnoticed from social activities. After the Manns moved into the house in 1941 he wrote Davidson: "In times of such deeply depressing events there is a special spiritual meaning to this harmonious house and its surroundings."

The private stair from Mann's study to the bedroom with an ocean view-deck where he enjoyed pacing. Photo: Gottlieb.

Dining end of the **living room, Sabsay house,** Los Angeles, 1940. Photo: Julius Shulman.

But in the beginning of the relationship Mann had held Davidson somehow responsible for "the bad manners" of the architectural profession in America. It seems that Richard Neutra kept writing and telephoning Mann begging for the commission. "He showed me a letter from Richard," Davidson said. "Richard asked Dr. Mann how he could be satisfied with less when he could have the best. Dr. Mann said that Richard wanted to use him for publicity and he didn't want any."

Greta's and Mrs. Neutra's friendship survived this and other trials. Davidson was not so understanding. An apology of sorts came from Neutra. He added a note in English at the end of his wife's letter to Greta: ". . . I am sad because I had by accident learned that you doubted my true sympathy for you both. I do not know whether what I say here can overcome

suspicions but life is not worth anything if good human beings doubt each other. There is enough real enmity around. I do not know what Dione may have written, Greta, with the sincerest intentions, but all I said was that in the role of struggle and keeping the noses over the flood, fellow men become competitors, especially when their endeavors and their possible patrons are similar. In a happier order just this would make them cooperative, but fate seems against it. . . . Faithfully, Richard."

There were several other houses completed before the war brought about a shortage of materials for civilian use, including houses for Sabsay and Branch. One larger project completed in 1942 was the Wilshire Medical Building. The commission came through the remodeling of a larger medical building, much admired for the circulation and the built-in furniture.

Little recognition was paid Wilshire Boulevard in the new building, except for a not too successful free-form canopy over the street entrance. The building was oriented as much to the parking lot at the back, and importance was given the side entrance. The layout of the interiors of the long rectangular space was planned to be controlled by one waiting room, with the circulation and lighting introducing various innovations which led to wide publication in medical periodicals.

The recognition of the parking lot reversed an earlier indifference to it in a project called Curbside Market, a large glass-walled building whose parking at the curb would soon have been inadequate for the growing population and increased traffic.

Arts & Architecture Case Study House, West Los Angeles, 1946. A view from the street. Photo: Marvin Rand.

The south patio of the Case Study House. Photo: Julius Shulman.

The postwar years of 1945-50 established modern architecture in Los Angeles. One factor leading to the eclipse of eclectic styles was the Case Study House program of *Arts & Architecture* magazine. John Entenza, publisher and editor, initiated the program to build, furnish, and landscape a series of eight houses which Entenza hoped would be of practical assistance to the average American in search of a house he could afford. One of the eight architects selected was Davidson.

As the war was ending Davidson had bought five acres of land running from Barrington Avenue in West Los Angeles down a long flat stretch to a slope which ended in a chain link fence marking the boundary of the Veterans Administration grounds. A narrow road was cut from Barrington to the two acres at the end, which Davidson reserved for a house and office for himself. Three shallow lots along the side of the road were sold, and the fourth, a trapezoidal one on Barrington was the site for which he designed the first Case Study house. The client was a Dutch émigré who had owned the Bee Hive chain of department stores, one of which was designed by J.J.P. Oud. The project was abandoned when the client bought a large house in the Hollywood Hills, which

Davidson remodeled for him.

"So we had a Case Study plan and no client," Davidson said. The plan grew out of the wartime restriction of 1200 square feet for single-family dwellings, still in effect in 1945. His house, however, was 1100 square feet.

The plan is experimental although the materials traditional— redwood siding and stucco. It is a plan without halls, yet with a clear circulation pattern laid down in a series of interlocking loops. This was possible because of the truss roof and no load-bearing interior walls. All four rooms had doors to the outside, the main bedroom and the living room to a shared patio, and the second bedroom (which could be study or home office) to its private patio; the kitchen opened to a service court which doubled as a private entrance to the second bedroom/study/office, with its own bath.

The entrance area is screened from the living room by cabinets with obscure glass above. Behind the glass is the dining space, and separating this from the conversation area of the living room is an aisle directly from the front door to the patio. The passage to the second bedroom is along a bookcase wall in the living room. A remarkably legible circulation plan for a small house, with a double-functioning bedroom cut off from the rest of the house.

He managed to combine several functions in the passage to the main bedroom by placing a dressing room off the entrance area. It is lined on one side with a wardrobe closet and the other with dressing table and tiers of drawers. It serves as a place where guests may drop their wraps, and it leads to bathroom and bedroom, perhaps the neatest plan ever devised for a small house.

The house was finally built on the Barrington site for two of Entenza's associates on *Arts & Architecture*, Robert and Flora Brown Cron. The plan was used four other times, first for a Case Study in La Canada. Davidson did not include the other three examples in his building list because he did not supervise construction; one was for the two Dr. Billings on Bonhill Road in West Los Angeles, one for an attorney, a paraplegic, for whom certain changes in the plan were required.

Before Davidson could get started on his own house he built two houses on adjoining lots in the Italian Riviera section of Pacific Palisades. The clients were Mrs. Paul Kingsley and her son Joseph and his family. The site, a slope facing the ocean, was an old lemon grove, and most of the trees were saved.

The houses are below street level, and over the entrance court is egg-crate trellising

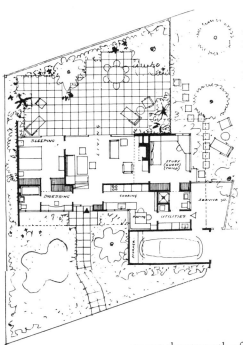

Case Study House plan. This 1100-square-foot house is without any halls.

Joseph Kingsley house, Pacific Palisades, 1946. The circulation is by a long gallery on the entrance side and along a glazed wall on the terrace side. Photo: Julius Shulman.

to cut the strength of the northwest sun on the planting beds. The houses were similar in another respect: major rooms (living room, dining room, breakfast room, and master bedroom) open by sliding glass to the view terrace on the southeast: the Joseph Kingsley terrace is at ground level and Mrs. Paul Kingsley's raised several feet above, with steps down to a lawn stretching to the lemon grove.

Davidson holds in his composition with six-inch parapet walls at the side, which seem extraordinarily thin in contrast to a Neutra terminal wall of masonry which rides above the roof. (It was Frank Lloyd Wright who cautioned the architect to watch out for his terminals!)

In the Joseph Kingsley house Davidson enlarged on his scheme for a house without halls. He uses a wide gallery off the front door, leading at one end to the kitchen wing and the other the bedroom wing, lighted by high strip windows on the entrance side. The gallery is separated from the living room by obscure glass panels above a music cabinet and a built-in sofa angled to a fireplace. A dressing room serves as a hall to the master bedroom, lighted by an obscure glass window facing the terrace.

After Mrs. Paul Kingsley's death the house was turned into a grand neo-

Kingsley living room. The built-in sofa backs up against the gallery. Photo: Julius Shulman.

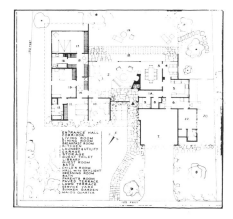

ENTRANCE HALL
CORRIDOR
LIVING ROOM
DINING ROOM
BREAKFAST ROOM
KITCHEN
LAUNDRY & UTILITY
GARAGE
STORAGE
GUEST TOILET
GUEST ROOM
HALL
CHILD'S ROOM
HALL WITH SKYLIGHT
DRESSING ROOM
BATH
PARENTS' ROOM
PAVED TERRACE
LAWN TERRACE
SERVICE YARD
SUNKEN GARDEN
MAID'S QUARTER

The raised terrace of the Mrs. Paul Kingsley house is next door to her son Joseph. Photo: Julius Shulman.

Corbusian mansion by an architect-developer who, after selling it, moved on to aggrandize a simple, elegant house in Santa Monica, sold by the Cesar Pellis when he assumed the duties of the dean of the School of Architecture at Yale.

Davidson once said that he was not happy with the way he had handled the layout of his own house, planned at the same time as the Kingsley houses, but not finished until 1947. "I was busy on other things," he said. But he liked the floor plan. Of floor plans in general he said, "I never had a plan I wanted to change—only details."

From the street the Davidson house is indeed different from his others. A double garage continues on the same plane as a blank garden wall, broken by a door to the entrance garden to the house; outside the wall is the large drafting room and office. I myself had liked the long planes, the integration of the office into the composition by the simple device of resting the overhang of the office entrance on the garden wall, and butting the other end of the overhang against his typical high thin terminal wall.

He never disguised the wall with a stonefacing. "It is not because 'form-follows-function.' Form-follows-function doesn't make good architecture. When I was young I had an argument about this with the architect Gordon Kauffmann. He said it didn't and I objected. He was right. I was young."

I was never sure whether it was the incised rectangular opening to the garden

The Kingsley terrace from the dining area. Greta Davidson, Mrs. Kingsley, and this writer are in the deck chairs on the slope to the lemon grove. Photo: Julius Shulman.

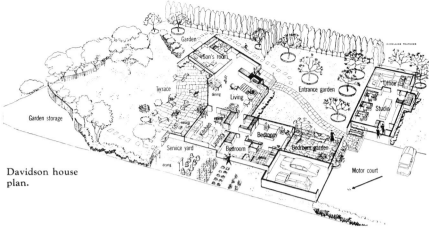

Davidson house plan.

he was unhappy with, or the contrast between that and the amenities of the planting which gave the office the appearance of being the house. However, inside the wall was a long curved path to the front door, passing a grape stake enclosure around Greta's bedroom court. The entrance court was planted as a citrus grove, and a fork off the entrance path led to a private entrance to the son's quarters, which had their own private patio.

Nor had Davidson really liked the solution he arrived at in the entrance hall, but I argued that he could not otherwise have had the conversation corner separated from traffic—an absolute necessity to him. The wall between entrance hall and living room is the reverse side of a fireplace wall which defines the intimate space. As in the Vigeveno house, he angles the living room fifteen degrees, narrowing it down as it reaches the kitchen; the angled wall is

The entrance to Davidson's office. Photo: Julius Shulman.

Davidson house and office, West Los Angeles, 1947. The office is at the right; the door to the entrance court is at the center of the wall. Photo: Julius Shulman.

sliding glass opening to the patio.

I was in this house so often that I know well the way it was used. Of a late afternoon I might take in a visiting architect, and we sat at the conversation end of the living room. In the bookcase-cabinet wall below the west windows (facing the entrance court) was a delightful low cabinet whose door dropped down to form a counter. Here drinks were poured from bottles stored inside, or a pot of coffee was plugged into an outlet in the cabinet. Into a surprisingly small space had been fitted cups, saucers, glasses of various sizes, bottles, cans of nuts and biscuits, a box of sweets—and always the wonder at how it all fitted in! And Greta, seated in a low straw chair by the cabinet, dispensed drinks and laughter. (My husband called her affectionately "The Little Princess.")

There were the formal dinner parties for some visiting notable with ten around the Eames table in molded plywood Eames chairs; there were the buffet cocktail parties during the holidays with a caterer slicing slivers of smoked turkey and ham, the scene enhanced by a Christmas tree on the terrace and candles on the lawn.

The most memorable times were the noon breakfasts on the terrace, sitting on the built-in round-the-corner seat or in canvas chairs at the long table covered with brightly striped Mexican cloth. At one end of the table was the door to the kitchen, and Greta brought on platters of fruit, of scrambled eggs and sausage, and last an almond coffee cake, with J.R. manning the coffee urn plugged into a wall socket. There were always one or two doctors at the breakfast parties, some of the dozen or more who had houses by Davidson, many of them psychiatrists. We would sit over breakfast for two hours, then walk down the garden slope or sit in the lawn chairs and talk. There was still another place to eat, a breakfast table in a corner of the kitchen, facing the terrace.

Food and tact and cheer went with the house, and the planning of a variety of places to eat was an act of thanksgiving. Color was another blessing. It was used so subtly that one was aware of it only when it reached a high pitch, then the eye traced it back through gradations and con-

The Davidson living room. The entrance hall is behind the fireplace wall. Photo: Julius Shulman.

The Davidson terrace. An outdoor dining corner is shaded by an overhang. Photo: Julius Shulman.

trasts to the sources in grayed blues, lemon, or rose.

This was the man who never sought commissions, who could reply when I inquired if he wanted to work for Gropius: "He didn't ask me." But as I think of it now, Gropius was only six years older, and at the end of the First World War may have had less work than Davidson.

I shall never forget sitting with Greta in her bedroom garden, so cut off from the sounds of the house and office, watching a hummingbird sipping honey from the bright flowers of the canary bird bush. Or, after they had moved to Ojai, listening intently as I read aloud to her the last chapter of my book *Vienna to Los Angeles*. She would nod judiciously, "Yes, yes," then stop me at times, "Too gossipy." I would delete the passage and then continue. I had wanted her to hear it because she loved Dione Neutra; yet she had urged me to write it, saying, "The record is getting muddy. You must clean it up."

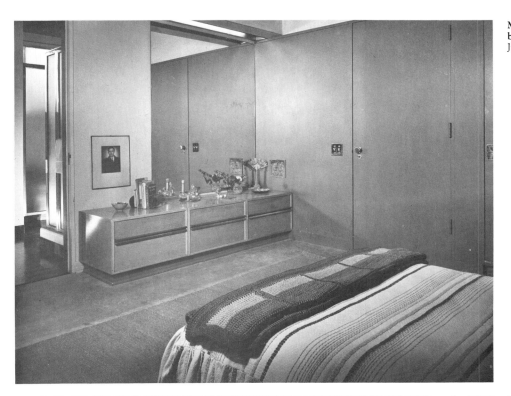

Mrs. Davidson's bedroom. Photo: Julius Shulman.

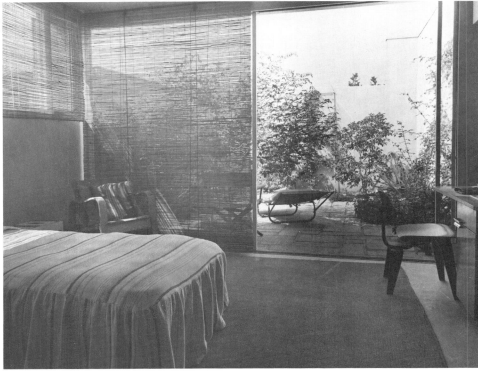

The patio off Mrs. Davidson's bedroom is separated from the entrance court by a grapestake fence. Photo: Julius Shulman.

The house expressed better the simple elegance of European living than any I knew in Southern California. It was not an American way of life in the sense that an Ain or Harwell Harris were. Harris's shells were expansive; Davidson's interiors were. Davidson had grown up in large houses with servants (the children had a governess and a maid); his plans recalled this, sometimes only symbolically.

By the mid-1960s the quiet Barrington Avenue was lined with apartment houses, and ones on both sides of the Davidsons cut off much of their privacy and some of their light. The house was sold to a developer and was destroyed. The last time I saw it Greta was sorting things to discard in her bedroom, a room running through all the subtleties of flesh tones and pink browns, rising here and there to a vibrant Mexican pink.

Then Davidson built a group of four two-story attached apartments not far away, and they moved into one. The eight-foot-high sliding glass on the south looked out on a small, walled garden with bromeliads and tuberous begonias hanging in baskets from a small Chinese elm.

Other houses built by Davidson in the late 1940s were a small one for Floyd Crosby, a cinematographer, enlarged in 1954 for a psychiatrist. With the enlargement, the house made a hinged half circle around a swimming pool. It was one of the houses with the front door around a corner from the street, which Davidson never hesitated to do if it eased the plan; in this case it allowed for an interior court off the psychiatrist's office.

The Sam Taylor house, 1947, resembled the Thomas Mann plan, but it was the children's rooms which were set at an angle to the terrace side of the house rather than the writer's study. The wing is also raised half a level above the terrace, following an upslope on the site. The Madeleine Goss house of 1948, on sixty acres in Duarte, was another two-hinged wall scheme, facing a pool at the foot of a rocky slope.

The Osherenko house, 1949, was a large house for the publisher of a fashion magazine, *The Californian.* During this period Davidson's exteriors were unassertive redwood or plaster skins over a wood frame, the entrances were marked by a wide overhang supported by posts or pipe columns; roofs were almost flat; the front doors were flanked with panels of obscure glass, with light from the interior illuminating the entrance; a terrace on the southeast was partially roofed, with trellis extension; glass areas were usually set either four feet or eighteen inches above the floor, reaching almost to the eight-foot ceiling height, except for room-height sliding glass to terraces. The plan had right-angular projections or angled off at fifteen degrees. Most of the interior walls and ceilings were painted plaster; the floors were rubber tile or carpeted. The cabinetwork was exquisite, and built-ins were innovative, readily lending themselves to excerpting from the whole for publication. A look at published stories on Davidson houses indicates more interest in the terraces than the facades, more interest in details than overall views.

This was at a time when there was a growing emphasis on form. Other 1949 houses were R.M. Schindler's Tischler house, rising restlessly from the street, from heavy garage fascia to off-center heavy pylon which appears to support the living room glass, and *does* support the high dormer; there were the Case Studies of the same year by Charles Eames, with factory glass walls facing a meadow and framed in exposed steel columns; the Eames and Saarinen house for Entenza, with its universal space visible through the glass wall facing the sea, the freestanding sculptural fireplace, so often copied, contrasted sharply with Davidson's simple rectangular openings in the wall, framed only with strips of marble. There was the 1949 Wayfarer's Chapel of Lloyd Wright, with its delicious geometry and its glass set between the roof ribs of wood. There was Craig Ellwood's steel-framed panel house, lifted above the ground on slender steel stilts; there was John Lautner's circular Foster house with a curved wall of horizontal siding.

Davidson's typical usage and atypical details survived the changing sensibility, but in 1951-52 he moved more into the spirit of the day in his Dann house. (The first plans were drawn in 1950.) It is a collage of rectangles and squares on different planes, of different materials and

Dann house, in the hills above Sunset Blvd., Los Angeles County, 1952. Photo: Julius Shulman.

transparency; some are extended, as the brick windbreak wall, and the high cypress rail, a windbreak for the balcony. The scale is lost by the height of the rail and the two-story height of the glass of the entry hall, which conceal the second story floor level. As the rail turns the corner the balcony widens to eight feet, running the length of both bedrooms, and the rail lowers to bring in the panoramic view of the city and sea in the distance. With the small lot dropping sharply on one side, the only outdoor living and garden areas are the balcony and the patio, the latter space held in by a retaining wall. It is a house which the eye encompasses easily, compact and strong in form. Indeed, form was the determinant, not the floor plan, as was so often the case.

There were many changes in the fifties. Davidson began to use post-and-beam construction, and his roofs were pitched. Post-and-beam was popularized during the late forties and the fifties by the USC-Pasadena School—so called because many of its practitioners taught architecture at USC or lived in Pasadena. Theirs was mainly a panel-post system on a four-foot module, panels of solid or transparent materials filling in the spaces between four-by-four posts. Post-and-beam reduced the number, or eliminated altogether, interior bearing walls, and was a more direct approach to achieving a flexible plan than the enclosed truss in the Case Study houses.

He also followed the growing practice of bypassing the plasterer by using exposed two by fours for the ceilings; however, his was not the typical tongue-and-groove decking which had been profiled to conceal the imperfections in the common Douglas fir. Instead Davidson used two by fours with spacers between; his usage and the more typical one were both economy measures, for they allowed the insulation and roofing materials to be applied directly to the surface. At the same time as the development of the new ceiling treatment came the growing use of "dry wall" (prefabricated plaster wall panels). The two together almost eliminated the need for plastering. This was a time as well as cost saving, for the seven-day wait between the coats of plaster added two or three weeks to the construction time of a house.

The post-and-beam construction favored very much the free use of Davidson's gallery plan. The freedom to place walls or half walls where he wanted led him to widen the gallery and use it more intensively for built-ins—desks, cabinets, guest closets, book shelves, settees. The gallery was the key to the circulation, being a passage from the front door to service wing, bedroom wing, and living room. He continued to separate the living room from the gallery by panels of glass above built-in cabinets, and he was faithful to the two-axis living room, which assured the privacy of the conversation corner. Another feature entered his design—fireplaces were bolder and were of stone, often extended to constitute a wall. The hearth was raised and often turned a corner, with the surface used for seating.

His most interesting houses of the fifties were for doctors, three of them psychiatrists and one a psychotherapist. The first of his houses for a psychiatrist was the remodeling and additions to the 1946 Crosby house for Dr. Furniss, already mentioned. The major problem in the plan for a psychiatrist is the separation between entrance and exit for patients, solved in the Furniss house by a small court through which patients exited while entering through a door on the opposite side of the office. But another requirement put additional pressure on the plan, separate quarters for the doctor's parents, with an entrance to the street. The rooms were attached to the main house at an angle to give privacy and a view of the pool. Another addition was a two-bedroom guest house, which completed a half circle of structures around the pool.

A house in 1957 for Dr. Egeberg posed a site problem—a 75-foot frontage with a drop of 80 feet from front setback line to the end of the lot. The shelf at the front was only wide enough for a drive to the garage, so the carport and 3000-square-foot house ride out over the 20- to 30-foot drop, supported on heavy timbers as long as 30 feet from footings to floor level. Rooms lined up single file stretch 66 feet on the entrance level and 44 feet on the lower level for four bedrooms. Continuous cantilevered balconies and an inset dining balcony offer spectacular views. Davidson had wanted steel columns to ease the

The recreation room added to the Hindin house, Los Angeles, 1953, marks the beginning of the turn to post-and-beam construction. Photo: Julius Shulman.

plan but the client preferred to put the money in square footage rather than a more flexible plan in which outdoor spaces cut into the rooms rather than lining them all up on the south. Without access to gardens the house was essentially an apartment in the sky.

The 1957 house in Bel Air for internist Dr. David Rabinowitz is on a canyon rim with 100 feet of fairly level land. Davidson pushed the house forward to save the level space at the back for terrace and open garden. The 2300-square-foot house stretches to the side setbacks, forming a rectangle with two projections; one is the family room, which separates children's play yard from adult's outdoor living.

Davidson had no opportunity to develop the adjacent gallery plan in the Egeberg house but stretched his skill in the Rabinowitz one. It is an extension of the living room, almost a room in itself. The stone fireplace which backs up to it, is flanked by three-foot high cabinets without glass above, thus making the fireplace freestanding and the two spaces interlocking. Along the wide gallery are desk, settee, and the many cabinets and shelves typical of earlier galleries.

On the living room side a nice drama is played out as forms build up from the colorful rubber tile floor to the long wide shelf at hearth level, capped with concrete slab covered with bright pads and cushions,

Addition to the Dr. Munk house, West Los Angeles, 1957-1975. Its new owner added a bedroom reached by a glazed picture gallery. Photo: Marvin Rand.

to the fireplace of Palos Verdes stone, then on up to the finely proportioned white plaster hood. The hood folds over at the top to continue as a skylight, the hood and skylight so alike in dimensions that one seems a reflection of the other. Indeed, as the south sun enters through the skylight, throwing shadows of glazing bars on the white surface, the hood is something of a sundial whose shadows tell the time.

The post-and-beam construction with posts at intervals of 9 feet in one direction and 21 feet in the other allows many half walls; a freestanding cabinet separates the living room from the kitchen, with book shelves and small bar on the living room side, and on the reverse it forms a passage from carport entrance through the end of the kitchen to the family room. Over all the spaces floats a ceiling of two by fours with spacers between, visible from any of the social rooms as a continuous textured surface.

It took a little doing to bring the program and site into equilibrium in the Margit Munk house in West Los Angeles. The long, narrow lot stretched along a canyon on the east, and the best place for a living room terrace was near the front of the lot. Mrs. Munk, a psychotherapist, wanted her office semidetached from the house, so the trellised entry garden near the end of the lot split the office from the house. Another of Davidson's long treks to the front door! On the way one passed the high windows of the living room and a fenced service court off the kitchen.

One result of this scheme was a living room tapering on the canyon side from 25 feet to 16 feet; sliding glass opened to a terrace, with steps down the canyon side. The house, finished in 1957, was sold to a screenwriter in 1975, and Davidson was asked to enlarge it by 1000 square feet.

Next to psychoanalysts' requirements of sound-controlled offices set apart from the rest of the house, the writer working at home runs a close second as a destroyer of a neat floor plan. Add to this Davidson's insistence on terrace or patio on the east, northeast, or southeast. If the Munk plan was odd the one for Mark Justman, the screenwriter had few contemporary precedents outside of Charles Moore's antic

plans. But both the Munk and Justman exterior might have profited from Moore's virtuosity. Davidson had spent too many months of 1920 and 1921 drawing capitaled and fluted columns out of hunger not to see a bare unchamfered four-by-four post as a blessing.

The Justmans departed from the Davidson typical living room arrangement of built-in sofa at a corner, with a circle of chairs light in weight and color, with flashes of vivid color; instead there are two heavy Tobia Scarpa sofas of dark leather and matching chairs in the middle of the room. Very strange indeed to see the center of gravity of a Davidson living room shift to the middle.

The new master bedroom and balcony are lifted above the slope, and to reach the bedroom from the living room Davidson used a 22-foot-long glazed picture gallery 6 feet wide. An innovation arising out of necessity, it has the baroque character of many of his staircases. Paintings on the far wall of the gallery are visible from the living room through the glazed wall. It is the most successful part of the addition. Davidson had opposed Justman's wish to have south light in the bedroom, and the gallery was a compromise. He wrote Justman after it was completed: "The final acceptance of the southern silhouette of the addition gives my mind repose—but not as a winner of a competition."

The 1958 house for the psychiatrist Dr. Robert Johannes Jokl has a plan somewhat like a Juan Miró floating shape. Although the large almost level lot, which backs up against hills, gave Davidson more scope, it presented the problem of an open storm drain cutting the lot in two. No enclosed structure was permitted over the drain so a simple bridge of planking is access to the garage, and a lightly railed footbridge leads to the covered walk to the front door. This redundancy of two bridges close together has the effect of slowing the approach to the house; Davidson spurned such artificial time pauses in the approach to a house unless forced on him by the site.

The office wing, angled off the front of the house, consists of a guest room and a study which opens to a patio with a translucent fence. At the cross bar of the approximate **H** plan is the living room, tapering from twenty to sixteen feet in length, and from twenty to twelve in width, the total space uninterrupted by supports. The openness was possible by the post-and-beam construction on a modular grid of eight by twenty feet. The grooved roof decking of two by fours is of the more common but stronger Douglas fir, the changes of direction of the beams and decking reflecting the odd shape of the living room.

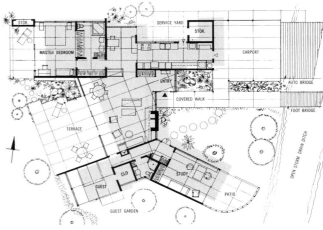

The Jokl house plan assumes an **H** shape to accomodate the many functions. A trapezoidal living room stretches between the end verticals.

Jokl house. Viewed from the motor court are the foot and motor bridges across the storm drain. Photo: Marvin Rand.

The beams continue out to the recessed patio off the living room, these supporting a bamboo screening to cut the west sun. A most complex house whose exterior suggests none of the intricacy.

The last of seven houses over the years for a psychiatrist was the 1957-59 Dr. Hannah Fenichel house in Brentwood, a three-level house on a downslope on a site dropping in slow stages some 25 feet, with an additional drop of 8 feet to a swimming pool. In the the street level of the 3500-square-foot house are only a master bedroom and entry. A slow ramp leads down to the middle level small sitting room, large kitchen, and dining balcony over the double volume living room. The ramp and stairs on the canyon side are glazed, giving a fine view of the canyon.

The house had two later owners, both families with children, and Davidson was called in to fit other bedrooms into the unusual organization of the plan. But the two most interesting features of the house were preserved, the glazed stair and ramp, and the strongly vertical living room opening to a many-sided deck overlooking pool and terrace.

In 1965 the Davidsons's own special way of life continued in one of the townhouses he built in Brentwood. In their 40 years of marriage they had lived together in perhaps two dozen different houses or apartments in five cities, only two of which Davidson had designed entirely to suit themselves—not the case in the townhouse, for the four 1000-square-foot units back to back on a small lot had to please three renters as well as himself. It had been a blow when they sold their apartment in Berlin, but the loss was greater when they were crowded out of their Barrington Avenue house. They had suffered through two wars, disastrous inflation, the Great Depression—and now the destruction of the house they loved.

They stayed six years at the townhouse, then after an operation Greta lost sight in one eye and had limited vision in the other. They moved to a small house in Ojai near their son and his family. They were both 82. It was their last move.

I visited them in Ojai several times. Once Davidson said sadly that he had never had an opportunity to design a house on an unlimited budget.

The Fenichel and the Osherenko houses were as close as he would come, and neither was his best work. Both lacked the simplicity and friendliness of his most successful houses, the Fenichel house suffering because it was for one person only, its small sitting room used mainly as a television room, its large living room reserved for large gatherings – something of a showplace. The virtuosity of the Osherenko house may have been its undoing. Davidson could resist ostentation but not the problem of designing novel storage spaces, or special lighting, or a new kind of half wall. In the Osherenko master bedroom were bedside tables with every manner of electrical gadget; the head of the bed was a long panel with storage cabinets and drawers on the reverse side – the cabinets forming a doorless passage to the bathroom.

He had done other adventurous built-ins, in the Beverly Hills house the Italian architect Leonardo Ricci designed for his brother, with Davidson commissioned to do the working drawings and built-ins. Sometimes Davidson had not restrained the client, as in a remodel of a house for the writer Irving Stone; Davidson's well-detailed small bar was blown up to a size that killed it. He was delighted when Stone was quoted as saying he had designed it.

But he usually had his way. Or there was a compromise he could live with. In a letter to a client in the 1960s he gave several examples "out of my 65 years of experience" when the clients' wishes prevailed and ending, "I still experience regret when I give in."

Once in Ojai when I mentioned the disparity between the exteriors and interiors of his houses, and he replied impatiently, "The outside is masculine, but at the heart of the house is the kitchen and boudoir. They are feminine."

The Jokl house
living room looking
toward the breakfast
room and the
kitchen. Photo:
Leland Y. Lee.

But also feminine was the proximity into which he brought people, the tight warm areas with cool intervals between. This, I thought, came from Greta's habit of touching her friends lovingly—pressing a hand and holding it for some moments, touching some clever detail of the dress worn by a friend. ("She sees with her hands," my husband had said.)

There was still work to do in Ojai—the remodeling of the Munk house, two remodelings of the Fenichel house, and many small jobs for old clients.

He had said once, "You have to work harder than you ever think you can when you are young just to keep even." He did not stop until he was 88. Sitting one day in the living room answering a letter from an old client he called out to Greta in another room, "What was his wife's name?" When she came in several minutes later he was dead.

Harwell Hamilton
Harris, 1903- . Photo:
Robert Imandt.

Harwell Hamilton Harris

Harwell Harris was pure Californian. His paternal grandfather, Benjamin Butler Harris, arrived in California in 1849[1] and after several months mining gold, opened his law office in Mariposa. His maternal grandfather, Joseph Hamilton, a colonel in General Longstreet's division, settled in California at the end of the Civil War. His mother, born in Orange County, spent most of her girlhood in a house on a homesteaded quarter section between Vermont and Hoover, and Adams and Exposition, bordering the USC campus. His father, Frederick Thomas Harris, could recall the early days in San Bernardino when the twenty-mule team came through.

His Uncle Harper owned a parcel bordering Sunset and including Laurel Canyon, which had two springs to provide water for his orange grove. Frank Lloyd Wright later built the Storer house on the orchard site.

Harwell was born in a town hardly twenty years older than himself—Redlands, started by a water company, settled mainly by easterners of means, and given stability and a cultural and aesthetic purpose by the Brothers Smiley who, as they bought up land, founded institutions. They built the first public library in 1898, a Richardsonian Romanesque building with turns of plan to delight a child, and many touches of courtesy; they established Redlands College, and built an amphitheater for outdoor concerts. Smiley Heights was a horticulturist's delight with its thousand different species of trees and shrubs.

The region was the inland desert, the fertile soil a decomposed granite that with the coming of water blossomed into the Citrus Belt. Redlands, and San Bernardino where Harwell attended high school, were the packing and shipping centers. They were part of the chain of cities of the plain, hemmed in on the north by the San Bernardino Mountains, on the south by the San Jacintos. The plains were dotted with hot springs which brought winter visitors in search of health; as they stepped down from the Pullmans of the early morning Santa Fe bound for Los Angeles, dry, still air was alive with the perfume of orange blossoms.

". . . neither town nor country, neither rural nor urban, it is a world of its own," wrote Carey McWilliams of the Citrus Belt.

Harris was 40 in 1943 when he left California for the first time. He went to New York, where he was deeply impressed by Rockefeller Center—a kind of project which fitted his ideal of "a rich program full of complexity." By 1980, Harris regretted most in his career the abandonment of a commission to develop a tourist center on a Malaysian island, a problem so fresh and complicated that it stretched his talent.

"When you are young," he said, "you want the permissive client. When you are older, you want complexity. It forces you back on your originality."

His father (Frederick Thomas) was an architect, born in 1875 in San Bernardino, a town laid out in 1852 by the Mormons after buying the 37,000-acre Lugo land grant with the intention of establishing a way station between Salt Lake City and the Pacific. They were gone less than a decade later but their legacy was wide

1. *The account of his trip west,* The Gila Trail, *was published by the University of Oklahoma Press in 1960.*

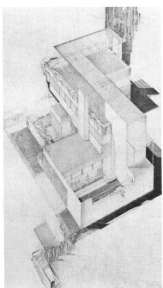

Harwell H. Harris.
Project for a house
while a Neutra
student, 1928.

**Fellowship Park
house, Los Angeles,
1935.** By 1935, all
traces of the heavy
masonry forms of the
International style
had faded in the
lightweight Japanese
pavilion with modular
sliding screens and
exposed wood
framing. Photo: Fred
Dapprich.

Harris favored a plan in which one arm commanded a view, as in his famous inverted gable house for **Havens, Berkeley, 1941.** The deck, rising twenty feet above the slope, faces the most cherished views of the Bay Region. "More sky house than earth house," the architect called it. Photo: Man Ray.

streets on a square grid precisely ⅛ of a mile apart. The legibility of the grid, with its numerical and alphabetical streets, Harris said, "predetermined my affinity to the unit system of design."

Fred Harris had a love of ranching, and before he was twenty had sown and harvested crops on his own stubborn piece of land in a canyon. The profession of architecture served later to support his various ranches. His Wesleyan spirit engaged in holy battle to make bloom the sorriest of soil. Architecture was easier, ranching more adventuresome.

Fred Harris's architectural training was in a large office in Los Angeles which designed in Americanized English Renaissance, Richardsonian Romanesque, and Mission Revival styles. The office was still in existence in 1934 when his son, aged 31, designed his first house.

Harwell's mother, born May Julia Hamilton, was a graduate of the State Normal School (on the site of Goodhue's Central Library); before her marriage she drove each morning by horse and buggy the six miles to the little schoolhouse in the community of Watts, where she taught all four grades. Once part of the Dominguez landholdings, there was always a Dominguez child in each of her classes during her six years of teaching.

Los Angeles at the turn of the century had many established architects; younger ones looked for expanding communities in which to develop a practice, often moving on to a new community after satisfying the more pressing need for public buildings. Fred Harris had a further need to satisfy, that of ranching. "In the desert side of Los Angeles," Harwell said, "ranching was a habit."

The growing demand for citrus fruit in the east was reflected in the expansion of fruit packing and shipping in Redlands, where Fred Harris opened his first office in 1900 – about ten miles from his birthplace. Among his early commissions was the First National Bank Building where he had his office. The style was what Harwell called "traditional business block."

Redlands had begun to enjoy national importance because it was the setting of some of the popular novels of Harold Bell Wright, pastor of the First Christian

Church, and one of Fred Harris's commissions was for a Mission Revival mansion for W.F. Holt, "Father of Imperial Valley," who was a character in the novel, *The Winning of Barbara Worth*.

When Harwell was born on July 2, 1903, the Harrises lived in a frame house whose furnishings were typical of their station: the upright piano with selections from *The Bohemian Girl* and *Lohengrin* on the music rack, a leather-bound copy of *Pippa Passes* lay on the stencilled runner on the library table, the lamp was Craftsman, the vase Art Nouveau. Beside the usual Morris chair was a backless curved Roman chair on which no one ever sat. On the wall was the Sistine Madonna and a portrait of Richard Wagner.

The books on the shelves that interested Harwell were *A Museum of Antiquities*, which he usually opened to the "Ruins of Pompeii," reproductions of the drawings of Charles Dana Gibson, which he copied, and *Around the World with a Camera*, with illustrations of European cities.

Many of the schools he attended in his earlier years had been designed by his father, but his knowledge of architecture extended no further than visits to the building sites with him to hold the horse while his father went on a tour of inspection. This ended in 1911 when they bought a Studebaker.

Harwell was more interested in reading than in buildings. The "passion and romance" of architecture touched him first through reading Louis Sullivan many years later. But he was aware of houses: he felt "more comfortable" with bungalows than Gothic revival houses. He did not think of bungalows as architecture, and was grown before he heard the names of Greene and Greene. He was vaguely aware of the rightness of certain indigenous building practices, and the concessions structures made to climate would one day find their way into his style. He had grown accustomed to the long line of eucalyptus used as a windbreak for citrus groves, and later he used tree-lined drives for a house in an orange grove, a fig orchard, and would eventually build houses in almond, pecan, olive, and avocado groves.

He knew his father first in the role of rancher. They spent summers in a large apple orchard near Beaumont, living in a portable house, and in 1911 when his father moved his office to El Centro, they lived year round on a ranch two miles from town. In an area below sea level, in temperatures going as high as 125 degrees in the summer, his father directed the Fresno scrapers, leveling the 160 acres of sandhills. The water for the corn and alfalfa they planted came by canal from the Colorado River.

El Centro was laid out by W.F. Holt of Redlands, and in 1911 it was just emerging from the primitive frontier settlement. Holt had brought Fred Harris in to design a block of store fronts, some office buildings, and a small opera house; later Harris designed a high school and the elementary school Harwell attended. The family stayed four years, then war was declared, and as Fred Harris's work fell off rapidly, they moved to San Bernardino.

The move was propitious for Harwell, who was just entering high school. He discovered a friend who had read as widely as he. His English teacher, a classmate of his aunt at Stanford, turned the students' ambitions toward becoming writers. His history teacher was a retired college professor whose belief "that history embraced everything man had ever done or thought" created an intellectual excitement new to Harwell. He was introduced to the theory of natural selection; he learned how the legal system worked by sitting through a trial in the local courts the first summer.

At eighteen he entered Pomona College, which was dull compared to his high school classes. He had learned, however, to direct his own education, and he found his way to Ibsen and Shaw and Whitman.

"Shaw freed me from many conventional ideas," he said, adding that the end of the war revealed "a whole new world of thought and expression in the act of being born—in poetry, painting, sculpture, music, mathematics, psychology."

His father died while he was at Pomona and his mother moved to her sister's in Los Angeles; Harris decided to spend a year there in art school. The new director of Otis Art Institute was Karl Howenstein, just arrived from Chicago. With him, Harris was again in the presence of a man whose real interest was ideas. In the

Howenstein house, there was talk of Jung's theory of the collective unconscious as a resource of the artist, of the theory back of nonrepresentative art, of Clive Bell's "significant form."

He began to model in clay. "I built my forms with small bits of clay rolled between my fingers, adding one pellet at a time to a piece of sculpture. It enabled me to look ahead and keep the form in mind. It invited form to suggest itself and, seemingly, to realize itself. This anticipated the procedure I later followed with architectural form. The unit or module replaced the clay pellet as my building element, and through it I could feel my way into architectural forms and inhabit them. I could lead them or be led by them. . . ."

He found in Los Angeles the intellectual stimulation lacking in Pomona. New theater groups were springing up. At the Potboilers' Club were productions of *Emperor Jones, RUR,* and *The Adding Machine.* With the wife of a visiting philosophy professor from the University of London (H.W. Carr), he saw Pirandello plays at the Pasadena Playhouse. In Mrs. Carr he met for the first time someone who had known personally one of his idols. She had met Bernard Shaw at age sixteen in the British Museum – and now Harris held a Christmas card to her written in Shaw's own hand!

He enrolled in a Saturday painting class at the Art Students League on Second and Spring Streets. The class was taught by S. Macdonald-Wright, one of the first American painters to work in abstract images; he had been a founder of the Synchromists Group in Paris, and his work was hung in the 1913 Armory Show.

Some of the theories of the Synchromists were useful in architecture – familiarity with the major and minor scales of color harmony helped in creating mood or in making forms advance or retreat. The Modernists in architecture were chary of color but Harris was never afraid of it. J.R. Davidson used color mainly in planes, but Harris also attenuated the plane into line. In the Hawk house (1939) it was a gold line suggesting a cornice beneath the hipped ceiling. Harris's palette was subtle and sophisticated. In the Laing house (1935) he overcame the reluctance of the clients

against stucco walls of pink-tan, eggplant colored floor coverings, and vermillion trim around the windows.

His turn from sculpture to architecture came slowly. One day in 1924, he found Karl Howenstein in his office writing a letter to an architectural journal about the death of Louis Sullivan. Howenstein talked to him about his year in Sullivan's office. When Sullivan's *Autobiography of an Idea* appeared months later, Harris was fascinated by the personality of the architect. But at the time he had just discovered Maillol and Brancusi, and was finding his way into ancient Chinese sculpture. He was encouraged when a portrait head of his was exhibited in a group show at the San Diego Museum. Any thought of returning to Pomona College had faded. His mind was on the universality of form – form "on a truly grand scale in Spengler, form in Beethoven's Ninth Symphony, the formless form in *Leaves of Grass.*"

A positive step toward architecture came when a fellow student of sculpture, Ruth Sowden, told him she and her husband were building a house designed by Lloyd Wright. She was surprised that Harris did not know the names of Frank Lloyd Wright or his son Lloyd, and she advised him to see Hollyhock House on Olive Hill.

He was stunned when he saw it. His eye and spirit and intelligence moved around and through the forms of the house as if he were seeing into a stone he was carving. The house spoke to the sculptor in him.

"Hollyhock House seemed born, not made. With this experience I realized what architecture could be. Gradually I realized that Hollyhock House was born in the mind of a man, and whatever else that man might be he was an architect."

The experience was unsettling. This new evidence lay in his mind for weeks as he continued sculpture. But he was not the same. He found a copy of Wright's 1911 Wasmuth Portfolio in the Los Angeles Public Library. Like dozens of others in many parts of the world he became a disciple. There was no decision to make. The house and portfolio of drawings had made it for him.

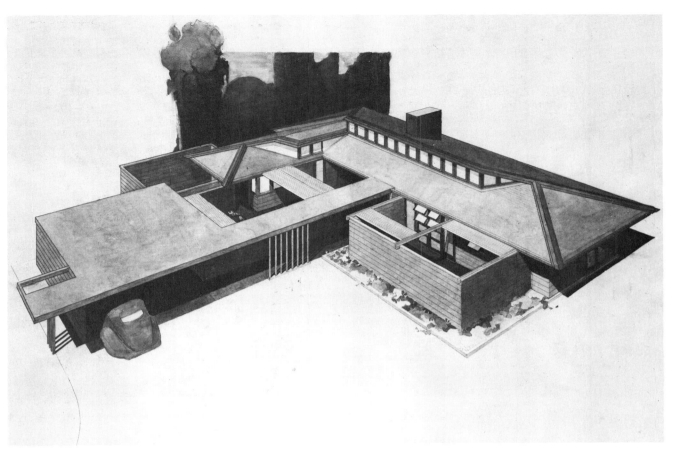

The 1942 model Solar House for Libbey-Owens-Ford controlled the sun by reflecting it, filtering it, and intercepting it, one device a hinged fin which rotated with the sun to prolong the shade.

He applied for admission to the School of Architecture at Berkeley and was accepted for the fall of 1928. He had certain doubts as he considered his age—25; at 25 Sullivan had been made a full partner with Dankmar Adler!

In the meantime a Japanese student at Otis told him about an apartment house of concrete and glass then under construction on Marathon Avenue. It was altogether different from Wright's hollowed-out volumes on Olive Hill, but just as different from any other apartment house he had ever seen. Both were in revolt against tradition.

He noted the architects' address on the sign and went to the office on Kings Road of Schindler and Neutra.

Harris has written the story of that first visit to the house of R.M. Schindler, a moving account of the interrelationship of house and architect, and the new way life

was lived inside it. "If any building can fire one with the passion for simple living and high thinking, this is it," he wrote.

The world of architecture seemed smaller and closer at hand when he learned that Schindler had worked four years for Wright, and Neutra, who shared Schindler's drafting room, had known Wright at Taliesin.

Harris told Neutra that he was entering architecture school in the fall, but Neutra proposed that he study engineering at night school and work for him during the day, assuring him that he would learn more than at a school that taught the Beaux Arts system.

Harris started at once. On a drafting board resting on a trunk he began drawing details of the Lovell house, ready to rise on a steep lot on Dundee Drive near Griffith Park. This unique steel-framed house supplemented well the engineering

courses he was taking at Frank Wiggins Trade School.

Neutra's lecture series at the Academy of Modern Art, "A Practical Course in Modern Building," brought other apprentices, one of them Gregory Ain. They worked on Neutra projects in the house in Hollywood where F.K. Ferenz had established his academy. The projects were Rush City Reformed, Ring Plan School Project, Lehigh Portland Cement competition for an airport, and CIAM projects.

Neutra had proposed that they form a chapter of CIAM (Congrès International d'Architecture Moderne) with Harris as secretary and himself as delegate to the third congress, to be held in Brussels late in 1930. The subject of the congress was Rational Planning.

Harris said that he learned more on these projects than he could have on working drawings. "Of all the lessons I learned from Neutra, integration was the most important. How one thing calls for another, how one thing excludes another, how two things produce another. . . how a design becomes alive and unique once it is part of a real world; how as part of the real world it grows and develops, becoming a natural rather than an arbitrary thing." He added that he and Ain had learned in a few weeks what would have taken years if left on their own.

After Neutra's departure, Harris became an instructor at the newly formed Los Angeles College of Architecture and Engineering, started by one of the professors at Wiggins Trade School, M.T. Cantell, an English architect. Harris followed Neutra's methods of teaching, and the buildings the class designed were similar to the CIAM projects. When Harris found a client, the duplex he designed for him (never built) was steel framed.

Steel was his tribute to his teacher. It was his tribute to revolt. He would remain a Modern, but he soon learned (as did all the Moderns during the 1930s) that steel and concrete were not the sole criteria.

He had known from the first that the Moderns in Los Angeles worked in isolation, were held in contempt by the School of Architecture at USC. Their contact with students was only through schools they themselves set up. Neutra was content to teach history at such a school. The small band of Moderns was fortunate in having *California Arts & Architecture* in which to publish its buildings. But an issue devoted to California Modern (January 1935) met criticism in the East as well.

H. Van Buren Magonigle, D. Arch., FAIA, writing in *Pencil Points* (March 1935), dismissed the movement in California as "a flurry." Modern houses, he wrote, looked alike wherever they were built, and nothing about them suggested a home. "They do not seem to be built for real people leading real lives." He characterized Neutra's interiors as "gas pipery," and tarred with guilt by association the two FAIAs on the Board of Advisors of *California Arts & Architecture* — "Though it is none of my business I can't help wondering what such men are doing in that *galère*."

When Harris's staunchly Modern design for a second client ran into trouble with financing, he took the plans back to Neutra, who had signed them originally, because a licensed architect's signiture was required. Neutra suggested they collaborate, but the project fell through. Harris found a third client, and this time he kept him to himself. His first study for the house had a tubular steel frame, and walls and roof were of three-foot "bubble stone" panels reinforced with steel lath. When the loan was denied, Harris first changed the material to stressed plywood sandwich panels, then to redwood siding over a wood frame. The flat roof became hipped. He ceased being the student and became the architect. The rebuff from the bank had thrown him on his own resources, and he brought into play all he had stored in his eye and mind of houses for hot climates. In doing this, he arrived at a style uniquely his own.

To Harris's surprise, the house received unusual attention. The 25-year old who had worried about entering architecture too late had, at 31 distinguished himself.

Harris's art represented a consciousness at once purely American and western. Except for his late work in North Carolina, and the few small works in the East, the body of it was in California and Texas, the new ground which had developed free of the Colonialism of the East.

It helped to have grown up outside a major city in the West (as had William Wilson Wurster) for he was in the habit of finding his own way among ideas. Like many an easy-mannered provincial, he was the soul of revolt.

But he could be sly. He disguised a roof so there was barely a trace left of the plan below it. When he was denied a flat roof, he covered an **L**-shaped plan with a rectangular roof composed of three hips cunningly joined.

He could take a square plan and revolve the roof 45 degrees, then clip off the edges of the hips on four sides to turn the roof into a gable and make the hip a ridge. Beware of reading his plans from the roof!

He could take an almost square room and use every trick, including an implied aisle down the center, to turn it into a long narrow space.

He could interrupt the slope of a shed

roof to flip down two panels in the ceiling to form a symbolic halo over a library at the end of the room. It was really a little gable; it was really like a little echo of the exterior gables—like the word *lilac* in Whitman's cortege-slow tribute to Lincoln beginning, "When lilacs last in the dooryard bloom'd," which echoed in that purest of dissonant lines: "But mostly and now the lilac that blooms the first."

He could let a clerestory meander over a roof and then design patterns of ribs on the roof to combine high and low relief.

He could distract the eye from the altar

in a chapel by placing the gable ends on the side, then dissolve them into screens.

"By doing the most natural thing you do the most revolutionary," he said once. But natural to him was often like pulling forward a submerged theme and letting it dominate the carefully orchestrated whole.

One of his draftsmen recalled: "He wasn't a man to whom you would lightly offer a clever solution. He could lead you through the whole process of his reasoning. He knew exactly why he did everything."

Harris's houses of stucco owed more to Wright than those of wood, but the **1935 De Steiguer house, Pasadena,** was his sole tribute to Wright's Prairie style. Photo: Fred Dapprich.

43

Harris's first house was in 1934. The cost was $3720. The client was a buyer of women's dresses at Bullocks Wilshire.

These facts are worth considering because they tell something about the economy of the early 1930s. The great number of bank failures in the country had prompted President Roosevelt to declare a bank holiday when he took office, and although this gave confidence to a frightened nation, as well as stabilizing banking, it did not turn the economy around. The ensuing social legislation put millions of unemployed who lived without hope into "made" work, thus preventing ruin, perhaps rebellion.[2]

The 1934 money could buy much more than in 1929, the year of the market crash. The shift in fortunes created a new moneyed group, and for the first time architecture was available to it—not least of all because architecture came down from its high horse to meet it.

These were the shifting realities when Harris designed the Lowe house in Altadena. (His associate was furniture designer Carl Anderson.)

"I doubted that I would ever again design another building," Harris wrote. "This would be my first and last executed project. I went about its design with a solemn resolve: it must be a summation of all I have ever thought or felt about life and architecture."

The brave new material he called for had little appeal for the bank, snowed under with foreclosed houses, and worried about the resale value of experimental ones if the borrower's payments lapsed.

The "bubble stone" was a material Maybeck had adapted from an invention by a J.A. Rice for a cottage: burlap impregnated with a mixture of cement and a foaming agent was attached to the frame. No, said the bank. And no to the subsequent proposal: plywood panels cored with aluminum foil membrane—the foil, used

Lowe house, Altadena, 1934. From the living room looking toward the dining alcove. (Assoc. Carl Anderson). Photo: Fred Dapprich.

in Neutra's research house, was a development of Frigidaire for insulation of refrigerators. And no to the flat roof.

Harris said that the choice of the twelve-inch redwood siding was the client's, the choice of the roof was the loan company's, the circulation owed something to Wright, and the fenestration owed something to the Japanese. The **L**-shaped floor plan was his.

The entrance, deeply recessed, was reached from a path past the carport, and between the carport and front door was a fifteen-by-fifteen-foot roof opening lighting the entrance garden. The recessed entrance, incidentally, was used effectively in Eric Mendelsohn's Gleiwick house on which Neutra had worked, and Neutra, Harris, and Ain found it a useful way to enter a house when the living room was oriented to a patio at the rear or to a view. The blank wall of the bedroom wing flanked the entrance walk, and high strip windows lighted the bath and dressing room.

The two bedrooms were given individual patios by projecting one of the bathrooms to divide the garden space. The glass walls of the bedrooms slid back so beds could be pushed into the open on

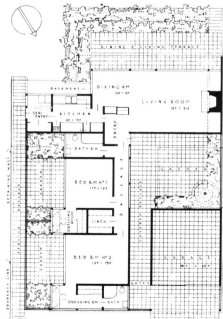

Lowe house plan.

2. Some of the made work saved many historic buildings that were falling into ruin, and the establishment in 1933 of Historic American Buildings Survey by the Department of the Interior served to document them with measured drawings, photographs, record of structural changes, and chain of ownership. HABS in its 50 years of existence has been in the forefront in the preservation of our national treasures.

the hot summer nights in Altadena.

The living room established procedures which were to be almost constant in Harris's California work – a cornice line above standard six-feet-eight-inch doors, concealing curtain track, and the sixteen-inch strip above treated as part of the hipped ceiling by covering it with the same fiber panel. The module then and ever after was three feet. Although he constantly cut away at the cost, one thing he could not give up was the boxed-in soffits, which continued the ceiling line out to the edge of the overhang.

The broken rhythm of the fenestration and change in character of the light are unique to this house: three-foot sliding glass to the view terrace, and three-foot translucent screens in the dining end of the living room. The doors are divided by horizontal bars, the bottom quarter a solid kick plate, the divisions above of clear glass. The translucent screens are of cloth used in greenhouses, and the wood muntins are attached to the cloth by a mixture of beeswax and resin. These were made on the job by ironing hot wax onto the fabric.

When the house was published in *California Arts & Architecture*, the photographs were accompanied by his essay, "In Designing the Small House." Basic to the design were: rooms should not be halls; and traffic lanes should be set off from quiet bays. Don't crowd too many activities into a room in the belief that this saves space. Group the openings so solid wall and window wall give scale to a room, and plan walls in scale with the openings. Create the feeling of space by opening one room into another. Make one wall of a room glass facing a garden. Keep the same finishes and floor coverings throughout. Keep the furniture line low and the pieces movable.

When the house received an honorable mention in the annual *House Beautiful* competition, Harris allowed himself to hope that his life as an architectural designer had been extended a year or two. But no new client appeared so he looked for a job as a draftsman; when this failed, a call came from the head of the economics department at California Institute of Technology.

Professor Laing had a small up-sloping lot in Pasadena, and he wanted a house with a living room large enough to accommodate 25 or 30 seminar students, wall space in the room for 150 feet of book shelves, dining room space to handle large, informal buffet suppers, all rooms with glass to the south for sun and the north for a view of the mountains, a garage with space for a woodworking shop. The budget for this was $5000. Professor Laing expected to make his own furniture in the workshop.

This reprieve promised to be more complex than his seven points for the good small house.

He used stucco to save money, and this automatically brought him closer to Wright. The two large stucco fins at the front, one screening the deck off the living room from the street, the other the stairs to the front door, were framed with wide bands, a Wrightian touch.

The budget gave out before landscaping, and as the house needed the accents of plants, and the slope was in danger of slipping, Harris managed to get the great authority on native plants, Theodore Paine, as a consultant. Paine chose eucalyptus citriodora, ceanothus, natal plum, and oleander, with evergreen grape as a ground cover. The total cost, including his fee, was $25.

In the meantime, Pauline Lowe had asked Harris to replace the sliding glass in her living room with hinged doors, and he stored the ones he removed on land he had bought on Fellowship Parkway above Griffith Park. A misnomer, the parkway was only a five-foot lane rising steeply from a dead-end street. The land was once a private park, with picnic grounds in a dell, and a sign "Audubon Society" hanging from a tree branch. There were small tent houses and prefabricated houses in the park, dating from 1917, and on his own five small lots was a disintegrating portable house. It reminded him of the portable house in the apple orchard in Beaumont.

Before the winter rains, Harris went up to look at the glass panels and saw they would have to be used soon; then he examined the portable house and estimated that there were enough usable posts to frame in the sliding panels. He was less concerned at the time about how the structure would be used than in salvaging the material. "Maybe a place to go and sit," he said.

Thus began a small house which caught

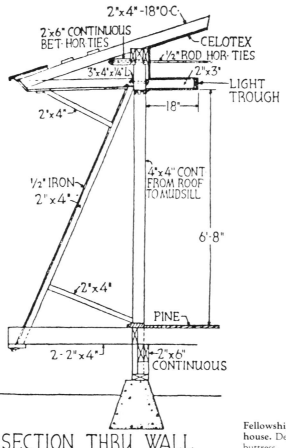

SECTION THRU WALL

the imagination of a generation of architects.

The site for the 12-by-24-foot pavilion was a long, narrow shelf of sandstone below a seven-foot bank, dropping off sharply eighteen feet on one side. There were several live oaks, and the leaves they had dropped for many years left a fine mulch in which ferns and moss and ivy grew. He did not excavate or step the house up with the slope; he lifted a platform above the contours. The four-by-four posts extended from the footings to the eave line, and he inserted two panels in the six-foot openings between the posts—they were set in place so they could be easily removed. He was several panels short of filling in all the openings, so he made the southeast corner solid.

Below the floor line the posts varied three feet in height; the highest corner,

Fellowship Park house. Detail of a buttress.

Fellowship Park house. The living room panels snap out to make an open pavilion. Photo: Fred Dapprich.

on the view side, toward the west, was shaded by a live oak.

For horizontal stability, Harris doubled the floor joists at each post and cantilevered them three feet as outriggers to receive a wood brace which acted as a buttress. Paired with each brace was a ½-inch steel rod so the brace could act in tension as well as compression. The six lightweight buttresses were a handsome decorative feature.

Harris's roof and ceiling were hipped, the hip line leveling off at the soffit; the wide boards of the soffit were spaced to vent the roof. A lesser architect might have mitred the corners, but Harris butted the soffit boards to give a play of planes.

When the construction was underway, Harris liked what was happening and decided it would be a good place to live; he added two bays to accommodate kitchen, bath, and dressing alcove. The total area was still under 500 square feet. The total cost of material, beyond the panels and salvaged wood, was $430. Plumbing and electrical brought it up to $2430.

The building was almost finished when Harris's attention was called to the $2500 grand prize winner for the General Electric small house competition; Schweikher and Lamb of Chicago had won with a plan almost identical to Harris's Lowe house. George Oyer, editor of California Arts & Architecture, published the plans side by side and editorialized on the plagiarizing of a plan for competition purposes.

Pauline Schindler, writing in *Aperitif* (Vol. 1, No. 6, 1935) quoted a dozen instances of Schweikher and Lamb's cribbing from Harris's essay, "In Designing the Small House," for their official text. Her comment: "There is no law against the theft of an architectural idea. Once it is published it becomes social property, and this is well. But to sell again such social property as a fresh creation opens an ethical question."

The *Architectural Forum* published the two plans with a letter from Schweikher and Lamb. They credited as the sources of their design Mies van der Rohe, Frank Lloyd Wright, J.J.P. Oud, Andre Lurçat, and "untold others," adding, "The history of architecture is in itself part of the bibliography."

The editor of the *Forum* invited Harris to send in recent work. This had a promising sound to an architect who had put off installing the plumbing fixtures in the Fellowship Park house because of cost—he also had to move them himself by wheelbarrow from the street and up fifteen steps. The photographer who had done Harris's two previous houses offered to work on contingency: no fee unless the house won an award.

Harris had learned from Neutra the principles of architectural photography, as well as the importance it played in publication. Harris followed Neutra's habit of going with the photographer to direct the shots. (It was because of the emphasis on architectural features that Southern California developed early, high-quality architectural photography.) The photographs of the Fellowship Park house are some of the most remarkable ever made.

Harris had removed the panels between the posts for photography, and where the floor fell off into space, he placed a large ginger pot that had belonged to his grandmother. The rush matting on the floor, woven in squares, suggested the modular base of the scheme; this, and the shoji-like panels, and the light through the bamboo screen hanging from the edge of the eave, added to the Japanese character. But it was the exclusion from the room of everything that did not reinforce the calmness that was unique.

So it was that early in his career Harris was more often linked to Japan, which he had not visited, than to Wright or Neutra. But in California, a closeness to the Orient had existed since Commodore Perry opened Japan to foreign trade; and products of Japan were sold in shops—bamboo furniture, screens, shoji panels.

In accepting the Fellowship Park house for publication, the editor of the *Architectural Forum* suggested that he enter it in the first annual Pittsburgh Glass Institute competition. By the time Harris heard that the house had won an award, he had already received an honorable mention

Fellowship Park
house plan.

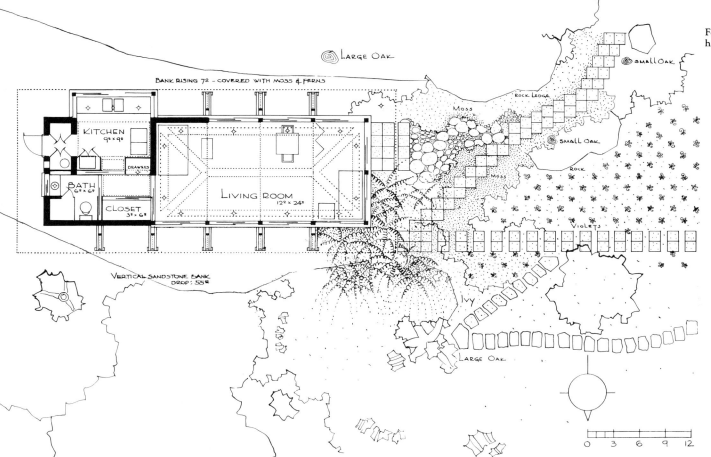

LARGE OAK

BANK RISING 7° - COVERED WITH MOSS & FERNS

KITCHEN
9° x 9°

DRAWERS

BATH
6° x 6°

CLOSET
3° x 6°

LIVING ROOM
12° x 24°

VERTICAL SANDSTONE BANK
DROP: 55°

SMALL OAK

ROCK LEDGE

MOSS

SMALL OAK

MOSS

ROCK

VIOLETS

IVY

LARGE OAK

0   3   6   9   12

for it in the ninth-annual *House Beautiful* competition. He was still not a registered architect nor a member of the AIA, but the Southern California chapter gave him an honor award for the house.

How did one account for the acceptance of Harris on both the popular and professional levels? During the 1930s, the young became interested in modern design, and a good small modern house of wood was rare. In Harris's favor were pitched roofs and the absence of the usual metal tubing furniture. (Neutra and Schindler were considered unacceptable to *House Beautiful* readers.)

The professional magazines saw Harris as a gifted designer in the Bay Region style. William Wilson Wurster was another in this tradition of Maybeck and John Galen Howard. Los Angeles critics saw Harris

as someone who bridged the years between Greene and Greene and the 1930s, using wood more directly and economically, but with grace and elegant detailing.

It seemed that the further Harris departed from Wright and Neutra, the more successful he was. The Laing house, with its strong suggestion of Wright, received little notice; he was more praised for his Fellowship Park house. His 1936 De Steiguer house of redwood and stucco had the lines of a Wright Prairie house—the long horizontals, the roof expressed unequivocally as hip, the adjustment of house to the countours of the site. One purely Harris feature, however, was a three-sided clerestory on an adjoining structure facing a cross street. The structure, used as a shop, had a minimum of glass toward the street to give it a domestic character, and interiors were lighted by the odd-shaped clerestory.

While the De Steiguer house was in preliminary drawings in 1936, Gregory Ain proposed that he and Harris work together on what commissions he could bring in. For eight or nine months there was an unofficial partnership – none of the four houses they planned together was ever built. Ain had left the Neutra office some months earlier with two commissions, the addition to the Galka Scheyer house and the Edwards house, the former then under construction. His marriage had broken up and he seemed unable to work in his apartment. Harris, quiet and reflective, was at ease working alone; Ain's talent was enlivened in a milieu in which intellectual sparks flew.

As work was low in the Harris office, he had enrolled in another course in engineering, and he used some of his freshly gained knowledge when they were designing together the Lewis Gaffney house for the Silver Lake area, with Ain leading him on. It was a feat of engineering of which both were proud. Harris himself took the drawings into Plan Check at the Building Department, and was delighted to see that all the computations were correct. The checker rerolled the prints, handed them back and asked drily, "Why all that engineering on a house?"

"That was the last time," Harris recalled, "that I ever over-engineered a house."

In 1937, Harris was married to Jean Murray Bangs, a graduate in economics from the University of California in Berkeley. She is known to historians for her early writings on Bernard Maybeck and Greene and Greene, published in architectural journals.

Two fine small houses were built on the edge of canyons in 1937 and 1939. One was for John Entenza, who had met Harris after reading about the plagiarized Lowe plan; earlier he had designed a house for Estelle Gramer, Entenza's father's law partner. The Gramer project was abandoned when Mrs. Gramer bought Neutra's Plywood Model House, built for Architects' Building Materials exhibit (1936), and moved it to Westwood.

Entenza had been a writer on an experimental film project, and was interested as well in experimental architecture. By 1937, when Harris was designing the Entenza house, George Oyer had turned the unprofitable *California Arts & Architecture* over to his associate Jerre Johnson, who asked Entenza to be guest editor when she took a leave of absence to have a child. (Subsequently, Entenza bought the magazine and soon dropped *California* from the title.)

The 1937 Entenza house was as close to the International style as Harris would

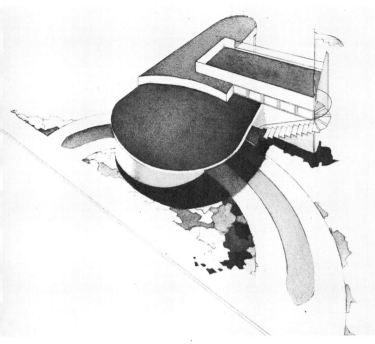

Entenza house. A
bird's-eye view.

Entenza house. A
view of the canyon
side. Photo: Fred
Dapprich.

ever come; it was a reminder of Neutra's 1936 house for Josef von Sternberg in the use of metal and the circular form. Neutra had an elliptical metal screen around a patio on the entrance side; Harris used a circular drive-through with a corrugated aluminum fascia.

The Entenza site was a ledge off a narrow winding street at the bend of which was Neutra's guest house for the Malcomson house on the street below. The crispness of the Entenza house came from combining metal with plaster. An exterior stair to the roof deck was composed of a single steel stringer, metal treads, and a pipe handrail; the circular aluminum fascia ended up as an elliptical line by a change of radius. In contrast, the Neutra house was a plaster cubic form building up as it approached the curve.

Because of Entenza's unusual height

Harris departed from his typical delicate scale in the design of the house. The area was hardly more than 600 square feet, but the large scale prevailed in room sizes as well as details. The 18-by-24-foot living room extended through two nine-foot openings to a view deck the length of the living room. (The sliding glass was hung from barn door tracks.) The heavy fireplace wall on the street side had recessed strip windows above, and the massive chimney stack at one side was a visual barrier from the entry hall. The large bedroom terminated in a semicircular glass wall overlooking the canyon and ocean.

Traces of the drawing board clung to the design, as can be seen in the bird's-eye perspective—the transformation of circle to ellipse in the entrance canopy; the circle meeting the straight line of the bedroom; the curve of the stair to the deck.

In contrast, the bird's-eye perspective of the second house on a canyon edge (Granstedt house) had the delicacy of a Japanese print. The gray-violet color by which Harris so often stretched a rendering into infinity was used here to delineate the steep bank at the edge of the site. There was a preoccupation with roof in both renderings.

The Granstedt roof was three-dimensional lineal sculpture on a white composition surface. Harris emphasized the hips of the roof with broad dark lines, and springing out from these were ribs scored in lighter lines. The crown of the roof was a five-sided clerestory—in search of a dark space below. Ain was capable of designing a clerestory that simply lighted interiors; Harris brought to it an analytical love of line. A roof to him was abstract sensation; read alone, it was a message to the sky.

On the wide, shallow lot below street grade, Harris set a simple rectangular plan, with major rooms facing the canyon on the south. There were 27 feet of glass opening the living and dining rooms and a studio to the view. The studio, which served as a guest room, opened by folding doors to the living room. On the street side, the entrance hall, bath, dressing room, and kitchen were lighted by the wandering clerestory.

Harris took advantage of the label *Japanese* attached to him by framing a view from the living room of a "little Fujiyama" across the canyon. In black-and-white photographs, the deep turquoise of window and door frames is lost. Oddly enough, people remember the calmness of his interiors rather than such interesting color combinations as dark olive window frames with raspberry red accents.

A dressing room and a second bath were standard practice in small Harris houses under $6000 at a time when one bath was usual; in Granstedt's dressing room was a Schindlerian dressing table—a narrow wall-hung shelf with drawers turned a corner and broadened into a wider set of drawers.

The kitchens were an insight into the way storage space is actually used; the typical approach to the modern kitchen then was unbroken vertical and horizontal

Granstedt house, Los Angeles, 1938. The major rooms face the canyon view. Photo: Fred Dapprich.

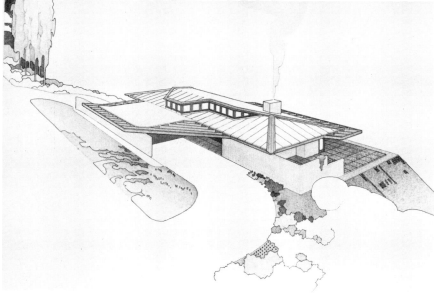

Granstedt house. A bird's-eye view.

52

Granstedt house.
Living room. Photo:
Fred Dapprich.

Granstedt house.
The dressing room
cabinets are a
Schindler touch.
Photo: Fred Dapprich.

lines, with cabinets and drawers as deep as possible so that everything on the counters could be swept into them. The clear surface was more important than convenience. Harris's kitchens were neither laboratories nor sentimental catch-alls. He broke the symmetry and continuous line to provide cabinets and drawers in the width and depth needed for things to be stored. I know of no one else who designed cabinets the depth of two standard cans or one large one.

In the Clark house in Carmel (1937), a **T**-shaped plan opened the house to the views of the valley to the east, the beautiful Carmelite Monastery on the southeast, and Point Lobos on the southwest. The terraces were on the lee side, but facing the beach where the winds sweep off Point

Lobos was a large window wall around the corner of the living room.

The roof was white, as in the Granstedt house, the window and door frames the turquoise color of the sea. Coarsely woven curtains of yellow-green framed the seascape during the day. The crimson stain on the redwood soffit, repeated on the living room cornice, blended into the pink-tan of the interior walls; the rugs were patterned in yellow-green and violet-red.

Soffit vents to the attic and vents up the chimney crossventilated the rooms. The chimney vent created such a draft that doors had to be propped open. Harris tried numerous kinds of ventilation over the years (never the attic fan which sucked in the dust); one inspired solution was vents on either side of the roof ridge in the State Fair house, Dallas (1954).

53

A complex plan evolved in 1938 in the Bauer house in Glendale. It went through five studies. First Harris discarded the L-shaped plans, with equal and unequal legs, because the twenty-foot setback requirement did not allow the bedrooms and living room to open to the patio. Then he began revolving walls at 45 degrees; he shortened the house by revolving the dining bay, which also allowed for a door to the patio. The plan fell into place as he revolved a third wall, the entry hall.

Harris returned to the L-shaped Lowe house plan in the Pumphrey house (1939) on a flat site at the bend of a steep road in Santa Monica Canyon. But the house is two-story, of stucco, and a separate studio is entered from the walk to the front door. The vertical surfaces were stucco and outsloping planes of balconies were lapped redwood boards, a practice Harris always followed.

Two houses on downslopes were the Joël house (1937) and the Hawk house (1939), both entered from the top level. The Joël living room was placed below the entrance to gain a better view of Silver Lake, and the shed roof covering both levels ended in a heavy sculptured form. Large-scale elements—a big window pressing against a fireplace—were concentrated in a corner below the heavy dark cornice which divided the room horizontally.

The Hawk house living room, more delicate in scale, opened to a canyon view on two sides, and by pleated doors to a patio carved out of the slope. Indeed, the three-level house is part of the slope. In a dressing room in the Hawk house was a lacquered Japanese-like gold and orange wallpaper, a patternless paper giving the impression of pure color enameled on the wall.

Harris's most successful house for a slope was for Lee Blair, an artist, in the hills between Laurel Canyon and Cahuenga Pass, with a wide view of San Fernando Valley. The site was a 45-degree upslope with a 30-foot rise from the street to the first level; to the third level of the house was another 25-foot rise.

In vertical sections, the house steps up the hillside in full steps, the middle level at right angles to the other two levels. The second and third levels open to roof decks

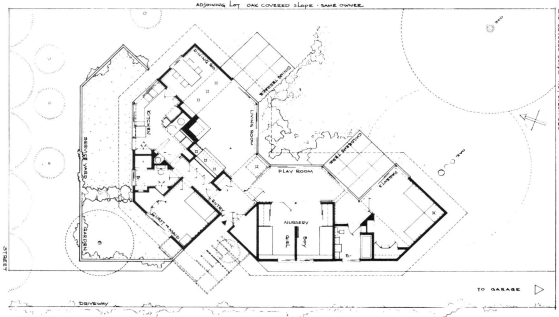

Bauer house plan. The ends were angled to face the living and bedrooms toward the patio.

Bauer house, Los Angeles, 1938. Living room. Photo: Fred Dapprich.

at the front and hillside gardens at the back. The site was sensitively read. Every live oak was considered, every view, every glimpse of morning sun and evening sunset, and the valley at night blooming with light. Yet the land was little disturbed except for the stepped retaining walls of the bedroom level. The spots for terraces on the living room level left the slope a strong presence. Harris managed hipped roofs flattened at the center for view decks.

In 1938 two Chinese brothers, aged twenty-one and twenty-four, came to Harris with a grand scheme for a restaurant in New Chinatown, rising then in picture-book splendor, while authentic streets of Old Chinatown were being ripped out to

Blair house, Los
Angeles, 1939. Photo:
Fred Dapprich.

Blair house. Living
room. Photo: Fred
Dapprich.

Blair house plan. All
three levels open to
gardens and decks.

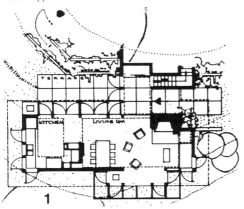

1

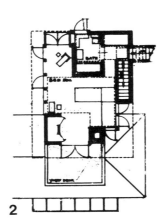

2

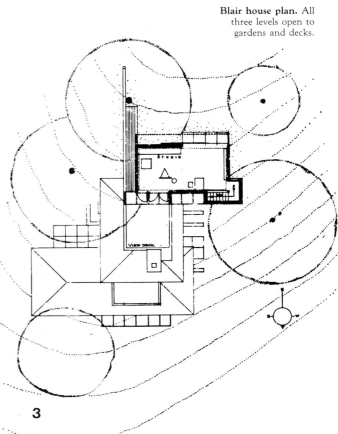

3

Grandview Gardens Restaurant, New Chinatown, Los Angeles, 1940. At a $1.39 per square foot, Harris performed a miracle of rich illusions. Photo above: Fred Dapprich. Photo below: H.H. Harris.

Grandview Gardens Restaurant. Looking toward the outdoor dining court. Photo: H.H. Harris.

open a plaza around the central railway station. The older Chinese approved of this progress, the younger ones held sentimentally to the past—except for the two brothers.

They wanted a two-story restaurant, Grandview Gardens, which would wrap around a court filled with bazaars. They had the taste not to ask for a bedragoned building like others in the new compound, accepting instead Harris's vision of the spirit of the Chinese in California. Plans were drawn, chairs, tables, dishes, and matchbooks were designed and approved, all within the ample budget. Then the 1939 Sino-Japanese War broke out, and the students' money was all tied up in China.

Their enthusiasm undampened, they canvassed friends of their family; when they got commitments for only $15,000, they asked Harris what he could build with that.

The second floor and the court for bazaars were omitted, the refined materials and special details went next. Harris used single-board walls of fourteen-inch unseasoned redwood, lapped an inch on each side, to produce a rhythm of fourteen-inch board and twelve-inch batten.

"A slow-moving wall," Harris called it. "Undulating, slow, monotonous; ideal background for lively action; it makes the moving foreground more moving, the still background more still."

But in this slow-moving wall Harris introduced slit windows in alternate boards, extending from table height almost to the eave line of the hipped roof. The low building was dramatically heightened by a superstructure in which gables, like refolded paper, sprang from a square base. Two staffs at the entrance, playfully built up of spaced and tripled and artfully dwindling two by sixes, 24 feet tall, with flying streamers from their tops.

There was a problem in holding together a single wall without studs. Roof loads were carried by paired two by sixes and walls were tied together at twelve-foot intervals by pairs of two by twelves spaced to house the lighting. Rolls of insulating blankets faced with aluminum foil were crushed to create thousands of tiny reflectors to spread the light. The silver light bounced softly on the tables.

Near the entry were cocktail lounge and tables for dining, at the back a small night club with dance floor, and tables in a walled patio.

Grandview Gardens was immediately successful and soon enlarged. Alas, not by Harris, who with imagination and balloon staffs and insulating foil and single slow-moving walls had built it for $1.39 per square foot.

By 1941, Californians knew what to expect of Harris, but the Havens house in Berkeley came as a shock. Complex roofs were expected, not inverted gables. He had built for other steep slopes, but the Havens house was a tour de force.

Berkeley was more intensely built up in 1941 than most of Los Angeles, and flat lots were scarce; also the view from the site was spectacular—Golden Gate Bridge, Alcatraz, Mount Tamalpais. For a lot with a 35-degree slope, off a narrow road, with hardly any shelf, the engineering was not esoteric. This was because the house was built into the floor rather than the walls of the slope. Guest parking was on a platform the width of the narrow lot, and the garage, with servants' quarters below, was detached from the house. The house itself was pushed forward of the slope and supported on footings; the stepped retaining walls became planting wells.

The house was reached by a bridge in the shape of an inverted gable, the louvred sides of which blocked the view of the bedroom terraces and badminton court below. From the entry hall the living room was concealed from view by a freestanding guest closet; light flowed around it, even touching the handsome intricate circular stair to the bedroom level.

The upswept ceiling above the high glass wall opened the living room vertically and horizontally to the most treasured views of the Bay. The view reached in to the seating area at the low side of the room; as a twenty-foot drop from the living room deck to the canyon below called for a strong rail, a transparent chain link was used. The glare of the west sun was cut by slat blinds dropped from the edge of the soffit, or by sailcloth curtains. Direct light came from clerestory windows on the east.

Whenever Harris found the best solution to be a steep shed roof, as in the earlier Joël house or the later Wyle house, he managed to set up a countermotion to interrupt the line and distract the eye. The inverted gables of the Havens house were really a consequence of the shed roof; aesthetically, they disguised the flat portion of the roof and the steep shed; structurally, they acted as lateral bracing, much as the buttresses did for the Fellowship Park house. A stripped-down view of the Havens structure reveals similar triangulations, which transmit forces from member to member, and tie into the masonry wall. The lateral bracing for the Havens house became a decorative feature when the obtuse-angled gables were filled in with redwood boards with copper edging.

Havens house, Berkeley, 1941. A side view of the house. Photo: Man Ray.

Havens house.
Above: The living room opens toward the most famous views of the Bay. Below: Seating around the fireplace on the low side of the roof slope. Photos: Roger Sturtevant.

Harris explained the gables poetically: "It is a sky house more than an earth house." The gables "lift the beholder into the sky."

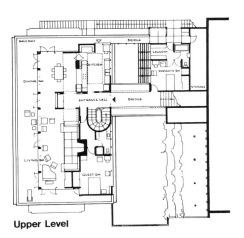

Upper Level

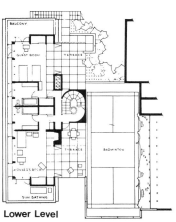

Lower Level

Havens house plan. The upper story social rooms are level with the street.

Havens house.
Sectional view.

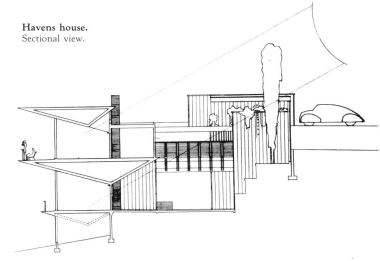

Of the five commerical and institutional buildings designed during the 1930s, only one was built, a Buick salesroom and service department in West Los Angeles (1937). The salesroom was a circular building of brick under a lamella dome, the repair department under a lamella vault. Both were framed with interlocking diamond-shaped elements. As these were the first built in the U.S. by the Summerbell Roof Structures, they moved saw and drill to the site to check calculations as work proceeded. Harris was not given control over production, and many changes weakened the design.

In 1952, he designed a second, more successful vault of diamond-shaped components, the National Orange Show Exhibition Building in San Bernardino. The site was a sandy river bottom which would support no heavy buttressing so the vault sprang from the ground and was tied together below the walls. The vault "leaps over the walls, and the ties below the ground take the kick," Harris noted. Inside the building were screen walls for exhibits. The temporary roof of canvas bathed the interiors with a luminous light, and Harris suggested plastic for the permanent roof; he was disappointed when corrugated metal was used.

An unbuilt project that Harris was sorry to give up was the Pottenger Clinic for tuberculosis patients in Monrovia. He used the same folding glass doors as in the Lowe bedrooms so the patients' beds could be rolled out into walled courts under the stars at night. It brings to mind Irving Gill's use of an open skylight in his Oceanside jail, so prisoners could see the sky and feel the rain!

He designed several pieces of furniture during the 1930s, a rigid frame chair for the Kershner house, a side chair and arm chair of rattan, and a two-column table. But in 1938, he deferred to Alvar Aalto for furniture for the Bauer and Blair houses. Unable to find any on the West Coast or through a distributor in London, Harris appealed to Aalto in Finland. The first result of this contact was that when Aalto was in the United States the following year he came to Los Angeles to speak at the Art Center.

Lek house, La Jolla, 1942. The court off the living room of this solar house. Photo: H.H. Harris.

Harris recalled a memorable drive with Alvar and Aino Aalto and William Wurster in Wurster's car. They stopped to see Wright's hexagon house in Palo Alto before driving down the peninsula, ending at Harris's Clark house in Carmel. Aalto was delighted to be in the land of Jack London, whose books he had read as a boy. After he and Aino were married, she read aloud in English all of London and Mark Twain. Aalto asked many questions about the foods eaten when supplies ran out on London's trips into the wilds. Wurster stopped the car for them to see the spectacular sunset over the Pacific and Aino begged to touch it. She had, she said, touched all seas from the Baltic on.

When Harris received the commission in 1957 to design the U.S. Embassy in Helsinki, he spent a summer with the Aaltos, and at a dinner to introduce him to the Finnish architects Aalto toasted him as "the most important architect in the United States after Frank Lloyd Wright."

Harris's plan for the embassy ended in a bureaucratic snarl. In Washington, the three-man commission of the Office of Foreign Buildings first deleted from Harris's plans the subterranean bomb shelter required for all large buildings in Finland; then they added living quarters for twenty staff members and their families. This addition pushed the embassy so close to a Finnish government building that a snowplow couldn't pass between them. Snowplow circulation seemed a very arbitrary requirement to the committee – but in the meantime, the committee had made new changes; then there were counterchanges. The commission after many months decided that they could get along for the present with the consular offices. The building was cancelled.

The Birtcher house had several things in common with the Lek house in La Jolla, both begun as the war started. They were versions of the Eric Mendelsohn plan, brought to America by Richard Neutra, with one essential change, the motor court at the front of the lot.

The firmness of faith that architects had at the beginning of the war in the power of technology to free us from the motor car was present in Harris's comment on the motor court: "Assuming the continued use of the automobile in some form or other, a large parking area for guest cars is provided close to the main entrance."

The word *minimum* had begun to appear in many contexts soon after war was declared, but Harris rejected it for the Birtcher house. "To begin with minimum, is to end with minimum," he said. The house, planned for expansion, laid down the circulation to allow for additions which would not nullify the scheme. Wings, one room deep, sprang from a central core, with clerestories to give cross lighting and ventilation for future rooms. "Additions of a leaf, a limb, or a segment to enrich rather than complicate the pattern," Harris said.

The Lek house, was made up of loose forms pulled together by a continuous line of clerestories. The Birtcher house was something quite different; on the street side large simple forms built up from fascia to fascia, to two, closed flat-roofed superstructures. It was a composition of lapped boards for fascias and the lower of the two superstructures, but the higher mass, the mechanical core of the house, became a strong vertical element, with a rhythm of battens at three-foot intervals. The appearance was of a thin-walled water tower, or even the walls of bamboo and peeled saplings of indigenous African houses. Harris obviously liked this wall construction, for it carried over into late work in North Carolina. It spoke of Harris's extraordinary clarity, although it left out his subtle twists and turns. For instance, the surprising rectangular coffers piercing the 30-inch eaves extending over the Birtcher deck and terrace.

Several of Harris's houses were photographed by Man Ray, among them the Birtcher house. His eye found the hard forms; he freed a house from nature and it stood isolated, as if in the strong shadowless light of Greece. It is quite a feat to separate a Harris house from its setting. No wonder the softer, more comfortable photography of Maynard Parker was preferred by the editors of *House Beautiful*. Man Ray's low, sleek sports car was often parked in the foreground, another strong shape. A close-up of the car would have shown the mousetrap dangling inside the

Birtcher house, Los Angeles, 1942. Photo: Man Ray.

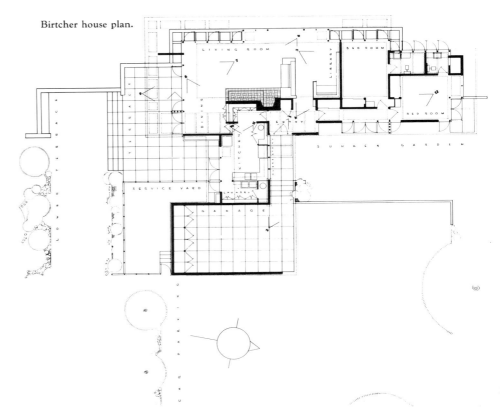

Birtcher house plan.

rear window—a parody on the pair of baby's bootees that graced car windows in the 1940s.

Wood was Harris's material, and for the most part his architecture was skeletal rather than wall. In *Arts & Architecture,* in May 1939, he recounted the advantages and disadvantages of the material. "Wood swells, warps, burns, and rots. It is as variable, unpredictable, and unreliable as the human creature it shelters or warms. Why, therefore, after centuries of effort to eliminate the uncertain from his life should wood persist?"

He then listed the virtues. "Weight for weight, it is stronger than iron in most situations. Allow a slender strand of steel to take the pulls in a structure, the wood will take the pushes and bends. . . ." The carpenter can "shape, surface, and join it," he continued "with a few power tools, a good eye, a steady hand, a methodical mind, and a love of wood greater than his love for his tools. If only someone would teach wood to breathe," he added. He mulled over the fact that steel in the beginning followed wood forms but now wood follows steel forms.

By 1942 there were many restrictions on building. The War Production Board permitted construction of new single-family dwellings only in defense areas as shelter for war workers, at a minimum sale price of $6000, or rental of $50 a month. Common materials were hard to find, and materials vital to war work could not be used in home construction.

In the months before Pearl Harbor, Harris had four draftsmen, each working on a different house. By 1942, his office dwindled as the draftsmen entered the service or went into war plants. In March 1943 the Harrises left for New York.

It was his first trip outside California except to cross the border into Baja California. He was overwhelmed by the enormity of the city. He met people for the first time whose work he knew well through magazines. The editor of *Architectural Forum,* Howard Myers, asked him to lunch with Frank Lloyd Wright, who was then working on the early plans of the Guggenheim Museum. They had met the year before through Paul Frankl, a furniture and industrial designer in Los Angeles. Mary Frankl had invited him to dinner and asked him to fetch "Frank and

Olgivanna" on the way; she asked him not to talk about the war because "Frank is an anglophobe," which made it hard on his son Lloyd, with whom the Wrights were staying, because Lloyd was an anglophile.

Harris lost the opportunity to fetch the Wrights because his car was a 1925 DeSoto with a rumble seat—so Charles Laughton and Elsa Lanchester drove the Wrights. (Harris broke into his narrative to remark, "Laughton has a Monet.") When Harris and Wright were alone for a few minutes Wright put his arm across his shoulder and said, "Harwell, when your hair is as white as mine you will be a great architect." (Harris's voice made one feel the presence of Wright, the weight of his arm, and the tremendous weight of the prediction on a young man.)

New York during the war years was the center for experimentation and planning of postwar products. Funds were available in abundance for research on new materials and new uses for old ones. Most of the research was aimed at housing, recognized as the field in which there would be the greatest postwar activity. Even before leaving for New York Harris had participated in several of these projects, as there was always some effort to spread them geographically. He was second to Neutra as participant from Southern California.

In 1940 Harris designed one of sixteen "America at home" rooms for the New York World's Fair. (The subtitle "South of the Golden Gate" located Los Angeles as an appendage of San Francisco.) Harris's complex plan separated dining bay from sitting area by low storage cabinets, book shelves, and sofa. In the July 1940, *Pencil Points'* Talbot Hamlin praised the exquisite proportions of the geometric shapes and the subtle harmonies of colors and textures.

One project was the Solar House for Libbey-Owens-Ford (1942). Starting with the **L**-shaped plan for the Lek house, he devised ways to control the sun by reflecting it, filtering it, intercepting it, absorbing it, and harnessing it. One of the devices was a hinged fin which could be rotated with the sun to produce a longer period of shade.

The magazines entered the postwar housing race in 1942 with the *Ladies' Home Journal* House, followed by the *Woman's*

Home Companion House and *Mademoiselle*'s House in 1944, and in 1945 *Good Housekeeping* House. Harris worked out schemes for all of them, mostly expandable houses which could start with a few hundred square feet.

The Revere Copper and Brass Corporation's project in 1942 for an expandable house (Segmental House) was a nine-stage plan beginning with a full-sized kitchen, a small living room, a bedroom, and bath. Stage two added a two-car garage; stage three doubled the area of the living room; stages four and five added children's bedrooms; stage six a parents' bathroom, stage seven a guest room, and stages eight and nine added a parents' sitting room and a third child's room. In the end the **T**-shaped plan had become a long-armed cross. The spirit and realities of the late 1940s and 1950s was in the plan: togetherness, large families, cheap land in the suburbs, a plentiful supply of cheap labor.

In 1945, Harris explored for industrial designer Donald Deskey some new architectural uses for porcelain enamel. The client was a group of six porcelain enamel companies, and Harris's most promising suggestion was a four-by-eight wall board armored with sixteen-by-sixteen inch porcelain enamel steel plates, spaces a saw's thickness apart so the wall board could be cut into any multiple of sixteen inches and the joints between panels would look exactly like the joints between the plates. Any homeowner who could handle plywood could handle porcelain enamel steel.

Also for Deskey, Harris designed a packaged utility core and a number of small house plans to illustrate the versatility of the core. On a tract in Kalamazoo, Michigan, Borg Warner's Ingersol Division built one of the designs, and one each by Alden Dow, George Fred Keck, Hugh Stubbins, Morgan Yost, and Edward D. Stone.

Much to Harris's liking were two mind-stretching projects, one an adobe house for *Sunset* magazine, the other a log cabin in Sitka, Alaska. (The latter was built after the end of the war.) The projects crystallized in Harris's mind the difference between the closed and open form—the mass as op-

posed to the spider web.

He worked with small units, the adobe brick, and the green log slabbed on two sides and linked with dowels. His ideas in shaping the two materials came from sculpture. He set up these rules: Don't butcher a material; don't fragment it. Make whole forms of it that accommodate the openings. Don't mix vertical logs with horizontal logs; logs don't shrink vertically. Carry all loads on horizontal logs. Columns and even mullions in a wide open wall can be made by stacking logs and turning them at a right angle to the glass. When he wanted an opening he turned a corner and projected a bay. Openings were not cut in the stepped-out bays, just the solid end wall omitted and the space filled in with glass.

"When I wanted an opening I made a whole wall of glass," he said. "I made the wall twelve or so feet wide and constructed it of lightweight material. The side walls of the bay had the same settlement ratio as the load-bearing walls."

(In his Kings Road house, Schindler had also distinguished between mass and openings; no holes were cut in the concrete panels. When he wanted an entrance he dissolved a corner; he stepped it back and covered it with a dark redwood canopy which extended beyond the concrete walls. The glazed areas were in long recessed sections lightly constructed of redwood, with a line of clerestories above.)

Between 1942 and VJ Day in 1945, Harris had designed 27 buildings with only a demonstration house and a headmaster's cottage built. At this time he was eager to put up an office for himself below the Fellowship Park house and see his designs built. "To be expressed," he wrote, "an idea must be built. To be built, it must be particularized, localized, set within a region." Just as he was ready to leave, a call came from Dean Hudnut at Harvard offering him a post. But it had been too long since he had built anything.

Some of Harris's draftsmen had kept in touch with him during the war—Gordon Drake, the imaginative young man who had survived the war and received awards for his first house, only to be killed in 1952 in a senseless ski accident. When Drake

Ralph Johnson house, Los Angeles, 1948. Living room, second level. Photo: Fred Dapprich.

went into the service he wrote one of the idealistic letters that only the young can write, thanking Harris for all he had learned from him, for the Fellowship Park house where he had discovered how things were put together. Drake had worked on the Lek and Havens houses, and during leaves from the service he would turn up at the construction site of one of them to watch it going up.

When Harris reached Los Angeles, Drake was there, and he worked on the plans for the office. But by then he was ready to start his own firm doing low-cost housing with an engineer he had met during the war.

Another draftsman, Harry Harrison, had come to him from Neutra's office. Emiel Beksky drove out from Chicago in January 1941, and his first job in Los Angeles was with Harris—brief, for he stopped in December after Pearl Harbor. After the war he worked in the office of Quincy Jones (later Jones and Emmons). There was a great deal of work then in the Harris office. "He put the four of us on different jobs. I was on the Birtcher house and Sox house in Menlo Park. Harwell was a mild-mannered man, one of the greatest guys you could know, but we were a little afraid of him—definitely not a man you offered ideas to."

Harris said of his office in general: "I enjoyed having someone take the responsibility in the operation of the office, but I've never shared the design. There are those who are good at organizing an office who often want to decide how much time we can afford on a job, whether it is wasteful to spend as much time as I want to. Once I had an engineer in the office who concentrated on getting clients. I don't want to work that way. Most of my early clients came in with copies of architectural magazines with my work in them. That made it easier. They knew in the beginning that what I suggested would be worth considering. I would like the help a partner could give me but when you accept one you have to accept the other things I would rather not have. It would be wrong for me. I can't recommend my way of work. It's not a way to get rich."

He felt sure, however, that he had given up nothing he really wanted. "I think if there had been more money I would have built more things for myself." But he wasn't sure.

He was sure, however, at the end of 1945 that he wanted real clients again. Several important houses were built in the last years of the 1940s.

Harris grew up in the panel period, and the panel was at the base of his unit system. The panels Harris used most frequently were ones of fiber (Celotex), long available. Interior and exterior plywood panels were produced from the 1930s, but glues developed during the war made exterior panels more impervious to weather; Harris also liked Cemesto panels, composed of cement and asbestos.

There was a prejudice against panels. They were considered a cheap substitute for dimension lumber. "They looked like a product of the austerity program," Harris said. During the 1940s when austerity was a virtue the witty William Wurster remarked, "I use plywood panels because they *look* cheap." (They cost more than traditional wood.)

Harris's early module was three feet as opposed to the typical four feet, which accommodated four-by-eight panels. Harris said the three-foot module felt better to his eye. "Also the door unit in a four-foot panel butchers the rhythmic pattern, unless a side panel is used." He divided his rooms horizontally at door height by a continuous fascia, behind which were the curtain

Ralph Johnson house. A view from the street. Photo: Fred Dapprich.

tracks. The twelve-inch band between the four-inch fascia and ceiling took care of the twelve-inch scraps; it was also an element in the rhythmic play.

All of his materials were in multiples of three. The one-foot square grass matting he liked to countersink in the floor was ⅓ of a unit; the twelve-inch board of his board and batten walls was ⅓ of a unit; the three-foot panel a full unit, the six-foot windows a double unit.

The unit was the space, the unit line (or division between spaces) the accent. He called the accent "the dominant element in our consciousness, the space being only an interval between the accents or beats."

He manipulated the units to create emotional effects. He multiplied them to hasten the movement; he subdivided them to slow it down. The accent could be strengthened, made insistent, weakened, disguised, or merely implied.

An example of the way he used the rhythmic patterns is the living room of his most famous postwar house, that for

Clarence Wyle in Ojai. The unit measures are easily identified: the tile on the hearth = ⅓ unit; the redwood boards of the wall = ⅓ unit; windows = double unit; ceiling panels and panels above windows = one unit; a pair of glass doors = double unit.

The accent is subdued in the panels above the windows; it is strengthened in the wood battens running in one direction on the ceiling, and in the opposite direction the accent is insistent. The board and batten exterior walls have a ⅓ interval, with a double interval between the posts of the loggia. These intervals are marked with heavy accents.

In the Havens house the accents were expressed in greater variety. Panels of Flexboard (asbestos cement) were bordered on both sides with small brass tacks. The mullions of the glass panels of the ceiling were strengthened by being doubled and deepened. The special rhythm in the Havens house was the alternating 2-3-2-3, with heavy accents made by the thick posts, and a light accent by the slender mullions.

Ralph Johnson house. The detail of outriggers pays homage to Maybeck. Photo: Fred Dapprich.

Wyle house, Ojai, 1949. A play of gabled forms. Photo: Julius Shulman.

"Several rhythmic patterns may parallel one another, as when the wall presents one pattern, the ceiling another, the floor still another, all related by adherence to the same basic unit. Or one unit pattern may be laid on top of another, as when the pattern made by the building framework appears in front of a pattern of wall or ceiling panels. Sometimes the background and the pattern are merged in a compound rhythm," Harris wrote in *Perspecta 2.*

The pent-up energies of the war years, waiting to be released, gave a particular intensity to two postwar houses. The Ralph Johnson house and the Wyle house, built a year apart, were explorations of the gable form.

The Johnson house paid tribute to Maybeck, all the more sincere because of the free interpretation of Maybeck's trellis extensions for gables and the play of large and small members in the projecting floor joists. But the skillful imbalance of parts, and the dissonance, came from Harris.

The house, on an upslope, was stepped back from the garage with sundeck above, and a two-story gabled form placed off-center had a projecting bedroom wing on the right. The glass panels and windows in the gable end decreased the mass to a toylike superstructure. The living room (mentioned earlier) disguised the square plan by strong verticals and heavy beams leading the eye through the glass to the gable peak. Maybeck's narrow high rooms "with lots of space up there" were truly so— Harris's were a visual deception. Instead of the usual fiber ceiling panels, Harris used narrow boards, but stopped short of Maybeck's trick of varying the width and staining some of the boards blue or red.

The Wyle house grew out of the cruciform plans of the expandable houses, but the important rooms were at the ends of the arms where each could have three exposures. Each arm had arrived at its destination, with no further place to go.

The house was a family of gables, but it would be hard to say which were the parents. The entrance was a gabled pergola,

partially roofed, perhaps the only symmetrical gable. On the street facade gables originated in the long shed roof, the highest one so off center that the short face served only to slow the long sweep to a gentle close—inside as well as out. (Harris called it a hockey stick gable.) The lower gable also sprang from the shed roof, borrowing one plane from it and generating the other. Complicated as the roof was, the plate line remained a steady six-feet-eight and the fascia was constant at seven feet. The weighting of the forward arm of the cross plan to gables was not reflected in interior ceilings; the living room was under the shed roof except for the dropped luminous ceilings over the alcove and the piano. There was, however, the gratuitous gable created simply by flipping down a ceiling panel. It was a symbolic pediment over the bookshelves and desk in a jog in the wall. The same sort of jog in the master bedroom left the fireplace almost freestanding and produced nooks on either side. The treatment of the living room firep[lace] also had a certain symbolism. Crow[...]

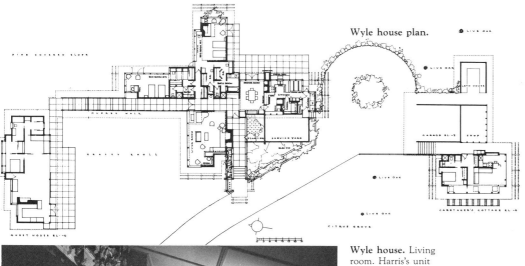

Wyle house plan.

Wyle house. Living room. Harris's unit system is clear in the panel and window dimensions. Photo: Maynard Parker.

Wyle house. Bedroom. Photo: Maynard Parker.

with a row of clerestories, and with the shaft at the side, it recognized that a fireplace is not the major source of heat. It functioned, but essentially it was form—a piece of wall furniture.

The Mulvihill house (1949) and the English house (1950), with their continuous wall and roof planes, were less taut, the Mulvihill of vertical redwood, the English in Beverly Hills a play of stucco masses. In the **T**-shaped English plan, the garage wing with bedrooms above was linked to the house by a short entrance hall between motor court and terrace. The two-story living room on the northwest extended along the terrace and blocked off most of the prevailing wind. Harris devised two six-by-six-feet-eight rolling plate glass baffles to shield the dining end of the patio, and he recalled a dinner on a December evening on the terrace to celebrate the return of Igor Stravinsky from Paris, with the baffles and the heated pavement turning the evening into June. The swimming pool at the end of the terrace had solid walls with strip windows above to further discourage the northwest wind.

The artist owner, son of the founder of U.S. Gypsum, had a large collection of paintings. Plaster walls with high ceilings were used in the living room, light was filtered in from a row of clerestories and a five-foot parapet wall bent the light through a translucent plane to enhance the paintings.

The views of canyons and lake from the site above Beverly Hills were numerous, but Harris brought in unexpected glimpses of them rather than introducing any full scale. When the house was remodeled recently all views were welcomed, the protected dining terrace closed in, and a large concrete table built near the pool; indeed there were tables for outdoor dining on three sides of the house, all massive, one on the slope above the dining room. The intimacy is gone, and the wind blows free. Most of the large houses of J.R. Davidson met the same insensitive fate, the superb Stothart house spared because it is owned by Gifford Phillips, a distinguished collector of modern art.

English house,
Beverly Hills, 1950.
Terrace. The rolling
glass screen shields
the dining area from
strong winds. Photo:
Fred Dapprich.

English house. A
view from the motor
court. Photo: Fred
Dapprich.

English house.
Double height living
room. Photo: Fred
Dapprich.

The Fellowship Park pavilion, initially conceived as a plan to use up stockpiled material, became before completion an idea for a group of pavilions on other Fellowship Park lots owned by Harris. One pavilion was built, and that on a different site, but the pavilion idea surfaced again in 1949 in Redding, Connecticut as a 750-square-foot addition to a vacation playroom for Gerald Loeb. On the wooded hillside the pavilion was a level above the existing structure. Fifty feet of perimeter walls were filled in with removable panels of glass, translucent plastic, and fly screens, each type of panel with its own track; the upper channel was deeper than the lower so panels can be pushed up and slipped out. Four panel pockets along the walls provide storage space for ones removed.

Harris pioneered what he called the "tea-kitchen" in large houses, usually placed near the master bedroom. His first was for an unbuilt house for Arnold Schönberg in a new development[3] in the Italian Riviera section of Pacific Palisades. He also designed a "tea-shed," a ten-foot square panel prefabricated structure with a "petal" roof—diamond-shaped elements of the folded roof formed gables over each of the four openings. Harris described the tea-shed so minutely that I could taste the Darjeeling. I was disappointed to know it had never been built. The client was John Pennington, an English director for a Pasadena string quartet who held concerts each summer in his garden. The walls of the Pennington living room folded back so the musicians sat inside and the audience outside.

In 1946 and 1948, Harris planned two schools for the Palos Verdes Peninsula, the first an unexecuted design for Palos Verdes College on a knoll overlooking the ocean. Campus buildings were ranged along the sides of a rectangular layout. Among the features were marshy land at the center developed as a water garden, an academic grove opposite the classrooms and library, and below the crest of the hill were dormitories and faculty houses.

3. *The developer had been persuaded to offer distinguished musicians a free lot; among them was Schönberg, then living in Nichols Canyon. After Harris designed the house the developer reneged.*

Loeb pavilion, Redding, 1949. The glass panels snapped out as in the Fellowship Park pavilion. Photo: André Kertesz.

Loeb pavilion. Photo: André Kertesz.

The progressive Chadwick School was on land donated by the public-spirited Vanderlip family, who had also given land for Lloyd Wright's Wayfarers' Chapel. In 1918, the Vanderlips had acquired 16,000 acres of the Palos Verdes Peninsula and commissioned the Olmsteads to lay it out as a community of large estates, with a clubhouse and small business centers. The land planning and the establishment of the Spanish Colonial style made Palos Verdes unique as a development.

The site for the school was in the adjoining development of Rolling Hills, where less splendid ranch houses are on one-acre lots. The land for the school had previously been used for war refugee children, and some of the buildings were remodeled so the school could open at once. In these, and in subsequent buildings, Harris set a style of low-gabled roofs with broad eaves, wood fascias, and trellis extensions. Paths through the trees linked the buildings. The result was a loose colony of roofs stepping down with the rolling terrain, the gable ends turning in different directions. The early buildings had been placed around the crown of the hill, and later ones stepped down to a magnificent view of the whole San Pedro harbor.

Materials were then in short supply, and when the school was offered a gift by the chairman of the board of a company manufacturing building materials, Harris suggested a carload of Cemesto panels; thus most of the buildings are of concrete block and Cemesto panels, contrasting pleasantly with the heavy accents of redwood.

The most distinctive of the new and remodeled buildings by Harris was the 1951 Activities Building with indoor and outdoor stage. The major block was a long room with heavy-beamed ceiling, at one end of which was stage and dressing rooms. Projecting from the building were two low wings for seminar classes. Pleated doors opened the major block and wings to the protected court, which was the outdoor stage. Cut into the slope at the end of the court was a twelve-tiered semicircle with turf seats to accommodate an audience of 200 for graduating exercises or school plays. When the amphitheater was in use, the seats were gay with striped canvas cushions. The aisles of the amphitheater led up to winding walks to the upper campus. From the continuous windows in the Activities Building was a view down the hill to San Pedro harbor.

Activities Building, Chadwick School, Rolling Hills, 1951, with indoor and outdoor stage. Photo: Quinlin.

Activities Building plan, Chadwick School.

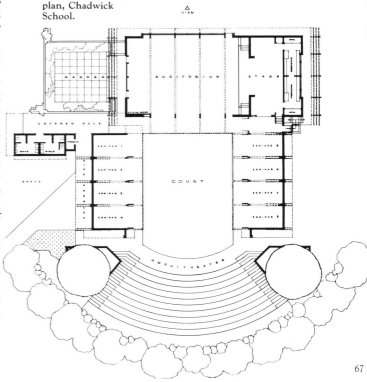

While designing the Alvin Ray house in Fallbrook in 1950, the Harrises were impressed by the similarity of the area to the California they had known before the First World War, and decided to build a house for themselves there. Fallbrook had become famous in the 1880s for a grand resort hotel, popular because of the proximity to hot springs.

A 100-foot-wide boulder on the Ray site was made a feature in the terrace, which with an avocado grove pushing close, gave a naturalness to the house of vertical redwood. A tribute was paid to the citrus packing shed of an earlier California in a long, high, gabled lattice arbor.

Harris's planning in 1951 for a combined house/office was organized around four trellised courts. His search in climate control continued in heat-absorbing concrete block walls, one of them a freestanding visual separation between the living room court and the drafting room yard. Before the house was finished he was summoned to direct the School of Architecture at the University of Texas, and although it was completed the following summer the Harrises lived in it exactly five days.

Harris had always enjoyed an exchange with students while carrying on his own practice, and from 1938 he taught architectural design at Chouinard and Art Center, then was a design critic at USC before leaving for New York; he lectured at Columbia before returning to USC in 1945. (Although still not a registered architect his reputation had grown steadily since his first house. He received his license in Texas.) He did not look upon the move to Texas as one that would keep him away from California long, but the decision proved to be momentous. It would cut him off finally from his practice in California.

It was momentous in more ways than one.

In California, Harris had seen with an eye different from Wright's what forms and materials were suitable to the climate. Wright's vision in the 1920s was of a semiarid land in which compact forms were at home, although even by then the natural climate of the Los Angeles Basin had become lush from the water "borrowed"

from other states; nor did Wright appreciate fully the difference between the dry and rainy season when he built the 1936 Sturges house with its long redwood fascias. The long boards twisted in the dry rainless season. The broken lengths used by the Greenes and Harris escaped such warping. Harris, native to California, had an intuitive understanding of the various pockets of climate scattered over the south, which shows in the condition of his houses.

In Texas, Harris sniffed a new air – or airs, for the climate varied from Austin to Houston to Paris, and as for Abilene, he called it "hot in summer, cold in winter, with terrible dust storms in between." The climates of Texas would lead Harris away from the spider web form and closer to the bee hive, from open to closed form.

There was another consequence of the move. His Texas work appeared less frequently in architectural and other journals. There were two reasons. Editors visited the Los Angeles area frequently in the 1950s because they could see a vari-

ety of good buildings within a radius of thirty miles, but in Texas, ten times thirty miles might turn up less good work. If found, there were at that time no photographers in Texas trained in architectural presentation.

The second reason was that young postwar architects were finishing houses in the early 1950s, and the editors happily turned to new names. Hence the list of published work of all the honored prewar architects took a sudden dip in the 1950s, and many good houses went unphotographed. This situation accounts for the photographic gaps in this book. Unless photographs were taken within four years of completion the house tended to disappear in the landscape.

In Texas, Harris's palette of materials changed. Wood was poor, the native yellow pine good only for framing. There was a soft salmon-colored brick he liked very much, and a golden-hued stone with shell deposits which had been used in the

Harris house, Fallbrook, 1952. A solar house for the inland desert. Photo: H.H. Harris.

University of Texas buildings. Panels of shellstone were available, and he chose these often.

"With brick," he said, "I began thinking in sculptural terms. I enjoy shaping something. I enjoy unbroken surfaces—geometric shapes, whether outside or inside. But then I also enjoy the opposite—something without mass, thin, the spider web. But there is another factor—the pattern of action within the building; the shape a person takes as he goes through a building, both the solid, closed building and the spider web. It's fun to work with both. . . . There are no limits to the elements in a building so long as they all fall in and work together to produce one thing. You're orchestrating something. That's what it comes to—something that has to find a form."

His forms in Texas grew out of new materials and a new climate.

Harris completed four buildings during his four years at the University of Texas. In the Cranfill house (1952) he projected a glazed gallery beyond the walls of shellstone panels—a variation of the rules he established for the mass houses of log and adobe. The 1954 Barrow house in Austin had a plan with two wings, one used for a real estate office. (The son of the owner was an architecture student who later worked in Harris's office.) The 1952 Lang house was in San Antonio, and the 1954 Texas State Fair House in Dallas.

Only one of his buildings during his four years in Austin was photographed fully. This happened when General Electric, which was planning a kitchen jointly with *House Beautiful*, suggested that the kitchen be a part of the Fair house. Thus the house became a *House Beautiful* Pace Setter House, and Maynard Parker was brought from Los Angeles to photograph.

Harris worked at top speed on the expanded plans, with the help of four graduate students, while the editors assembled all that was fashionable or startling in furnishings and accessories—somewhat to Harris's dismay. The materials, all donated, were stone for garden walls, redwood for exteriors and interiors, and yellow pine for framing.

The result was closer to Harris's California than his Texas houses, but the water

Pace Setter House for the Texas State Fair, Dallas, 1954. Motor court. Photo: Maynard Parker.

Pace Setter House. The ventilation along the roof ridge. Photo: Maynard Parker.

in the scheme was for the Texas climate: a walled entrance courtyard with a pool, and a walled court with a plunge off the master bedroom. Another cooling device (at a time before houses were air conditioned) was a line of vents at the roof ridge; currents of air drawn in under the eaves carried off the warm air through screened roof vents. The **L**-shaped plan was one room deep with cross ventilation, and in the Texas tradition was oriented to the prevailing winds.

The innovations in the kitchen were "a sit-down sink," two counters on wheels which could be rolled to new positions, and floor space broken up by two work islands. The passthrough for serving from kitchen to dining room was featured as new, but the louvred fence screening out the west sun on the dining patio was newer.

With so many cooks the house made few new statements. The editors described it as "contemporary" but "somehow it is not modern, traditional but somehow not

Grand Court, Dallas Trade Mart, 1958. Photo: H.H. Harris.

period." The crusading days of the 1930s and 1940s were over.

After four years at the university, Harris moved to Fort Worth to open his office. By that time he was also registered as an architect. His work ranged from 300 miles west of Fort Worth to 100 miles east, with several jobs in Dallas. The sum total of the Texas work between 1951 and his departure for North Carolina State University in 1962 was eleven houses, an apartment, two churches, a mausoleum, and a high, glass-roofed atrium court for the Dallas Trade Mart—this predated John Portman's atrium spaces. There were commissions from other parts of the country: the 1956 Motel-on-the-Mountain in Suffern, New York, the 1957 Kirkpatrick house, Southport, Connecticut, the 1960 Havens Memorial Fountain and Plaza, Berkeley, and a 1958 remodel of Louis Sullivan's famous 1908 Security Bank at Owatonna, Minnesota. (In 1964, the bank commissioned Harris to design a motor bank.)

Only two projects were executed in Fort Worth, but they are among Harris's favorites. There was, however, a steady flow of large projects to design for the developer Trammel Crow, one an office tower; not one was built but the volume kept the office humming for several years.

The J. Lee Johnson house, which Harris gave three stars in his hierarchy of choices, was an intricate weave of light and shadow, of wall and court/terrace, with circulation a pattern that swelled into room and narrowed into hall. Built of brick and stucco, it was inward-directed while welcoming every glance at or participation in the exterior world it so successfully framed.

70

J. Lee Johnson house, Fort Worth, 1956. In Texas, Harris turned from open to closed forms. Photo: Walter DeLima Meyers.

J. Lee Johnson house. Photo: Wayne Andrews.

J. Lee Johnson house plan. An interior court determined the cruciform circulation.

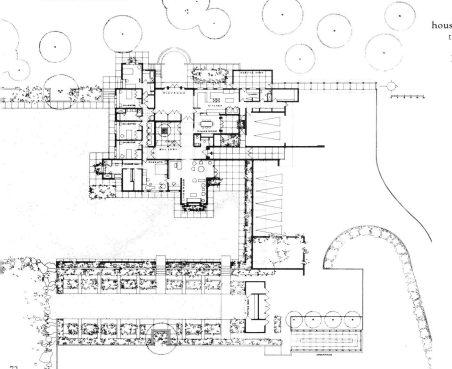

J. Lee Johnson house. The court off the dining room. Photo: Walter DeLima Meyers.

Eisenberg house,
Dallas, 1957. Entrance
drive.

Woodall house, Big
Spring, 1959. Interior
court. Photo: Paul
Lamb.

On entering the house one was immediately outdoors again, for the hall opened up in a central court which was the square hub of the cross-axial plan. The widening entrance hall running from front door to the double doors to the bedroom wing was crossed by a hall linking the living room to the playroom.

The cruciform plan of the Townsend house in Paris, Texas was also cut up with interior courts, although brick walls and hipped roofs gave a more traditional exterior. The Eisenberg house in Dallas (1958) was closer to the wall architecture of the J. Lee Johnson house; forms stepped horizontally and vertically. The brick was combined with redwood in somewhat the California way of using wood for canted surfaces and brick (stucco in California)

for vertical ones. The living room terrace, a deck of redwood with outsloping rail, rode above the downslope to a stream visible through the trees. The entrance side of the house stepped back along the curved drive, with walled courts off the entrance garden and dining room.

Between 1956 and 1959 there were two houses and a church for Big Spring, not far from the New Mexico line. St. Mary's Episcopal Church (1956) was of concrete block with off-center gables stepping down from the square tower to form a loose cluster. The Woodall house was organized around an interior court with a gallery along two sides. A wide channel of water at the perimeter of the court cooled the interiors without the disadvantages in this case of the typical one room deep plan.

Treanor house,
Abilene, Texas, 1959.
Motor court. Photo:
H.H. Harris.

Treanor house. The garden room without windows is lighted by glass at the perimeter of the roof, above the dropped ceiling. Photo: H.H. Harris.

When air conditioning was coming in in 1959, Harris used it in a completely closed-in "garden room" in the Treanor house in Abilene. The sun was excluded by prism glass blocks which reflected back the sun's direct rays while admitting light from other directions. The day lighting removed the feeling that the room was closed in. Lattice screens around the porches buffered other rooms from direct sun. Wide white fascias rose above the red-wood porte cochère and trellising at the entrance as the roof planes built up to the high garden room.

The Greenwood Mausoleum was designed after discarding ideas coming from many discouraging visits to mausoleums. The typical long stretches of corridors without natural light, with artificial plants substituting for nature, gave way to a square plan with a court in the center. The scheme reduced the corridors to under 100 feet, with openings at corners to courts planted with trees and shrubs. Harris used a cluster of court buildings, each complete in itself but capable of growth. The limit would be thirteen buildings linked by courts, with a total of 20,000 crypts.

In conceiving the plan he chose the unit, gave it a center, made the unit autonomous, clustered the units, linked them, developed the spaces between them, and linked interior with exterior space. "With each step the building formed itself. What began as a use-suggesting form continued as a form-suggesting use. As each form grew to perform easily and naturally the task for which it was intended, it grew to perform other tasks as well. Some forms have many accomplishments. For them, doing has become an act of being. They have become more important than what they do. They have become art."

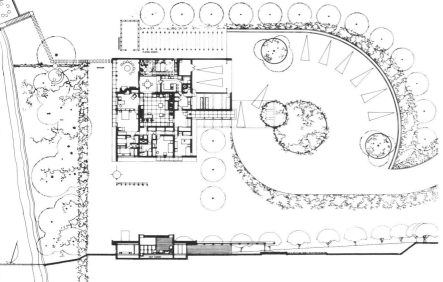

Treanor house plan.

Greenwood Mausoleum, Fort Worth, 1959. Photo: H.H. Harris.

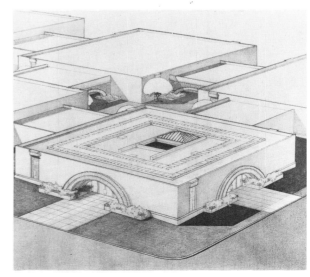

Greenwood Mausoleum. To expand the mausoleum, new buildings can be arranged around an open court.

The Unitarian Church in Dallas (1963) was a closed form for reasons other than climate – walls sealed off the sights and sounds from a heavily traveled street. The top lighting (borrowed from the Treanor garden room) was a twelve-foot band of prism glass around the perimeter of the roof truss. To enhance the quality of light entering the sanctuary the glass was set seven feet above the dropped ceiling. "Light streams down around the cloudlike ceiling like rain pouring off an umbrella. The

walls become a curtain of light, not so much enclosing space as marking the limits of one's interest," noted Harris.

The exterior forms were also limiting. The wide frame of ornament in high relief gave a scalelessness which reinforced the spiritual aspect. Projecting from the sanctuary was a long low block comprising entrance court and classrooms. The building owed something to Wright's Romanza period, but its spirit reaches back to the New England of Ralph Waldo Emerson.

In 1908, Louis Sullivan took banking out of shadowy grandeur by opening the walls with semicircles of light in his Owatonna, Minnesota Security Bank. He animated the interiors with ornamental grillwork and terra cotta, but over the years the remodelings steadily reduced the exuberance. In the 1950s when a more extensive remodeling was successfully opposed by architects and historians, Harris, whose devotion to Sullivan was well known, was called in as a consultant and remained as

the architect in full charge of the remodeling. He opposed such suggestions as a metal grid and plaster ceiling at the perimeter to light the tellers' booths because it blocked out the upper spaces. Instead, he worked out an open trellis in which lighting was integral, to be installed where light was needed. For the first time in many decades Sullivan was restored to his full glory.

During a lull in 1962 in the Fort Worth office Harris accepted a professorship at North Carolina State University School of Architecture. (The school was building up an impressive faculty; one professor was Matthew Nowicki who designed the arena at Raleigh in 1953.)

Harris expected to return to Texas after a year but as commissions continued his departure was postponed. Finally, in 1968, he built his own combined house and office. Now he is an emeritus professor at North Carolina State University, and at 79 he works in his office alone or with one

draftsman, at least one commission always on the board.

Two commissions of the Raleigh years involved planning clustered buildings on large pieces of land, both closer in spirit to the loose planning of the Chadwick School than the geometric clustering of the mausoleum. The first commission was for Raleigh's St. Giles Presbyterian Church, on a hilly wooded site. The decision to build in stages came from lack of funds to construct the most costly building, the sanctuary. The rapidly changing role of the church had upset so many established priorities that the congregation decided to build only what was urgently needed. An existing building was turned into a youth center, and three new buildings were constructed.

The layout was adjusted to the natural rise and fall of the land, and as many trees as possible saved. Fellowship Hall was placed on high land near the street, and down the slope was a structure housing the pastor's study, board room, and church offices; the third building was a **T**-shaped group of classrooms set among trees.

Fellowship Hall was designed to accommodate church services and all other activities until the sanctuary was built. It was a blend of moods: the sacred and the temporal. By the simple structural device of running the framing members longitudinally the gable was at the sides rather than ends. "I don't like the strong processional thing," Harris said. "This is a more comfortable shape."

In the enormous circular windows in the gables the intersection of a heavy framing member and a glazing bar formed a cross, which was silhouetted against the trunks and foliage of pines. On either side were tall slender panels of glass, emphasizing the height of the peak and the circular window. The window took on some of the importance of an altar.

The design inspiration for it and the sanctuary finished in 1983 came from A.C. Schweinfurth's 1893 Unitarian Church in Berkeley, which combined shingled walls with overscaled circular windows beneath a gabled roof. Schweinfurth's church, however, was something of a displaced Doric temple deprived of marble, standing at a busy intersection near the campus. The sanctuary seems not to have been designed but to have grown in its wooded dell. It is a spiritual presence.

The other commission was an unbuilt vacation resort village to cover the entire small island of Kinabalu, ½ mile off the west coast of North Borneo. Reached only

St. Giles Presbyterian Church, sanctuary. Of the same material and family of forms as Fellowship Hall, the sanctuary nestles in a dell. Trellised walks tie together the complex of buildings. Photo: Brian Shawcroft.

St. Giles Presbyterian Church, Raleigh, 1969-83. Layout, clockwise from top: Fellowship Hall, sanctuary, classrooms, youth center, offices and pastor's study.

by ferry from the mainland, the diversions were built in; around the 450-room hotel, in low buildings linked by gardens, were planned movie theater, bowling alley, discotheque, arboretum, and a floating restaurant on a lagoon.

**St. Giles
Presbyterian
Church,** Fellowship
Hall. Harris's
inspiration was A.C.
Schweinfurth's 1898
Unitarian Church in
Berkeley, combining
shingled walls and
bull's-eye windows
under a low gable.
Photo: H.H. Harris.

**St. Giles
Presbyterian
Church,** Fellowship
Hall. A view through
a bull's-eye window
toward the pines.
Photo: Louise
Andrews.

Harris studio house, Raleigh, 1968-77. A view from the living court through the glass wall to the sixteen-foot-high living room. Photo: Joann Sieburg-Baker.

Most of Harris's buildings in North Carolina were residential, although several churches were planned. The most adventuresome of the residential work was his own combined house and office. On the narrow sloping lot he managed two double-height rooms, one the office, the other the living room; above the drafting room was an open balcony for drawing and photographic files, and above the kitchen, bath, and bedroom were a small office and sitting room/guest room with a view toward the living room terrace. The entrance was at the second level, and the stairs down to the living room faced a two-story wall of glass. Beyond the glass was a high-walled court; paved with large glazed tiles— everything was in scale with the high wood wall and the huge opening to the living room, even the pots with blooming plants and the long tubular shade of Japanese paper hanging from the open web beams. This one bit of high-tech imagery was beautifully at home. The red of the open steelwork, supporting the Tectum ceiling and roof, was a chord which resounded in the room in the violet-colored door, the color extending up to an open web beam. The particular red-violet color dematerialized the corner while holding the eye. In North Carolina, Harris changed his palette of colors to acid yellows and true yellow, olive drab, and green-browns, which he used with grayed blues. Stronger colors appeared on movable planes like doors and in tracery like the open web beams.

In North Carolina most clients had a cultural orientation based more on the Colonial past. In Texas and California the Spanish Colonial tradition had been watered down, and Harris was one of several architects who created a new tradition. Many of Harris's clients in North Carolina were university professors from states where the Colonial past was alien so he could be more innovative. Contrary to typical practice, children's rooms and game or playroom were on the lower level in two houses, the social rooms and parents' bedroom above. In the Van Alstyne house in Durham (1966), the wide view of the countryside from the second level determined the location.

The Sugioka house in Chapel Hill (1967) was at the end of a cul-de-sac on a lot sloping down to a stream. The social rooms and parents' quarters were at the street level, and children's rooms below. Both houses were of wood, with hipped or gabled roof. There seemed to have been few of the wonderful Texas roofs which built up slowly.

The 1964 Lindahl house in Chapel Hill was close to the California ranch house in plan; like Ramona's Marriage Place in San Diego, it was a **U** plan around a court. Lindahl was a Californian, so client and architect spoke in a shorthand both understood.

In 1980 we walked around the house together, ending up in the court. Harris watched several leaves from the oaks and hickories on the site fall onto the white surface of the gabled roof. He seemed as sensitive to the chance gifts from nature as to his own contributions to the house.

The North Carolina houses were less exploratory than the Havens, Wyle, and J. Lee Johnson houses, perhaps due to the new climate, new cultural orientation, or a growing satisfaction with simpler solutions. But then just how simple was that glazed aisle facing a gallery around a court? Simplicity hid a rich complexity. At any rate, when our civilization has reached the end of the single-family house, Harris's complex or simple houses are the vital stuff the historians will feed on to reconstruct the treasures of the past.

"... the narrow
way lay right up the
hill, and the name
the going up the side
of the hill is called
Difficulty." Pilgrim's
Progress, John
Bunyan

Gregory Ain

The buildings of Gregory Ain came out of an attitude toward society that was intensified by the long, deep Depression of the 1930s. He had inherited his political philosophy from his socialist father, and during the Depression took an active part in bringing about social change.

He was set in the direction of modern architecture by his meeting with R.M. Schindler at age seventeen, and by Richard Neutra when he was twenty. Eclectic styles flourished, but Ain considered historicism a waste and individualism irresponsible. He saw in modern architecture a means toward social ends.

Most of his clients shared his concerns. His floor plans were conceived for the many rather than the individual, which accounts for his success in group housing, his most significant contribution to architecture. His theories began to crystallize in 1935 when he designed a prototype for housing agricultural workers. For group housing he tried pre-assembled bathrooms, prefabricated wall systems, precut studs, predrilled holes in studs for wiring. But his practical sense always drew him back to the custom-built carpenter's house because it was cheaper. Another factor was that most of his clients had unique sites, steep upslopes or downslopes, costing often no more than three or four hundred dollars. The prototype for mass housing developed early in the war by Konrad Wachsmann and Walter Gropius was based on factory production systems, and the *Arts & Architecture* Case Study prototypes were designed for flat sites. It remained for the merchant builders of the 1950s to find shortcuts acceptable to the building trades which could speed up mass production. The solutions of the merchant builders took no heed of the environment; one exception was the enlightened developer, Joseph Eichler, who chose excellent architects in Northern California, and Quincy Jones of Jones and Emmons in the south.

There was nothing clever or intricate in Ain's designs. Any carpenter could build them. They were constructed extraordinarily well, due to Ain's sense of obligation to the client and his choice of contractors who shared his goals.

His houses presented no sudden surprises, nothing underscaled or overscaled to delight or confound the eye; none of Schindler's sharp wit, suggesting that a house was built with a 4-H pencil rather than hammers and nails (Schindler actually used only 2-Bs). None of Neutra's implied metal columns, which were usually posts coated with aluminum paint. (When Ain and Harris worked for Neutra they thought of asking him: "What is the best material to build a steel house of?")

A house of Ain's could be easily recognized; even in a December pea soup fog one might have found his way to the Mar Vista housing project by the shape of the light from the windows. There were other guides such as his way of opening up a corner of a two-story house with glass. He didn't dissolve the corner; light was not the decoration, for the structural material was not delicate steel but usually two by fours that were emphasized by being painted a light color—one was the first Beckman house (1938).

Sometimes it was a glass cage projecting from the facade as in the Margolis house (1951)—not an arbitrary cage tacked on.

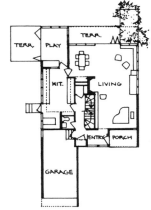

Gregory Ain's entry for the **General Electric** competition, 1935.

Ain's $4800 house of 1936 for a postman works as well today for a doctor. This and the 1935 plan for the General Electric competition (above), are examples of his servantless plan, which provides access to the kitchen from the entry and a way for a mother to oversee children while working in the kitchen. Photo: Marvin Rand.

The house is in a canyon off a narrow street, and the front yard promised to be a parking lot when there were many guests, so Ain made a gift of the front to a motor court, then projected the cage at one end of the facade, angling it in a gesture of welcome. The cage lights the entry hall and stair to the second story living room; the living room belonged on the second level anyway because there a south terrace could be cut into the upslope.

Another cage is like a nest of tables, one roof sliding out from another (Edwards house, 1936); the top roof is solid and the bottom one glass.

These details told more than just the way the light was brought in. They suggested the quality of the light in the Coastal Zone of Southern California. It is a soft haze, very different from the desert light in which the noon sun burns the sky almost white. The overcast sun in Los Angeles throws out an enormous amount of heat, and it is this rather than the light that made continuous windows on the south a grave mistake. Ain was always annoyed by the south-facing curtain wall office buildings along Wilshire Boulevard with their windows curtained all day.

He also knew the seasonal rains; he designed only one "butterfly" roof—two sheds draining to a valley between. The valley was sure to leak when the first heavy rains of the fall "surprised the roofs," Frank Lloyd Wright's expression for what happened when the first rains hit the roof of his Millard house.

He knew the various soils, from the stable decomposed granite of Hollywood to the wicked, layered formations of shale and siltstone in which the strata inclined out. Los Angeles was the only landscape he had known from the time he was three until his first visit outside the state when he was over forty. All his daily images were of sprawling communities welded together in the 1920s by the coming of the water from Owens Valley; of the spaces between the communities filling in over the years by the steady flow of new settlers, until Los Angeles was a vast continuous city almost to San Diego.

He understood how house styles changed and the climate didn't. He understood how houses were built because of the concentration of builders in the East Los Angeles area where he grew up. Many of the carpenters were Socialists, friends of his father. Ain went to high school with their sons; like many first-generation Americans, they followed their father's occupation. During the Depression years carpenters waited of a morning at the corner of Third and La Brea to be picked up by any contractor who needed an extra hand or two. By 1945 most of the fine Swedish and German carpenters had retired and been replaced by men trained to build barracks.

One builder true to the old type was "Shy" Kaplin, born and trained in Russia. When he put in the lowest bid for Ain's first house it seemed much too low. The bid was low, said Kaplin, because he liked the house. He constructed several of Ain's early buildings and commissioned Ain to design the Dunsmuir Flats, a remarkable plan that staggered four two-story apartments on a 49-foot-wide lot.

"Shy became enamored of each house he built for me and wanted to make gifts to it. He built the furniture as a gift for one of the bedrooms of the Edwards house."

Ain had a high regard for excellence and social conscience, inherited from his father, Baer Ain, who named his son for a Menshivist hero, Gregory Gershuny.

Baer Ain, son of a rabbi, was born in 1880 in a rural community in Poland that was annexed by Czarist Russia, and there as a young man he joined the Menshivists and dedicated himself to teaching peasants to read. After the 1905 revolution he was arrested and sent to Siberia. By then he was married to his cousin, Chiah, daughter of a well-to-do importer of woolens and flax from England, who by good fortune also had shipping interests. He arranged Baer's escape from Siberia to Hamburg, where Baer's wife and infant daughter awaited him at the dock. They sailed to the port of Philadelphia, arriving Christmas Day, 1906. From there they went to Chiah's successful uncle in Pittsburgh, and Baer was introduced to shopkeeping—to him a form of exploitation.

Living close to one successful in-law after another annoyed the socialistic Baer, and

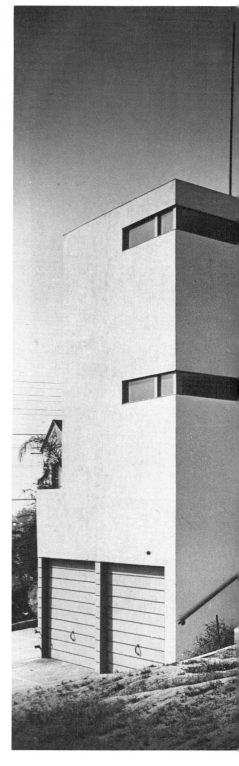

The Dunsmuir Flats tested all of Ain's skills and gave him the assurance that he was not just an architect by chance. Here he began to simplify framing and to devise ways to light all rooms from three sides. Photo: Julius Shulman.

after Gregory, the second child, was born in March 1908 he moved on to Kentucky, which proved even less congenial because of the treatment of the blacks. Gregory was three when the family settled in Los Angeles, with no relatives closer than San Diego. By this time there was a third child, Augusta, named for the German socialist, August Bebel.

In Los Angeles he settled into shopkeeping and the enjoyment of a circle of political friends among the large colony of Russian and Polish refugees. The family lived near Boyle Heights, already an ethnic community. Typical of Boyle Heights was the small frame house on a 50-foot lot, with a lawn and shade tree in front; the children of the original builders were by then moving across the river to more up-to-date houses and apartments. The houses were still neatly kept, but the sounds on the street were livelier; the business districts were transformed by a population which used the streets as a living room; men sat in cafes over a glass of tea and argued; the women gathered in knots in the markets; it was a verbal community. One could have smelled the change by the spicier odors. Brooklyn Avenue was the center of activity.

Baer Ain became a supporter of Job Harriman, a Socialist candidate in 1911 for mayor of Los Angeles. (He received 35 percent of the vote.) By 1914 the labor movement had been broken in Los Angeles, and a group headed by Harriman bought a thousand-acre tract in the Antelope Valley on Llano del Rio[1] to start a cooperative farming colony. Harriman was a grass roots liberal from the Midwest who had studied law. Ain put up $500 to join the colony, the full payment being $1500, the balance to be deducted from the $4 a day guaranteed wage. Only a third of the colonists had experience in agriculture but many, like Ain, chose it above the dozen or more occupations.

Gregory and his sisters attended the Montessori kindergarden or the public school. Ain taught Gregory to observe the earth formations and the stars, and the boy became intensely aware of shapes and

colors and began to draw. At night in their tent the children devoured books, played mathematical games, and were scolded by their father if they lapsed from formal English or into accents he considered impure. ("He was a linguistic snob," Gregory said later.)

When arguments started between the financial directors and the policy directors over the running of the colony, Baer Ain was impatient; the nightly doctrinaire arguments of the colonists began to unravel his nerves. After a year and a half Baer Ain had had enough and withdrew from the colony. From that time on he never attended a Socialist meeting.

The family returned to Los Angeles where they settled again into a shop, this time a tire shop near the county hospital. Henceforth his friends were from among the more philosophical socialists who took an international view of politics. A change in political philosophy meant only a change of cafes on Brooklyn Avenue; each sect had its own.

Ain became successful enough in the tire business to open a second shop in Culver City. Gregory, then in Lincoln High School, began to draw automobiles. His father blamed the capitalist schools and questioned the teachers about their political views. When Gregory brought home a table he had made in manual training class his father asked why he didn't build something useful like a garage. At fifteen, Gregory managed to build one. His father found fault with a window which did not fill in the space between the studs.

During Gregory's last year in high school a friend of his father's sent him to see a modern house on Kings Road in West Hollywood. The meeting with R.M. Schindler was decisive. Schindler explained the principle of the concrete, redwood, and glass house, and made Gregory at ease. He met Mrs. Schindler, and because of the Schindlers's involvement in left-wing politics, Gregory accepted modern architecture as an agent of social change.

Gregory said many years later, "There was another reason I liked architecture. It was the only field my father knew nothing about."

He announced when he graduated from high school at age sixteen that he wanted

1. *Dolores Hayden*, Seven Utopias: The Architecture of Communitarian Socialism, 1790-1975 (*Cambridge: MIT Press, 1976*).

to study architecture at the University of Southern California. His father insisted that he take a year first at UCLA (which had no tuition) studying mathematics and physics. He was determined that Gregory have training in the hard sciences and enter a profession.

Gregory enrolled in architecture in 1926 at USC. Instead of learning about design as he had imagined, he spent hours drawing classical orders in India ink. When his father saw the drawings he thought architecture a frivolous profession indeed, one that promised little opportunity for straightening out the world. In the summer he gave his son one of the tire shops to manage, with immediate and disastrous results. The youth clearly had no head for business.

The father may have had a presentiment that he was dying, for he made a last attempt to find a niche for his son. He appealed to two Culver City friends, licensed engineers, to give Gregory a drafting job on a city hall they were designing.

Baer Ain died as the job was completed. But Gregory had found his niche. He moved easily on to the Department of Parks and Recreation. There, with another draftsman, he started plans to remodel the Director's House at Barnsdall Park on Olive Hill. This had been designed by R.M. Schindler while working for Frank Lloyd Wright; Aline Barnsdall, Wright's client, had in 1923 deeded to the city eleven acres of Olive Hill, which included Hollyhock House and the Director's House.

"We were taken off the job before we could do any damage," Ain said. Instead, he was put to designing some benches for the beach at Venice. The handsome umbrella-shaped pergolas had seating around a central support. They still stand at the Venice Beach.

Ain met Neutra at Schindler's Kings Road house in 1928. When they were alone Ain said shyly that it must be a great experience living in a modern house. Neutra replied that only houses using industrial technology were truly modern. This idea so impressed Ain that when he received a notice that Neutra was teaching a course in modern building at the Academy of Modern Art in Hollywood he enrolled. As Neutra's Lovell house was then under

construction it became a laboratory for the students. Out of a group of a dozen who attended all the lectures grew Neutra's first apprentice program. The classes were held at night and the students worked on theoretical projects under Neutra's supervision. Among the students was Harwell Harris, a sculpture student at Otis Art Institute.

Neutra soon proposed that they form a chapter of CIAM (Congrès Internationaux d'Architecture Moderne), whose third international congress was being held in Brussels in 1930. The subject was rational city planning and housing. Harris, appointed secretary, sent in the dues for the new chapter, and Neutra had no competition for the post of delegate to the congress. Ain and Harris, too new to architecture to distinguish *avant* from rear guard, became willing participants. Under Neutra's direction they prepared the projects he would present at the congress.

Thus began one of the most vital and concentrated student projects ever attempted in the United States. It was the more remarkable because it came from a nonaccredited school—a nonschool, in fact—directed by a 33-year-old architect with no previous teaching experience, newly licensed, with one completed building (Garden Apartments with Schindler) and a second almost finished.

It was the initial step in Neutra's theoretical project, *Rush City Reformed*. The students worked on office towers in inner city blocks, linked together by upper-level bridges; a twenty-story apartment house on the beach, raised on pilotis, two rooms deep, which used up little land and gave each apartment a share of the view; row housing with a community center; one-story modular housing in gardens, built with lightweight sandwich panels of diatom (porous microscopic sea deposits). Another project grew out of the first study for the Lovell house. Neutra initiated then the procedure of assigning a project to one draftsman, who followed it through to the end. He assigned Ain the beach apartment and a prison. Ain describes the prison as a four-story building with a glazed shaft at each corner. "It was detached from the cell blocks, and one guard could watch three floors from his shaft." Ain came down

with the flu while working on it, and Neutra drove to his house with a small drawing board and the incomplete drawings for Ain to finish in bed. "Neutra could never see why you stopped working just because you were sick," Ain said.

It was a three-year course in architecture and planning squeezed into one. In directing the work, Neutra's own ideas expanded and crystallized, and it would be hard to believe that any delegate arrived in Brussels more thoroughly prepared to present ideas on the rational city. The Rush City drawings were traced crisply in ink, the Lovell house was photographed under Neutra's critical eye after the furniture he had designed for it was installed.

There was not just one set of drawings and photographs but several. Neutra had decided to travel to Europe by way of Japan, and he wrote architects and editors in the cities where he wanted to make stopovers to ask for speaking engagements and publication. This in itself was a lesson to the apprentices in how to generate interest in their work. The fact that early houses by Ain and Harris were well photographed is due largely to Neutra's influence. (An editor of *Architectural Forum* said Neutra was a welcome contributor because he always sent good photographs and documentation.)

After Neutra sailed in the spring of 1930 for Yokohama no other work had quite the immediacy or tension for the apprentices. By then both were committed to architecture, which they now saw in terms larger than the single building.

Ain's real apprenticeship had been his work at night on Neutra projects, but at the same time he held day jobs, one as a draftsman in the office of B. Marcus Priteca, designer of many ornate movie palaces. The salary from daytime work allowed him at age 21 to marry Agnes Budin, whom he had met at the Academy of Modern Art.

Of considerable importance in Ain's development were the weeks he worked in the office of R.M. Schindler. Ain said of this: "At the time, I was trying to get jobs of my own. Schindler could not help with that but whenever I dropped into his office he would put me to work for a few days. He didn't really need me, he just made work for me. I was paid 50 cents an hour. He was doing some low-cost houses I liked and I worked on some interiors. Schindler was different from Neutra—he had transitions from one volume to another, there were sequences of spaces. Neutra was more concerned with windows."

Between 1930 and 1932, Ain designed a number of buildings, none of them going beyond preliminary design or working drawings; only a few remodelling jobs were executed. He was still at a disadvantage in asking clients for his fee when a job was cancelled. He was spared from mastering this most uncongenial of tasks by the return of Neutra in 1931.

Ain worked for Neutra until 1935. The major projects in which he participated were Neutra's own house (1933), Beard house (1935), and smaller houses, one for Galka Scheyer, a client who annoyed Neutra by telephoning after midnight; when she wanted an addition to her house Neutra gladly turned her over to Ain as a going-away present.

Neutra's first big job after the Lovell house was the one for himself. It was not the all-steel tour de force the Lovell was, but compact and comfortable; the living room, facing the street, was raised above traffic sights and sounds for a view of Silver Lake. Ain learned much from Neutra's siting of the house; the broad expanse of the lake expanded the site. The Neutras moved in in 1933—and Ain and his wife with them. It was a move Ain would regret in time, as he had failed to note that Neutra was as hard to please as his father.

The Beard house promised to put into practice some of the innovations developed in the housing for Rush City. Beard, the son of historians Charles and Mary Beard, was the perfect client, approving all of Neutra's proposals. The framing was **H** columns and open bar joists, the same as the Lovell house; exterior walls were hollow panels faced with sheets of thin steel. Under the floor slab of diatom was a heating system which spread the heat through the hollow walls to warm the rooms. Ain's early houses incorporated novel heating systems on a smaller scale.

The two years of living under the same roof with a man as dynamic as Neutra made it hard for the Ains to have a life of their own. Added to this was the irregularity of Ain's $10 per week salary. There were several draftsmen in the office then (a few on salary) and several buildings on the boards, one the fine Von Sternberg house. The draftsmen speculated often on the chances a modern architect had to set up his own office, what the possibilities were of getting clients like Beard or Von Sternberg who allowed you to experiment. As Ain brooded over the lot of the modern architect the tensions in his marriage increased.

He knew it was time to leave. He was becoming surer of his abilities. He made suggestions to Neutra about the floor plan of the Beard house; when Neutra rejected them Ain drew an alternate plan for his own amusement and called it "Billy Whiskers." When he was developing Neutra's scheme for a small house for the General Electric competition he again was rebuffed for suggesting ways of easing the circulation of the plan. Ain began working at night on his own plan to submit. (Neutra's plan received one of the more important awards, Ain's a lesser one, for which he got an electric clock.)

Ain's General Electric plan followed a practice he stuck to: the entry hall was the key to the circulation. From it was always access to living room, kitchen, and stairs. In the General Electric plan there was even a door to the garage, and a lavatory near the entry. He was skillful in planning circulation without pressure or crowding. A prophetic feature of his competition house was a playroom off the kitchen, with folding glass panels opening the playroom to a play terrace. This was one of the first acknowledgements that children in a servantless house needed play spaces where they could be watched from the kitchen.

There has always been a lag between changes in living style and the family composition and the reflection of them in the floor plan.

Neutra and Schindler rarely reached the really democratic approach to the kitchen that Ain found at once. In Neutra's 1933 Kun house there is an outside stair down from the garage/roof garden level to the service porch off the kitchen; the

main stair from the roof garden lands in the living room. To answer the front door a servant (if any) would cross the social areas. The housewife returning from market would surely have taken the sheltered route through the living room rather than the outside stair. The assumption of servants runs through most of the Schindler and Neutra plans, while Ain assumed a servantless house.[2]

Ain was early to discard the service porch and put the washer and dryer under the counter in the kitchen. It was the rare Schindler or Neutra client who had a full-time servant, yet the plan implied them. During the 1940s when I would develop a rough floor plan of Schindler's, I omitted a wall to the service area and left a wide opening between kitchen and dining area. He always restored the full walls. Cooking smells seemed to worry the Viennese, and to have an undercounter washing machine in the kitchen was a no-no. Wright solved cooking odors by lifting his kitchen ceilings. Ain had no service porch in his own house (1941), and he left a pass-through between kitchen and dining area. Schindler missed the point when he used a glass panel over the kitchen counter of his Laurelwood Apartments. If it kept the kitchen smells in, it also opened the kitchen to view, which must have pained him, for he deplored the poor housekeeping of most of his clients.

But the owners of Schindler homes had grown up with servants, were educated, and were involved in political or civic activities, or held jobs. Their children were in nursery schools, and their "help" was the cleaning woman who came once a week—no work sharing with husbands. Also, modern houses were a badge of intellectual emancipation; the less venturesome and more domestic women preferred a Cape Cod or ranch house.

The floor plan has come far since Philip Webb's Red House for William Morris (1859), with its dining room down a long narrow hall from the kitchen, which in days when eating was hearty and courses numerous could have been a long haul for the butler. Yet the Red House is almost the beginning of the emancipated house.

In 1935, Ain signed a contract with C.H. Edwards for a small house. With this, and a second story addition for Galka Scheyer, he set up his own office. Scheyer, who introduced German expressionism to America, left a rare art legacy to Southern California. Born Emmy Scheyer in Braunschweig in 1889, she took up the study of art at age sixteen, but her interest in her own work lagged when she discovered Alexi Jawlensky in Switzerland in 1916. (He gave her the name Galka after a bird he had seen in a dream.) Henceforth her mission was to promote Jawlensky and his friends Kandinsky, Feininger, and Klee. She visited Klee at the Bauhaus while he was teaching there.

In 1925 she brought some 300 oils, watercolors, and prints of the "Blue Four" to America "where the brain was not yet tired." When a rare sale occurred she took her commission in a piece from the collection; to support herself she lectured and taught painting to children at the Anna Head School in Berkeley.

Greta Davidson remembered Galka as a refreshingly outspoken woman, "so ugly that she would not have her picture taken." Mrs. Davidson recalled a party at which the hostess remarked that something "could not be done socially." Galka retorted, "Everything can be done, even murder. And we must try to understand."

Claire Falkenstein who replaced Galka at the Head School when she moved to Los Angeles said that Galka had the same intensely dramatic gestures in the classroom as in her role as a madam in a UC Berkeley play.

Marjorie Eaton, a client of Ain's, said she took lots of pictures of Galka but the only one left was of her back as she directed a bulldozer excavating for Eaton's little theater. Eaton recalled Galka's many affairs but was offended to read that Schindler was her lover. "Never. He had great respect for her although they quarreled constantly. She wanted him to instruct her in modern architecture but always fell asleep at the lessons."

Galka's great love was her collection, for which she sacrificed much and regularly

---

2. Le Corbusier wrote in the 1920s that "in a decent house the servants' stairs do not go through the drawing room." But by the 1930s in Southern California stairs and servants (if any) were singular.

Galka Scheyer house, Hollywood Hills, 1935. This second floor space was added for guests and the exhibiting of European Modern artists. Photo: Julius Shulman.

replenished on trips to Europe. When Jawlensky gave her a series of oils of heads she gave five to her closest friends: Eaton, Greta Davidson, Walter Arensberg, her attorney Milton Wichner (for whom Davidson designed an unbuilt house), and Valeska (Lette Valeska, native of Braunschweig who used only her last name for her paintings and photographs in Los Angeles; after Galka's death at age 56, Valeska was appointed curator of her collection).

Both the Arensberg and Scheyer collections were offered to UCLA on condition a special wing be built for them; when this could not be guaranteed Arensberg's went to Philadelphia and Scheyer's was left in trust to the Pasadena Museum. The museum floundered

financially after completing a costly new building of questionable merit, and was "saved" by Norton Simon, who gave it his name. When he changed the emphasis from modern to old masters he disposed of some moderns to help pay for some million-dollar headliners. Sued by artists and former trustees of the museum, certain restrictions were imposed, but at the time of writing the fate of the Scheyer Collection is in doubt.

The formidable Scheyer knew what she liked in architecture as well as painting. She had met many of the Bauhaus architects and was at home with the Neutra style. The budget was small for Scheyer's second floor addition so Ain used stucco over wood framing, with four-by-eight plywood panels for interior walls. To bring

the walls into scale with the paintings he raised the ceiling height for the main space to ten feet, but he emphasized the standard eight feet of the plywood panels by inserting a metal channel between them and the two-foot strip above. Paintings were hung by a single wire from hooks in the channel. The numerous storage cabinets were dimensioned to the sizes of Scheyer's watercolors and prints. On the secluded hill much of the living was on a balcony shaded by a grove of eucalyptus, with views toward canyons and city. Scheyer could shower on the balcony by reaching through the bathroom window and turning the shower head toward the deck. On the walls of the bathroom hung paintings worth half a million dollars today.

Edwards house, Los Angeles, 1936. A view from the side street. Photo: Lynton Vinette.

The two-bedroom Edwards house is in the hills above Los Feliz Boulevard, on a small lot on a loop of a climbing narrow road. The major site problems were the double slope and the public view of three sides of the lot from the road. The entrance is over a bridge which passes the depressed service yard, effectively screened out by planting. The front door is set deep in the plan and at the narrowest point; from the entry hall are doors to service and bedroom wings and living room. The first view of the living room is toward a glass wall opening to the terrace. Projecting from the living room toward a swimming pool is the glass cage (mentioned earlier) which slides out from under a solid roof.

The social rooms are the only ones that do not face the public road. The bedrooms are protected from view by a hedge at the lot line, and the bedroom terraces are covered with an arbor leading to the swimming pool. On the entrance side are the blank walls of garage and a bedroom; but on the third public side, dining, kitchen, and service yard, the wall is pierced and shaped. Ain wanted a three-dimensional wall like a Schindler but for all the stepped up and down surfaces, and the deep recess of the kitchen windows, it still reads as wall. Schindler would automatically have followed the motion of pushing in a wall with a countermotion of pulling another surface forward.

The planter on top of the wall is a Schindlerian touch—Schindler liked high planters in which the plants were sure to languish. He disguised the horticultural failure with boughs just before the photographer arrived. If this was not lush enough for him, he drew trailing vines in India ink directly onto the photograph. (Neutra was known for photographs with an out-of-focus eucalyptus branch in the foreground hiding something he disliked.)

The house, severely damaged by fire, was bought in that condition in 1969 by Dr. Theodore Lindauer who restored it to the original. On a plaque near the entrance are engraved the names of architect and craftsmen.[3] The original cost of the house was $5500, the restoration roughly fifteen times that much. Certain built-ins omitted during construction of the original plan were now added, as the cabinets on the fireplace wall.

3. *The Edwards house was named a historic cultural monument by the Los Angeles Cultural Heritage Board in 1983.*

Edwards pool off the glass-roofed playroom/library. Photo: Lynton Vinette.

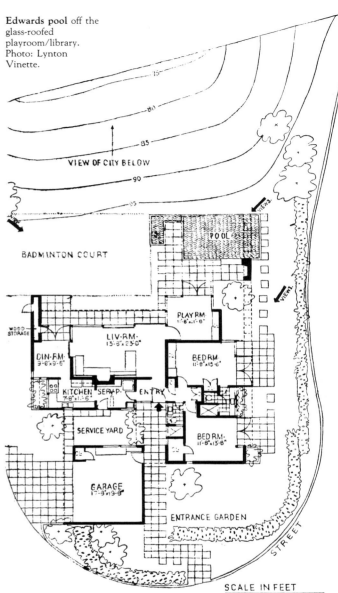

VIEW OF CITY BELOW

BADMINTON COURT

POOL

PLAY RM·

LIV·RM·
13'-6"x23'-0"

WOOD STORAGE

BED RM·
11'-6"x15'-6"

DIN·RM·
9'-6"x9'-6"

KITCHEN SERV·P· ENTRY
7'-6"x11'-6"

SERVICE YARD

BED RM·
11'-6"x13'-6"

GARAGE
17'-6"x19'-6"

ENTRANCE GARDEN

STREET

SCALE IN FEET
0 5 10 15 20 25

Edwards house plan.

Dr. Theodore Lindauer restored the **Edwards house** in the 1970s, making the playroom his library. Photo: Marvin Rand.

Ernst house, Los Angeles, 1937, is 200 yards up the hill from the Edwards. Photo: Fred Dapprich.

Two buildings completed the following year, 1937, were the Ernst house, up the hill from the Edwards house, and the Dunsmuir Flats for his contractor. Although the Ernst house is only 200 yards away from the Edwards, the rise is steep, and the site is a narrow shelf of land. The house is essentially a composition of big simple shapes, except for the one-story section of the front facade. The attached garage and entrance are of redwood siding, broken by two lines of horizontal windows the width of the siding, a detail which seems trivial beside the double volume plaster cube. Another face of the cube visible from the road is blank except for a high narrow window which splits the mass vertically. The low wood section is a reminder that Ain was one of the few of his generation who was never at home with the Wrightian idiom.

On the canyon elevation the glass is concentrated on one side, leaving the rest a blank wall. Ain begins here to treat walls as a grid of unequal rectangles, sometimes using color on the plaster within a rectangle to separate window wall from plaster wall. (See the 1949 Schairer house.)

The beams are extended over the glass areas to form a trellis, at the end of which is a planter box. Ain devised a way to water the vines which were to cover the trellis; irrigation pipes connected to the water supply were built in.

The plaster strip on the exterior wall between sash and clerestory pushes into the living room to become a high shelf for plants; the shelf is transformed into line to continue down the fireplace shaft, then it widens into a mantel. The metamorphosis from line to mass, was unmistakably out of Schindler.

A piece of paving glass was set in the floor of the entrance hall, and when lighted from below provided low illumination. This unexpected light disconcerted visitors — they carefully stepped over it.

**The living room of
the Ernst house.**
Photo: Philip Fein.

Dunsmuir Flats, Los Angeles, 1937. The north side is a tribute to the International style. The strip glazing lights the living room and entry. All rooms are lighted on three sides. Photo: Julius Shulman.

The Dunsmuir Flats of the same year is like one of the mathematical games Ain learned as a child. He set down a list of requirements extending beyond his hopes—"Just to see," he said. He did see. He saw something that affected the direction of his work and gave him a secure place in architecture. The only help he had from the site was the gradual upslope and the five degrees the sides varied from a pure rectangle. He made use of both by angling the building to the street and staggering the units back. The entrance corner of each unit hits exactly the four-foot setback line on the north. Each unit has its private entrance, lighted by a high continuous strip of glass on the north.

The entrance hall had access to the living room, the stair to the second floor, and a door to the service area, which led to a lavatory and the kitchen. One goal Ain set was to provide light from three sides for all rooms, accomplished in the kitchen by a clerestory above the entrance canopy. The dining space extending out from the kitchen has windows on the garden side and a panel of glass above the overhang.

Ain predated the merchant builders in reducing the number of elements in a structure. In the framing he carried four-by-four posts to the height of the building to form an uninterrupted girdle; he limited the sizes of wall openings to the four-foot intervals between the studs. This reduction brings a rhythm and an order that rules the building.

There is a change of mood from the north face to the south—the smooth thinness of the entrance side (north), the glass flush with the plaster, the only decoration

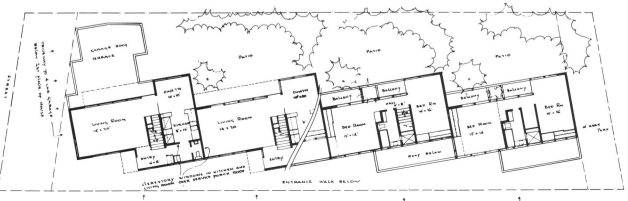

Dunsmuir Flats site plan.

The garden side of the Dunsmuir Flats adjusts to California living. Four units are staggered on the 49-foot-wide lot. Photo: Julius Shulman.

the continuous dark line of glass against white, the staggered blocks unified by the continuous glass (like a fascia), the glass disappearing behind the canopy over the low entrance, then reappearing. The mood on the south is openness—wide sliding glass, generous-sized sash and fixed panels, the wood trellises over the second floor porches. The rise of the natural grade placed one garden above the next.

In the four decades since the building was finished little has been changed; indeed, its structure defies change. It was locked into its site and locked into its moods, once and for all.

Shy Kaplin built it for himself and family, but the tenants in two of the units were friends of Ain—Robert and Dorothy Kahan, Rita and Max Lawrence. Mrs. Lawrence went to the Dunsmuir Flats as a bride, living there seven years, through two pregnancies, then moved to the Falk Apartments by Schindler, and after that to a planned community designed by Ain (Park Planned Homes in Altadena). Living so long in modern houses, the Lawrence children puzzled the Altadena teachers by putting flat roofs and large windows on all houses they drew. She recalled "the fun of being part of a new experiment. People came off the street to ask, 'Is it a house? What does it look like inside?' Greg gained his reputation from this building. Architecture students came often to photograph it, and they broke through the hedge to photograph the garden side. We lived there through the war years when you had to black out all windows at night. Not easy."

When Ain saw the building in 1979 after many years he was affected by the way it had been preserved. The new owner had known nothing of the historical importance of the building when she bought it several months before, and every week she discovered something endearing. She studied Ain's face for an explanation of her rapport with the building.

During that summer and fall when Ain and I visited his houses his spirits were low and he was intensely inward looking. He was surprised at the response to his work. The original owners whose faces had become dim to him treated him as if he

were a frequent visitor, for they had lived in his presence as long as four decades. He stood with his arms folded stiffly across his breast, his eyes moving over the rooms, slowly finding the intellectual process out of which some detail or felicity of plan had grown.

He talked shyly about the house, he talked about the little things. The owners talked about the big things—an exchange of roles from the time when the house was planned. Then it is the client who talks about the small things.

From 1938 on Ain usually had a collaborator. Before that he had shared an office with Harwell Harris. Upon leaving Neutra he had missed the stimulation of working in a drafting room with others. He did the preliminary design on all the buildings he listed as his own, often the working drawings, but the presence of a sympathetic colleague sparked his talent.

Harris had just finished his Fellowship Park pavilion and was working and living there in 1935 when Ain suggested sharing the work space. In exchange, he insisted on doing the working drawings of Harris's De Steiguer house. This association lasted less than a year, and during that time Ain brought in commissions for several houses on which they collaborated. None was built. Finally, Ain rented a small house in back of another on Kensington Road in Hollywood and set up an office.

In 1938 there was a collaborator, George Agron, a registered architect, which was an advantage because Ain was not licensed until 1943. Of the twelve projects they worked on together during 1938 and 1939, three were built, and after that Agron moved into the field of hospital design. There was another collaborator during the same years, Visscher Boyd, who had worked with Frank Lloyd Wright at Taliesin. Of their four collaborations, three houses were built, one the fine Tierman house.

Another collaborator was James H. Garrott, who with Ain was part of a group making proposals to the government for low-cost housing. (This brought about a sympathetic exchange of letters between him and Eleanor Roosevelt.) "One day I had to drop off some plans, and I was sur-

prised at the litter along the path to his house at the back," Garrott said. "I asked him if that didn't turn a client off. He was wounded. He couldn't imagine why clients cared where you lived if your work was good. He was so intense about his work that I don't think he ever noticed where he lived or what he ate."

Garrott at that time was moving to the Granada Building where many architects had offices, and he offered to share his space with Ain. It was Ain's first office, and he remained there until the beginning of the war. During that time, and later, Ain and Garrott collaborated on eight projects, all but two of which were built.

Ain's only partnership, Ain, Johnson and Day, began in 1946 and lasted five years.

Wood appeared more prominently in the 1937 houses, neatly in horizontal wood siding in the Goldberg house in North Hollywood, but manipulated in the Byler studio on Mt. Washington. In the latter he employed to little advantage the famous three-board corner detail Schindler took over from Wright and made his own—twelve-inch wide horizontal boards meet vertical ones in a mitred joint, the lapped boards producing strong shadow lines. Schindler used this large-scale detail above eye level to give a heavy half frame to a wall, but seen at eye level on the side of Ain's garage, and below eye level in the wide band below windows it is overweight.

Another house for a flat site, also of wood and stucco, has evolved because of the unusual activities of the owner. Richard Hoffman, a fine printer now retired from teaching printing at a state university, had acquired two historic presses and a library of fine editions. When the house was built in 1939 it was for a typical site (60-foot wide lot), a typical family (two adults, two small children), and at a cost typical of the contractor-built house ($5000); but the plan, materials, and orientation were not typical of the contractor house. A clerestory on the east followed the line of the steep shed roof in the living room, the high point a large brick fireplace; there were brick-paved terraces off the living room on the north, and the dining room on the

Hoffman house, Van Nuys, 1939. The north terrace is for the warm California summers. Photo: John Allen.

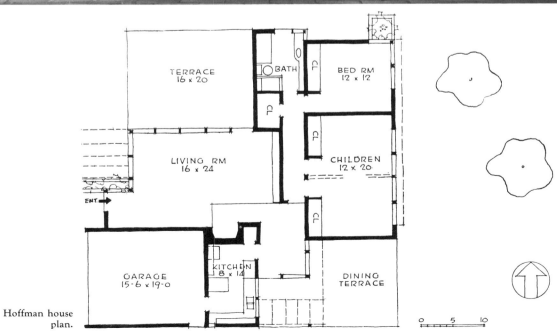

TERRACE
16 x 20

BATH

CL

BED RM
12 x 12

CL

LIVING RM
16 x 24

CL

CHILDREN
12 x 20

ENT.

CL

GARAGE
15·6 x 19·0

KITCHEN
8 x 14

DINING
TERRACE

Hoffman house plan.

0   5   10

southeast. On the street side (west) was the garage and trellises shading the end of the living room patio.

Now the garage is a printing shop, the original kitchen a library containing examples from the great presses of the twentieth century. The dining terrace was enclosed for a dining room, with glass facing a deep garden and a print shop with an open porch. On the porch is a witch's brew of cotton and linen which each Friday is miraculously transformed into fine paper. Something of the intensity and order of the original design remains in the intense pursuit of a dying art—fine printing.

When the plans had first gone for approval to the FHA, the garage on the front was denied. Ain telephoned the agency in Washington to point out the inconsistency of their reprinting in an official bulletin a sketch of his showing a garage

at the front. They agreed.

During this period Ain added a stage and amphitheater to Marjorie Eaton's adobe house near Palo Alto. Eaton, artist and actress, had asked Schindler to design the addition but he declined because the required steel courses did not allow shaping the material or introducing clerestories or large openings. (In 1939, Schindler was at the end of his cubistic period and had begun to rotate the plan by quarter turns at three levels, as in the Falk Apartments; this and screen walls were elements in his ultimate style.)

When Ain drove up to see the site, the walls of the house were covered with panels of black-and-white cartoons of Picasso's *Guernica*—Galka Scheyer had brought over the original to be shown in the United States, in Los Angeles at the Stendahl Galleries.

"Gregory saw that the diagonal rows of my almond grove were like the diagonal thrust in the *Guernica* cartoons. Diagonal lines are to me like a violin striking. They are the charm of the addition."

The module is the adobe brick. The high side of the shed roof is the proscenium, and with the glass doors folded back the room is a good-sized stage, with dramatic action flowing out onto a paved apron. The hillside was terraced, and drain channels installed for run-off.

Ain designed a second addition in 1959, and in 1974 built a "meditation perch" in a live oak, which he called "the pulpit." The house was selected as one of the ten most interesting ones around Palo Alto, along with Wright's Hanna house, Willis Polk's Georgian brick mansion, and the 1919 reinforced concrete house for Herbert Hoover by Clark and Davis.

The **1937-39 Scharlin house,** just below the crest of the hill, looks out over a valley to the east and west. On the long climb from the street it appears first as plaster cubes bound together at three levels by heavy trellises of wood.

Ain often set his front door at right angles to the walk, as if a momentary glimpse might be an invasion; the glazed wall of an interior hall is all one sees from the approach to the Scharlin house. There are more changes of level in the plan than is typical of Ain, resulting here in a living room with a ten-foot ceiling. The dining room, up three steps, is opened to a balcony on the downslope side, to a terrace on the upslope side, and by windows facing a grove of eucalyptus. The dining room is an early catch-all room that has outlived one name after another—play room, recreation room, family room.

Scharlin house, Los Angeles, 1939, with long views of Silver Lake. Photo: Fred Dapprich.

In the 1938 Becker house, Ain entered the stronghold of Schindler and Neutra around Silver Lake, really a reservoir, the only large body of still water in Los Angeles. It took two architects from a landlocked country to put it on the map—Schindler controlling the west bank by 1940 and Neutra the east by the end of the 1950s. The lower slopes near the Schindler houses on Kenilworth and Moreno were pretty well built up by 1938, but the Becker house is on a pinnacle of an upper slope. The house is unusual in its mixture of the Art Deco (curved wall) and the International style (metal pipe rails instead of Ain's usual parapet walls around decks). He never departed so freely from the right angle as here, with four curved walls. It was a striking composition when photographed with a red filter, the white stucco against a black sky, the wide-angle lens carrying the planes toward infinity. The dark redwood of the garage doors, set back from a curved white wall, gave a sleekness that Ain did not recognize as his own from the photograph. When I showed him his own sketch of the house, with a classic car in the drive, he claimed it—and related Neutra's story of waiting for the right light to get a picture of Sullivan's Carson Pirie Scott store which gave the illusion of glass and mullions on the same plane. The Becker house gives the illusion of being a fine little villa William Lescaze might have done above Lake Geneva.

Ain returned to the right angle, to wood trellises, and to solid balcony rails the same year for the Eisenstadt and the first of the A.O. Beckman houses. The Beckman house is on an old street with deep setbacks, and Ain placed the garage forward and to one side, staggering back the

Becker house, Silver Lake, Los Angeles, 1938. This is one of the few Ain houses with Art Deco curves. Photo: Julius Shulman.

bedroom wing and social wing. The vertical masses are staggered up from the low garage to the bedroom wing to the master bedroom on the second story. The entrance is pushed deep into the **L**-shaped plan, past the canopied walk along the bedroom wing; this he oriented to play terraces on the south and lighted on the north by strip windows above a covered walk. From the street, the bedroom wing appears to be a flat-roofed pavilion, the bays marked by posts and transom bars—a solution less modern than horizontal planes among its eclectic neighbors.

Brownfield Medical Building, Los Angeles, 1939. In the **H** plan, the crossbar is a waiting room shared by two doctors. Photo: Julius Shulman.

Two buildings of the late 1930s show how Ain molded form, one the Brownfield Medical Building (1938) in southeast Los Angeles, the other the Hural house (1939-40) for the end of a cul-de-sac street in the Hollywood Hills. The form of the medical building comes from giving the two doctors' offices different identifications. In the dumbbell plan, two staggered masses are joined by a narrow, transparent reception room, the glass wall at the back facing a court made by the projecting walls of the offices.

The forms of the Hural house grow out of a budget of $4 per square foot, a need for a dental laboratory with a separate entrance, and the west orientation. Three different studies were made to reduce the amount of excavation, each one pushing the house closer to the street. The only terrace is a narrow strip off the living room, shielded from the street by a low hedge, with decks above the garage and off the second floor bedrooms. Ain managed to integrate the garage level into the composition by broadening one wall into a mass, which he carries up to the level of the balcony parapet wall; this at the same time gives privacy to the deck off the den. The steps to the laboratory pass the service entrance and continue to the top level.

Much of the cabinetry in the house is unchanged: dressing table and chiffoniere in the master bedroom, wardrobe closets with sculptured pulls (there were always wardrobes of two heights), and bathroom storage of the right size in the right place. His large, tiled showers with a seat are rarely changed.

Hural house, Los Angeles, 1940. This three-level house is backed up against a hill at the end of a cul-de-sac. Photo: Julius Shulman.

A **freestanding fireplace** shaft extends through two stories and pierces the roof of the Tierman living room. Photo: Julius Shulman.

Micheltorena is a collector's street of small houses. It is part of the Silver Lake area facing away from the lake. The fifteen-minute drive to city hall and the courts recommends it to municipal employees, lawyers, newspaper reporters, social workers, and anyone working in downtown offices. On Micheltorena is Schindler's Oliver house (1933), the first of his cubistic style; John Lautner's own redwood house (1939) on a sliver of land, and his "Silvertop" (1957), almost the first of his large innovative houses of the period when he was turning away from redwood to concrete. Within a half square mile around Micheltorena on the west side of the lake is the richest lode of architecture in Los Angeles: nine Schindlers, an early Neutra, a Soriano, three houses by Ain, and his Avenel cooperative.

One side of Micheltorena slopes down, the other side up; all are problem lots which cost $300-$400 in the mid-thirties. From the upslope or the downslope is a magnificent view of the city. But up or down, a flat roof was prohibited. Schindler used pitched roofs effectively disguised as flat. Ain went another route.

The roof was the controlling factor in his design of the Tierman and Daniel houses (1939) and the Orans house (1941). The first two are unequivocally hipped, the last a composition of shed roofs on three planes.

The Tierman exterior gives little indication of the richness of the spaces within. It is one story at the street and three at the back, the 600-square-foot street level all one space except for a walled bath. The space is developed under a pyramidal roof with a pyramidal skylight at the center. (A square steel tie prevents the roof from spreading.) The skylight butts into the brick shaft of a five-sided freestanding fireplace, which acts as an axle which spokes out to entry hall, living room, dining bay, and kitchen. With one space opening into another, the shaft of the fireplace is visible from all points. From the front door the shaft forms one wall of the stairwell to the bedrooms below; as the shaft rises in the living room it is seen through the skylight presiding over the roof top.

The fireplace pulls the eye. You follow the angles up to the skylight. You work down the pyramid shape of the ceiling to the eave line. The plywood panels of the ceiling fold down to the sliding glass which opens the entire floor to the wide deck overlooking the city.

The central space is lighted by high glass extending from the entry around two corners, by the large square windows in the kitchen, and by the glass wall facing the deck.

Tierman house,
Silver Lake, Los
Angeles, 1939, has a
pyramidal skylight at
the apex of the
pyramidal roof.
Stepped cabinets are
used to screen the
entry hall from view.
Photo: Julius
Shulman.

Daniel house, Los Angeles, 1939. Two joined, hipped roofs capping a house on a double slope disguise the smallness of the interior space. Photo: Julius Shulman.

The modern architects of the 1930s spread their small budgets in different ways. Ain uses standard height doors to the deck and folded-down ceiling. Davidson would have scrimped on something else and used eight-foot-high sliding glass; in the 1930s he never spent such a sum on a fireplace—his fireplaces then were a simple opening in a plastered wall, and in the few cases where he used marble it was a band around the throat and a small hearth. Schindler's glass doors were standard height because his plate line was there; he used clerestories above.

Ain found ways other than solid walls to separate entrance from living. Here he uses a five-foot cabinet stepping down to four-foot shelves on the entry side, and against these he backs up an angled sofa which faces the fireplace.

Ain's fondness for narrowing or broadening a white plaster plane as it moves around retreating dark values had play in the Daniel house. But the lot is wider than the Tierman lot, and the steepest slope parallels the street, which gave him a good-sized canvas to work on. Here the dark

values are the recessed doors of the garage and the recessed glass on the second level. The astonishing feat is the double-hipped roof, the minor one over the bedroom section at right angles to the major one over the rest of the house. This produces a strange situation at the entry porch where part of the roof continues as an open trellis. The front door is literally inside the living space, separated from the built-in sofa by five-foot-high shelves—the shelves themselves part of the complicated built-in which incorporates the sofa. The impression is of all the furniture slipping to one corner of the room; the corner is one from which there are views to the south and to a deck on the east.

The built-ins suggest a concentration of activities—there is even a desk. One wonders how those desks were used that the modern architects liked to tuck into living rooms. They seem part of stagecraft, act one of a Victorian play in which a letter is delivered, the mistress goes immediately to her desk to answer it, and a response comes before the end of the act. The desk took the place of the telephone; yet in the photograph of the built-in is a telephone on a shelf within reach of the sofa. A desk seemed of little use in a living room in the 1930s; if truly useful would it not be cluttered? Yet Neutra had them, Schindler had them, and also Ain. Schindler traveled light, and so did Ain, they were not collectors, they were not sentimental; never any clutter. The desk to them was form, design.

(Of all pieces of furniture the desk is the least abstract; one's attitude toward it is based on experience, the experience of how a tool rather than a piece of furniture works. My mother had a neat little desk in the library that was form and design; in a room off the back hall that was called "the office" was her working desk, with her portable typewriter where she typed under a picture of Woodrow Wilson; across the room from it was my father's roll top desk with standard typewriter under a picture of Will Rogers. A desk to me is subjective, private.)

The third house on Micheltorena (Orans, 1941) falls more into Ain's postwar style than the ones with hipped roofs. The skillful stepping up of the shed roofs with the slope is reflected in the plan; the bedrooms are on a lower level, off a deck above the garage, the living space, half a level up, is oriented to a rear terrace. The twenty-foot-long glass wall to the terrace is ten feet high, but Ain held to standard height doors by using transom lights above. Working with larger elements Ain was still ingenious. A sun trap below the high windows on the street side funneled light to the bedroom hall below—the trap is a case from the sill line to the ceiling below, with glass top and bottom.

The Daniel house front door is in back of the built-in sofa along the low screen wall. Photo: Julius Shulman.

The unroofed section of the Daniel deck echoes the trellis treatment of the entry roof. Photo: Julius Shulman.

Ain's masterpieces of the hipped roof series are the Tierman house and the Margaret Hay house (1939) in North Hollywood. The central block of the Hay house is flanked by wings, the double slope of the site allowing one wing to be two stories; the lower floor, with separate entrance, was occupied by the son. The asymmetry of the facade is emphasized by a wide, dark stripe from a paved terrace to the eave line of the two-story section; rather than break the white mass with isolated windows, Ain incorporates them in the dark stripe. Otherwise the glass is in continuous banks. The illusion of depth is created by bending the vertical stripe into the strip glass at the top of the central mass; then the line dips down to a bank of large windows in the one-story wing.

The entry hall is half a level between the son's quarters and the main living space. The hipped ceiling covers the entire central space; the freestanding fireplace blocks a view into the living room, but the hips and ridge are visible from the stair; one hip extends down into a folded ceiling in the alcove guest room at the top of the stair, and hip lines continue beyond the glass wall as an overhang.

Ain used every irregularity of wall or turn in the plan for storage space, which was helpful to John Blanton, an architect who had worked for years in the Neutra office, in adding a room on the lower level.

He turned a long, narrow water heater closet between the stair and the bathroom into a hall to the new bedroom.

"It is a very subtle house," Blanton said. "It has everything, curtain walls, broken hipped roof, and shed roof. I have the utmost respect for Ain and was unhappy at the thought of changing the house."

Another hipped roof house was for Jan and Jocelyn Domela, an artist and landscape designer, in Tarzana. The strong wind and sun of Tarzana were tempered by a trellised walk from the combined garage and artist's studio to the house. The extended hip members protected a patio and shade gardens.

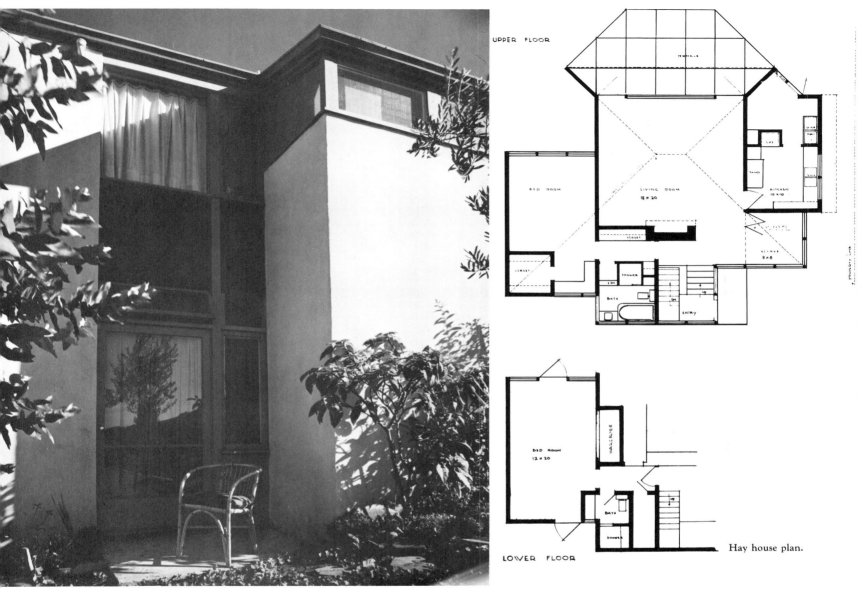

UPPER FLOOR

LOWER FLOOR

Hay house plan.

A two-story section
of the house contains
quarters for the Hay
son. Photo: Julius
Shulman.

In 1940, Ain received a Guggenheim Fellowship to study low-cost housing— two of his sponsors were Walter Gropius and Mies van der Rohe. This and another event were to affect the direction of his career. The other was his marriage to Ruth March,[4] an actress who was a protege of Katherine Cornell on the New York stage. Cornell's wedding present was a $2000 gift and a $2000 loan for a house which Ain could plan. They had already found a fan-shaped lot for $600 in Laurel Canyon, more than the $400 they could afford, but the half circular shape lent itself to a combined house and office. The lot was on a ten-year fill, and because of the age they were allowed to pour a resilient asphalt concrete slab which would spread the load. The skin was striated plywood panels glued to a four-by-four post frame. Ain liked the material because the striations hid the joints.

The plan has a long spine down the center with wings at the ends; the bedroom wing, with a lower roof, projects out on the canyon side, one blank wall screening the living room patio. Clerestories light the spine and the drafting room. The entrance to the office is near the parking area and garage, and the walk continues to the entry hall of the house.

"It was a mixture of skills and a willingness to try out one thing after another. My job was to design the boxes that the wing tips, the rudders, and stabilizers were formed in. We had to make our own containers—they looked like Renaissance machinery. The products were built up out of 1/40-inch laminations, nine to fifteen layers, and the autoclave was inflated with air under pressure. My real contribution was to find a way to put the air under pressure—something I worked out with the Nordquists. Marion Overby copied in plaster the template the Navy sent, and Margaret Harris imbedded wire in it— like a heating pad. They were inverted, the locks engaged, and the air pumped in. Before this, the plywood layers were painted with glue and held together with nails. Of the three contracts the Navy had given for plywood parts we were the only one that had worked out a way of doing

it mechanically. The others did tedious assemblage by hand."

Ain continued work in his own office during the three years at the Entenza-Eames factory, then for Evans Products which bought it out. However, because of the restrictions on strategic materials for civilian use, and the shortage of labor for civilian construction most of Ain's designs were unexecuted except for a job remodeling the facade of Gateway to Music on Wilshire Boulevard at the beginning of the war; in 1943 and 1944 there were not even projects.

During 1943, Ain took his examinations and was licensed as an architect— eight years after he had opened his own office. From 1943 he was active in the American Institute of Architects, which some three decades later elevated him to Fellow.

Ain called the 1930s as critical a time for the United States as the decade of the Civil War. "The Great Depression revealed the threat of unacknowledged and unsolved problems. The response of the architectural profession was the complete disavowal of the problem. Buckminster Fuller was the only one who responded in the form of architecture—as a field for imaginative innovation, not for ego-declaration—for the solution of a historical problem."

Ain's first work in social housing began in 1935, a year of unprecedented strikes among migrant workers in Imperial Valley. The standard wage was fifteen cents an hour and they were striking for twenty-five cents and for housing. A few growers provided shacks without sanitation, gas, or electricity. Most of the workers lived in the dilapidated cars which carried them and their families from cotton fields to lettuce fields to orchards, cooking on an open fire on the roadside, drinking from irrigation ditches.

Conditions in Los Angeles were only a little better in 1935. Half a million were unemployed, most of them white-collar workers—Los Angeles had few industries. As 1935 was the dryest year on record the caravans of jalopies from the Midwest soon swelled the number of unemployed. Single-wall shacks without plumbing or electricity,

4. *Born in the same Armenian village as painter Arshile Gorky, they were sweethearts in their youth.*

Bird's-eye view of the Ain house/office, Laurel Canyon, Los Angeles, 1941. The clerestory along the spine lights the house entrance and the drafting room.

built for a summer's vacation, now housed whole families. The recognition of the need for housing produced little until the end of the 1930s, then the Farm Security Administration of the Department of Agriculture built several camps with community facilities for migrant workers. As the regional offices were in San Francisco the architects were all from the north; Vernon DeMars designed many of them and Garrett Eckbo did the landscape planning. The FSA work was included in the Museum of Modern Art's "America Builds" exhibition in 1944.

The house was being planned when news of the Guggenheim Fellowship came, bringing the promise of a year in which to investigate low-cost housing. In five years Ain had designed twenty well-planned small houses for middle-income families, who without him would have bought houses "off the rack"—ones planned for the needs of families a generation earlier, or a contractor's model that could be turned in any direction on a lot regardless of sun and trees. He performed this service deep in the shadow of Neutra and Schindler, bringing to it a complexity greater than Neutra's and a simplicity greater than Schindler's. Ain was part of that small select group of the thirties—Harris, Davidson, Thornton Abell, John Lautner—which gave substance, variety, and surprise to the Los Angeles scene.

The Depression had ended and war was declared. The idealism of the Depression years (TVA is the proper monument to those years, just as are the proper words "My fellow Americans," coming over the air waves) was followed by the unity of purpose which marked the war—the last war in which the population as a whole joined together (exclusive, of course, of the Japanese Americans who were driven into tarpaper shacks in detention camps). Both the Depression years and the war years were ones in which Ain was spiritually at home.

In 1942, he was asked by John Entenza, editor of *Arts & Architecture,* which had published so much of his work, if he would take over the design of jigs and tools for a company which had just received a government contract for formed plywood parts. Ain had become interested in forming plywood while designing interiors for the U.S. Plywood Company in 1940, and had formed plywood in simple curves for radio cabinets.

The company, owned jointly by Entenza and Charles Eames, had been set up to research ways of forming compound curves for the Eames chairs. Eames and Eero Saarinen had won awards in all categories of the Museum of Modern Art's competition for furniture in 1938. The prototypes were all hand-formed, and Ray and Charles Eames had since their marriage in 1940 been exploring ways to mass produce it. In the Eames-Entenza factory, the experimental work was continued on double curvatures for chair seats and backs, and after the declaration of war the company expanded into plywood parts for the Navy.

Ain described the makeup of the office as "people who had talents in other fields joining forces." Besides Eames there was Margaret Harris, an English stage set designer who commuted by bicycle between a little theater in Hollywood and the factory on Washington Boulevard in Venice. She converted her stage set techniques to making covers for forming the compound curves—successful but primitive, Ain said. There was Marion Overby who had been an assistant to the sculptor Carl Milles, and Ray Eames who Ain called "a natural engineer with such a sense of structure that everything she touched became aesthetic." There were also two Swedish carpenters, Carroll and C.J. Nordquist, who had built Ain's own house, the Daniel, and the Hoffman houses.

Roger Montgomery writes in *Bay Area Houses* (Oxford, 1976), "Today the spirit of hope infused by the New Deal in its managers and planners and designers seems exotic, almost unbelievable. The experience of working in these agencies clearly transformed their lives. The connection between architecture and justice, good environment and good health, the integral relationship between physical community and social-moral community—these ideas seemed self evident and tremendously exciting."

When war was declared in Europe in the fall of 1939, the Dust Bowl migrants were a small stream compared to the mass migration. Tens of thousands came to war production industries. Thousands of housing units were built or converted in the first year of the war. (The movement of population was so sudden that many public schools had to operate in three shifts.) Few architects of note designed war housing; an exception in the south was Neutra and Alexander's fine Channel Heights Housing at San Pedro. War blasted the architect's world. Most of them were working as structural, mechanical, and piping engineers.

The AIA's Washington representative said, "In the past too much emphasis has been placed on the aesthetic side of architecture and architectural education."

Task #4, a "little" magazine for architects and planners, said editorially that architects were still considered picturemakers or the drafting arm of a real estate operator—aesthetes or facadists. "Survival is through social participation."

Students demanded a new curriculum. Women architects demanded equality. One wrote in *Task* that no matter how well trained a woman was she was put to cleaning up the drawings. "If you can figure the tension of a beam some man will do it over again—he will never believe you can add."

Catherine Bauer summed up the war housing experience thus: "The war has demonstrated the fact. . . that adequate housing is a basic problem of our productive economy, not merely a reformer's frill. The wartime migration simply threw a spotlight on the weaknesses and inflexibility of our traditional building enterprise."

Ain's first venture in social housing was a one-room concrete structure on a five-foot module, which could convert to the metrical system. (He revised his model later for defense housing for war workers, collaborating with Joseph Allen Stein on a model on a four-foot module.)

The structure was simplicity itself: four precast concrete corner slabs eight feet high and five feet long for a twenty-by-twenty house, the slabs spaced ten feet apart with a four-by-four post between. Other components were factory made partitions two feet wide and incorporating wardrobe closets and storage, and a prepackaged

Model of a factory-fabricated house, 1940 (with J.A. Stein). The window walls can be stacked and the reinforced concrete corners nested to truck to the site.

Room divisions for the factory-fabricated house are wall cabinets. The kitchen and bath are stamped out of metal and packaged.

seven-by-six rectangle stamped out plumbing and heating core with bath and kitchen back to back. The ten-foot openings between the concrete angles were filled in with prefabricated sliding doors, windows, and some solid wall.

Ain introduced for the first time a scheme he used in all his low-cost (and often high-cost) houses—a parents' bedroom which could be opened by sliding panels to the living room. In this case the **L**-shaped social space was lighted and ventilated on four sides. Furniture was built in, a dining table attached to the wall, and beds and sofa on platforms hung from the walls. Some of the ideas in the prepackaged plumbing unit, the precast angles, precut wood, and packaged doors and windows came from Buckminster Fuller's Dymaxion House, but were adapted to on-site hand labor in Imperial Valley. No house was ever produced for migratory or war workers but the project enriched Ain's vocabulary and brought him closer to certain contractor's practices which he adapted to architecture. For Fuller to accomplish fully his ends it was necessary to bring into use the standardization of the automobile industry. This was Neutra's ideal, but Ain knew all too well that each Neutra house was unique, not assembled out of Sweet's Catalog, and he brought no nearer the goal of mass housing. The modern house had simply, in Fuller's words, peeled off yesterday's exterior embellishment, to give it what Reyner Banham calls the appearance of mechanization.

An opportunity to prefabricate plywood parts came in 1938 when he designed a studio for the cinematographer Slavko Vorkapich on a wooded upslope back of the main house in Benedict Canyon. The skeleton was four-by-four posts and the skin a sandwich of four-by-eight plywood panels cored with two by fours. The same sandwich panel served for roof in the plan, but when built, composition roofing was applied to plywood. The floor was a concrete slab in which the plumbing was incorporated. The plan was six panels long by two panels wide: 24 by 16 with a pair of four-foot glass doors facing the treetops. A glazed entry hall was added when construction started.

Vorkapich guest house of prefabricated panels, Beverly Hills, 1938. Photo: Fred Dapprich.

"I wanted to try out a system of standardized parts that could be quickly bolted together for ultra low-cost housing," Ain said. "The structure went up in a day— but the wiring and plumbing were complicated."

As we talked in 1979 about the "complications" which developed in so many systems, we marveled at many of the old faiths. Scientific advances so often proved fickle, the most eerie being a combined heating-cooling system which was indeed a saving, but when used in a building for screenwriters, the hot arguments in the meeting hall raised the body heat and this,

combined with the heat of constant cigarette smoking, triggered the sensitive mechanism to shut off the heat and send out a blast of chilling air. The scriptwriters were irate—some of them writers of space age films where systems always worked.

The publication of the house for agricultural workers as a One-Family Defense House (*Architectural Forum*, November 1940) shows the superiority of the Ain scheme to others appearing in the same magazine; one designed by Navy engineers—if designed is the word—has the same square plan and almost the same square footage but without Ain's flexible

space, with less storage space, and the paltriest of windows in the living room. Also, the Navy's houses are set in barrack-like rows, the front doors a few feet from the common sidewalk. The text mentions that the roof can have several "treatments," and the same house can be set on posts for the tropics; no mention of a possible variation of the poor floor plan, yet there is evidence that a great amount of time and money went into the planning to reach the capability of erecting twenty houses in one day.

Ain developed a plot plan for a community of defense houses using two or three

Vorkapich guest house living room. Photo: Fred Dapprich.

basic houses, varied setbacks, and grouped houses separated by planting. He was already thinking in terms of relating houses to each other and to the land. He had tried several times to convince clients (Salkin and Tartar, 1948; Berg and Daniel, 1939) of the advantage of dividing a piece of land between them and placing the houses to obtain the greatest benefit from the gardens and the views. For three clients (Goldman, Salkin, and Berg, 1940) he designed houses which shared a swimming pool and common use of most of the land. The ampleness of the combined sites allowed Ain to vary the setback requirements, perhaps the

single worst enemy of good environment. The dictum that good fences make good neighbors was the rule in Los Angeles.

The Leshing project, which made use of the shared benefits of the land, was two typical one-acre lots in San Fernando Valley, one acre used for garages, with single apartments above, and the other acre for two-story town houses. The curve of the street allowed each unit to have an entry at ground level. This scheme was turned down by the planning department. Ain had hoped in the beginning to throw all the land between town houses and garages into what he called "a tantalizing

common green." The city was still unsatisfied after he turned the open space into private patios. The client gave up. The project was abandoned.

Ain worked on other plywood systems and plans on the Guggenheim Fellowship. (The first all-plywood house in Los Angeles was Neutra's Exhibition House, 1936; Schindler's all-plywood Southall house was built in 1938.) He tried thin panels of composition cement, a material then coming into favor; Ain proposed one called Transite for the walls of the Leshing project. He also specified Homasote as sandwich panels for walls—two panels framed with two by fours with a diagonal one-by-four let in for bracing. The wood extended beyond the edges on all sides to simplify nailing. Special screw-like nails were required to penetrate the composition cement, and to avoid this in field work he proposed the wood frame for nailing to the two-by-four studs.

As the war was drawing to a close, *Arts & Architecture* had a competition sponsored by U.S. Plywood Corporation for a "$5000 to $6000 house for the average American workman" which was "buildable now" and "afforded good living." Many of the entries were from young architects still in the armed service. Ain, as one of the jurors, sided against the others (Charles Eames, John Rex, J.R. Davidson, and Frederick Langhorst) on the first prize, a house by Charles D. Wiley which was placed two feet below grade—Wiley had been in the offices of Gropius, Breuer and Saarinen. The second prize, which had a packaged mechanical unit, went to Russell M. Andal; the third prize, which Ain thought should have had first, was Eduardo Catalano's plywood house. One honorable mention went to Harry Weese, another to I.M. Pei for a cooperative housing scheme, which Eames found the "most stimulating."

The jury's report was an occasion for Ain to predict accurately what would happen in postwar housing. "Tens of thousands of families now compelled by circumstances to occupy substandard dwellings will be in a position to start building as soon as priorities are lifted. . . . They will be unable to wait for an industrially manufactured product, or for some saner kind of land subdivision. . . . These first tens of thousands of houses will be built by methods not very different from those employed in the last prewar houses, in sub-divisions as they already exist. . . . If the problem's not well solved now by the architects, it will be badly solved later by the jerry-builders. . . . Too many architects in their zeal to promulgate new and frequently valid ideas withdraw from the common architectural problems of the common people."

Nevertheless Ain found the most interesting entry to the competition the

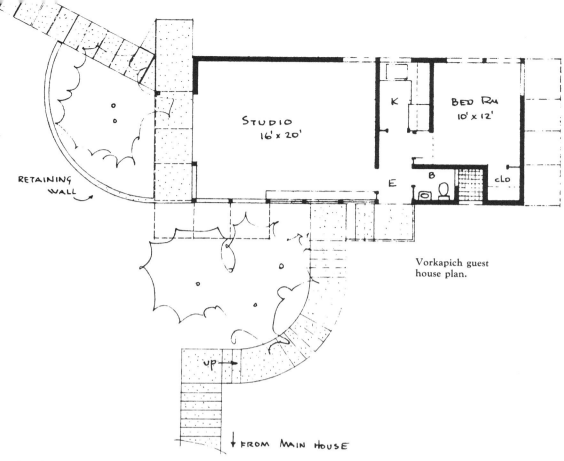

Vorkapich guest house plan.

Catalano house using molded plywood, a scheme remote from the common architectural problem of the common people, as well as unbuildable at that time in quantity. It was Davidson who pointed out that that mass-produced house was "still in the horseless buggy days." Eames put his finger on the ultimate aim of such competitions: "The most significant contributions may come from the most unpredictable phases of a problem, and the usefulness of this type of competition is most apparent when it makes possible presentation of important ideas which might easily have been choked off by the usual and more limiting program."

Even before this competition was announced, Ain was at work on his most ambitious project, 280 houses on 100 acres of flat land on Victory Boulevard in Reseda, a cooperative housing scheme called Community Homes. By this time Ain was a registered architect and had two younger partners, Joseph Johnson and Alfred Day. The partnership grew out of

a letter of congratulation in 1944 from Reginald Johnson (father of Joseph) on the cooperative, which he learned about from a story in the *Los Angeles Times*.

Reginald Johnson was one of the architects of the 1941 Baldwin Hills Village (Alexander, Wilson, Merrill and Johnson), a scheme in which houses are grouped around open greens. Johnson had long been noted for his elegant eclectic houses, churches, and public buildings. He invited Ain to lunch at the California Club.

"He was a surprise—this son of a bishop of the California Diocese of the Episcopal Church praising my work!" Ain gave one of his typical whimsical half grins. "This man I had always connected with privilege, patronage, was ardent about social problems. A man of great strength and vitality, great delicacy. He offered to help me with clients and in getting the FHA approval on the cooperative. I saw him again in Santa Barbara at a meeting where he got an award for a small house. He told me later that the plan was one for a gardner's cottage for a large house his office was planning. Then he recommended his son, recently out of architecture school, and his partner, Alfred Day, if I needed help on the cooperative."

So the firm of Ain, Johnson and Day was formed. "I did the designing, except for the jobs Joe Johnson brought in—he designed all of those. The partner who lived nearest a job oversaw the construction of it. I never included any of Johnson's designs in my list of buildings."

The partnership lasted five years. It ended during the McCarthy Un-American Activities hearings. "Some jobs we were hoping to get required government clearance, and my membership in various organizations would have ruled us out. So I resigned." (Joe Johnson said the partnership was dissolved because the volume of work was too small.)[5]

Robert Kahan who had lived in the Dunsmuir Flats, a CPA by 1945, put together the package for the cooperative Community Homes in Reseda. "The subscribers put up the money and I bought the land," Kahan said, "Most of them were young professionals—actors, doctors, attorneys, musicians, teachers; one was Saul Bass, the graphics designer, who later lived in Greg's Park Planned Homes in Altadena—before he was a client for an *Arts & Architecture* Case Study house in 1962. And there was Lena Horne, a black singer—Greg remodeled a house for her in Nichols Canyon."

On the board of directors was also Max Lawrence. He said, "When men were mustered out of the service many put their severance pay into a place to live. Any shelter was welcome, but after they heard Greg's ideas they were sold on a planned community, with cars separated from pedestrians, with green belt parks and small recreation spaces."

5. *The House Un-American Activities hearings spread fear everywhere. One earned a place in McCarthy's Subversive List not only by membership in the Communist Party but the Lawyers' Guild, Newspaper Guild, Engineers, Architects and Chemists Federation, and dozens of others; the names of petition signers were kept on file; association with known members of such organizations was as damning as membership. Mark Schindler, son of R.M. and Pauline Schindler, was denied clearance on sensitive government work because his mother was a "red." Both Ain and I were members of the Engineers, Architects and Chemists Federation.*

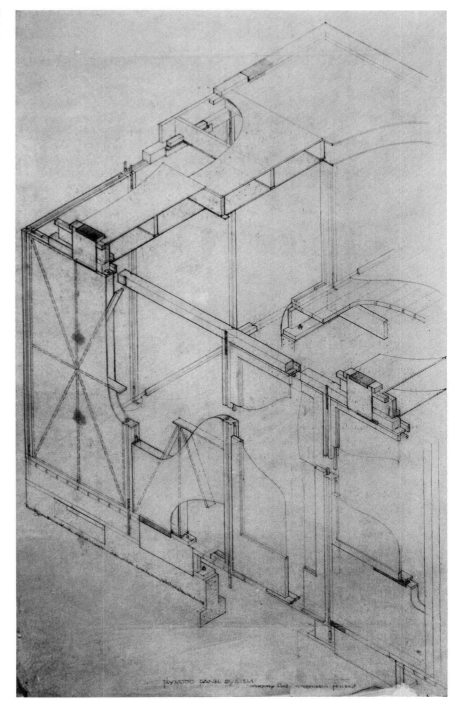

The first study of the panel system for the Vorkapich house was four-by-eight sandwich panels cored with one by fours between four-by-four posts.

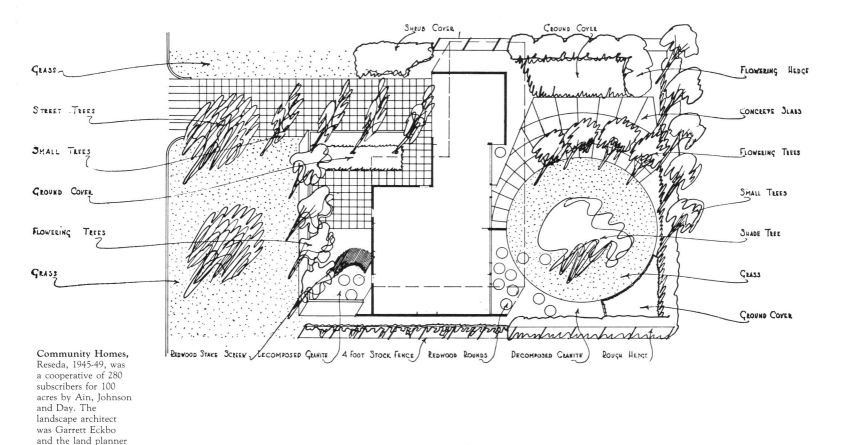

GRASS

STREET TREES

SMALL TREES

GROUND COVER

FLOWERING TREES

GRASS

SHRUB COVER GROUND COVER

FLOWERING HEDGE

CONCRETE SLABS

FLOWERING TREES

SMALL TREES

SHADE TREE

GRASS

GROUND COVER

REDWOOD STAKE SCREEN DECOMPOSED GRANITE 4 FOOT STOCK FENCE REDWOOD ROUNDS DECOMPOSED GRANITE ROUGH HEDGE

Community Homes, Reseda, 1945-49, was a cooperative of 280 subscribers for 100 acres by Ain, Johnson and Day. The landscape architect was Garrett Eckbo and the land planner Simon Eisner.

planned community, with cars separated from pedestrians, with green belt parks and small recreation spaces."

Most of the subscribers had grown up during the Depression when a house was a symbol of permanence. "This was their first house, they wanted everything. The decisions were all made by a democratic process, and the subscribers felt that their wishes mattered. No one had heard then of participatory planning but this may have been the first time it was tried."

The site plan, the work of Simon Eisner, was a grid laid down on an **L**-shaped tract, split on the long side by a wide strip park and on the short side by a narrow one; little finger parks broke up the plan to distribute recreation spaces everywhere, like rips in the fabric through which the

community could breathe. The Baldwin Hills green spaces encircled the houses; in Community Homes the green spaces were elongated, following and controlled by the grid.

The landscape architect was the talented young Garrett Eckbo (Eckbo, Royston and Williams), who like Ain preferred working at a larger scale than one plot – the street rather than the single garden. Eckbo transformed 57 lots on Wonderland Park Avenue by planting the street as a unit. (Some time after he went to Berkeley to teach landscape architecture and planning, his house and richly varied garden was bought by Governor Edmund G. Brown, Jr. who also saw beyond his own lot lines to the whole earth; but Brown, more a St. Jerome than a St.

Francis, was not blessed with a sensuous receptivity to the delights of a garden.)

Eckbo's planting scheme for Community Homes was "a backbone pattern of strong planes of tall forms of slender fan palms, Canary Island pines, Lombardy poplars, incense cedars, and eucalyptus which will dominate as years add growth. The master tree plan develops an expression in foliage, structure, and space . . . that accepts the good gridiron of loop streets and draws from the still rural character of the valley around it." The plantings varied for each street and lot – the ground covers, the hedges around the large **L**-shaped back yards, the trees giving privacy without too much shade.

There were four basic floor plans, Type B for instance, a two-bedroom plan in which the living room could be expanded through sliding doors to the parents' bedroom; both rooms had sliding glass to the trellised terrace.

Ain said, "Three or four years went to setting up the group, getting the land, the planning, then the meetings with planning departments of the city. They didn't like the floor plan so we revised it. Reginald Johnson helped us get FHA financing. Everything was fine. Then FHA learned that some of the subscribers were minorities—blacks, Orientals, Latins. They said it was a bad business practice. Furthermore, it violated Regulation X of FHA. The co-op board met and refused even to discuss it. We sent a protest to Washington—we said these people had fought in the war. They called our attention to Regulation X which prohibited mixing races. There was no way to win. So we had to dissolve the co-op. The price of land had risen so everyone got back more than he put in."

Some of the 280 subscribers were the clients for Ain's next cooperatives. However, a large number, all Caucasian, bought a hilly tract above Sunset in Brentwood and got Smith, Jones and Contini to plan the fine Mutual Housing.

Five years after Community Homes was disbanded and the property sold, Reseda was the lowest common denominator of tract housing— no green belts or finger parks, just houses set row on row as exactly as markers in a VA cemetery. In the cemetery, however, there was no Regulation X. Ain's prediction that if the architects did not solve the problem it would be badly solved later by jerry-builders proved true. But in this case the problem had been handsomely solved by Ain, Eckbo, and Eisner—not only the land planning, landscape planning, and floor planning, but also a social problem, integration. It was the federal government that lagged behind, certain that minorities (most of them professionals) meant economic disaster. By 1980, after Regulation X had been declared unconstitutional, came the bitter battle to achieve integration by bussing school children.

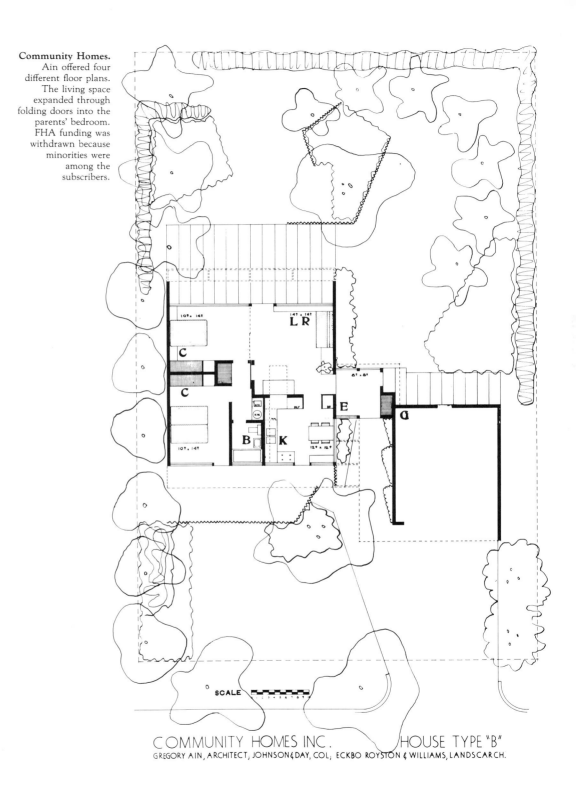

Community Homes. Ain offered four different floor plans. The living space expanded through folding doors into the parents' bedroom. FHA funding was withdrawn because minorities were among the subscribers.

COMMUNITY HOMES INC.   HOUSE TYPE "B"
GREGORY AIN, ARCHITECT, JOHNSON & DAY, COL; ECKBO ROYSTON & WILLIAMS, LANDSCARCH.

SCALE

PLANTING SKETCH: HOUSE TYPE B

One of the four planting schemes by Eckbo, Royston and Williams for Community Homes.

Several cooperatives were planned simultaneously by Ain for members of the Community Homes subscribers. "Ain was determined then to build nothing but cooperatives," Kahan said. "By that time he was well known and could have done large commercial building, he could have been a great success. But his heart was in social housing."

In the same year Ain planned Lucile Street Cooperative for nine families on two lots, and the larger Park Planned Homes on ten acres. The land, acquired from the Scripps estate, was below Foothill Boulevard, backed up against the moun-

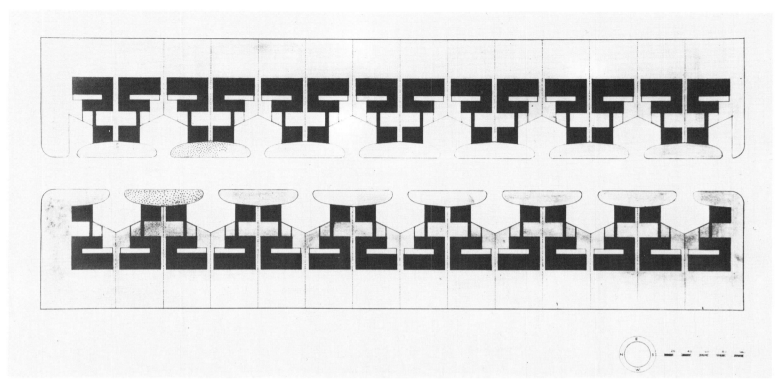

**Layout of Park
Planned Homes,**
Altadena, 1946. Sixty
houses were planned
for four square blocks.

tains. In the few years after the demise of Community Homes the cost of building had risen as much as land. The only thing to recede was faith.

Writing in the November 1945 *Arts & Architecture*, Ain warned that no miracle of plastic and electronics on a secluded acre of gently rolling woodland was possible. "Enough time and enough pages have been devoted to dalliance with hypothetical dreams," but the problem is still "how to make the most of a few truckloads of familiar, almost primitive building materials, put together by the familiar outmoded handcrafts, on a tight little city lot."

Ain and Kahan were partners on Park Planned Homes, Kahan acquiring the capital, negotiating for the land, and taking charge of all the scheduling and finances of building. Ain and Garrett Eckbo coordinated the land planning and landscaping with the design of the houses.

Sixty houses were planned (28 were finally built) for four square blocks on very deep lots on gently sloping land. A low concrete retaining wall separates the two driveways and takes care of the grade change. The garages, on the front, are paired, which creates a sweep of lawn between houses. The broken rhythm of lawns

and garages and different planting schemes for each house takes away the resemblance to tract housing.

The 1600-square-foot houses have three bedrooms and two baths, the living room facing a patio at the back. The staggering and the changes of level give visual separation. Ain used an inset clerestory which split the house laterally, the double line of glass bringing in both north and south light; sections of the glass can be pulled open by a cord to cool the rooms.

While the houses were being planned price controls were lifted and costs rose.

Inset clerestories for additional lighting and ventilation of the Park Planned Homes.

(The price of glass sometimes went up twice a week, and some contractors would work only on a cost-plus basis.) As the volume of building rose beyond all expectation, materials were scarce. There was a long pause in the changeover from military to new types of civilian goods; manufacturers shifted reluctantly to new products in demand after the war because they feared the "modern craze" would die out and they would be stuck with unsaleable products. But in short supply were such staples as nails and hardware.

To control rising costs, Ain revived shortcuts he had planned for war hous-

ing: precutting to reduce labor time, design of jigs for predrilling holes in the studs for wiring and ducts to pass through, all studs cut the same length, plumbing preassembled in identical units for all houses.

Kahan told the crews when they showed up for work that he did not want to see a saw on the job. "Leave them at home, no need for them." There was a revolt. The contractor said that if they worked without saws the hourly rate would be $8 instead of the standard $6. It was the same with the plumbers. They wanted higher wages to handle prepackaged units. And the electricians wanted to drill their

own holes in any part of the stud they liked, not follow a pattern.

The savings went out the window. The contractors demanded a cost-plus arrangement. The houses rose from $11,000 to $13,000.

Worst of all, thugs cruised the streets looking for stockpiled materials that had been purchased in quantity to save on cost. The lumber for the first houses was stolen almost at once. A night watchman was hired, but not before many of the packaged plumbing units disappeared. There were long delays in replacing them. Nothing

was bought in quantity again. Contractors drove from the valley to the east side to the beach scouring the area for two by fours. It was no good sitting at a telephone for it could take an hour to find a lumber yard whose phone wasn't busy. For two weeks there wasn't a stick of dimension lumber in town— no two by fours or six by eights. Jobs closed down and the carpenters went home. The mills in the northwest were on 24-hour shifts trying to meet the needs of the West Coast. The black market thrived.

Half of the houses were deleted from the plan of Park Planned Homes. People moved into the 28 before the interiors were finished. The profit on them was hardly worth the effort.

Today the houses show signs of wear, as do all houses built in 1946 and 1947—green lumber, poor nails, and hardware show in the twisted, long wood fascias, in the cabinetry, the hinges, the locks on the front door.

The neighborhood which would accept no blacks in 1946 was in 1979 predominantly black—one a realtor who said the houses fetched $68,000. (By 1983 that price has more than doubled.) After three decades it is still a unique neighborhood with its staggered houses and superb trees.

The nine-unit Lucile Street Veterans' Cooperative of 1946 fell apart, according to Joseph Johnson, because of soil problems. The soil report was late and footings were already started, but the unstable soil promised to raise costs so much that the project was abandoned. The families had waited through the long months of the demise of Community Homes, many of them living with in-laws or in substandard housing, with one child born and another on the way while they waited. The pressure to begin was greater as costs rose.

Avenel Cooperative,
Los Angeles, 1947.
Ten units were built
for motion picture
cartoonists. Photo:
Julius Shulman.

Ten families from among the initial subscribers, most of them members of the motion picture cartoonists union, pooled their resources for the more modest Avenel Cooperative in the Silver Lake district, where the streets and sewers were in, good schools existed, and the site fifteen minutes from the studios.

The Avenel land was two adjoining 60-foot lots, 140 feet deep, on a fifteen-degree slope. The grade was used to break the lot in two lengthwise. Little excavation was needed to prepare two pads, one eight feet above the other, and five of the row houses (with party walls) on the upper level looked out over the flat roofs of the lower five to a wide view of the hills.

The houses are set at an angle to the street, with no house directly behind another. The angle increased the depth of the 40-foot patio outside the living room and narrowed it outside the bedroom. Another outdoor space in the 960-square-foot house is the service yard behind a six-foot-high curved wall near the entrance. An Ain trademark on the street facade is the high glass concentrated at one side, and the large-scale surface play of light and dark values which give height and substance to the entrance of an intensively used site.

The party walls were not the saving Ain had hoped—the cost was still $10 per square foot. This, with the $2000 each subscriber contributed to the land and grading, brought the cost of each house to $11,000. Today one house is owned by architect Sam Reisbord who designed apartment houses, two of them in collaboration with Alvin Lustig, an important tastemaker.[6]

6. Lustig's design of art galleries, houses, and book jackets for New Directions, and his classes at Art Center, left an indelible mark on the postwar generation. He deserves a sympathetic biographer.

The terraces of the Avenel Cooperative faced an unobstructed view of the mountains. Photo: Julius Shulman.

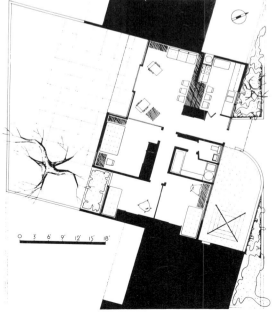

0 3 6 9 12 15 18'

Plan of the Avenel Cooperative units. Sliding partitions expanded the space.

Living room, Mar Vista Housing. The pass-through to the kitchen. Much of the furniture was built in. Photo: Marvin Rand.

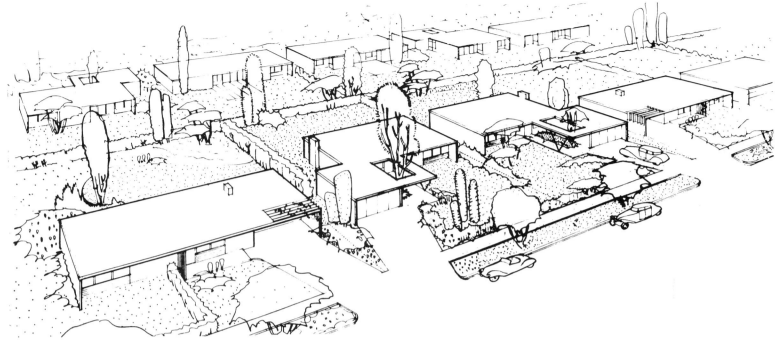

Mar Vista Housing.
One hundred houses
were planned for a
60-acre site by Ain,
Johnson and Day.

The best known of Ain's projects is Mar Vista Housing, which had the finest structure of a community. It was planned in 1947 for a hundred houses on a 60-acre site between Culver City and Venice Beach. The developer, B.M. Edelman, a convert to Ain's philosophy, backed him when the FHA requested in the name of "good business practice" that ranch houses and salt boxes be mixed with moderns. The agency saw no aesthetic advantage in land planning with irregular spacing of houses, rotation of the plan to introduce variety of form. They were prepared to insure the loan on condition that the houses be built in stages to test the acceptance. The first stage was 52 houses – which turned out to be the final stage. The average lot is 75 by 104 feet, with buffer gardens expanding the common green.[7]

Ain had better luck with systems here; the carpenters were willing to cooperate, and although time was lost on the first houses, the precut studs and fabricated built-ins were a saving in the long run. The cost of the 1050-square-foot house was $11,000 – a bargain considering all the amenities. But Venice Boulevard, the east-west thoroughfare three blocks away, is a street distinguished only for its unusual width. It seemed born to attract poor design, and is ever in the throes of replacing a depressed block with another potential

7. *Max and Rita Lawrence, who followed Ain from project to project, and who had one of the Mar Vista houses for a while, developed an interest in architecture through Ain, and ended by starting Architectural Pottery, a company which produced pots from designs of Los Angeles artists – their pots appeared in the photographs of almost every Arts & Architecture Case Study House, and were sold nationally.*

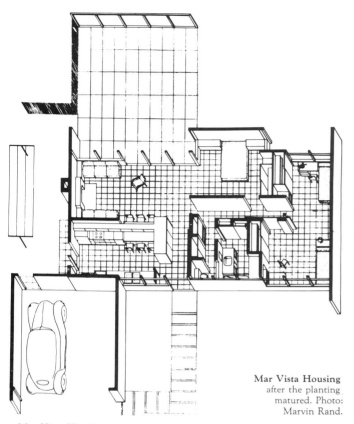

Mar Vista Housing
floor plan.

Mar Vista Housing
after the planting
matured. Photo:
Marvin Rand.

slum. The contractor-inspired house around Venice Boulevard was selling for $5000 then; in its typical plan the front door opens to a small living room with a dinette at one end by a corner window, a two-bedroom stucco box with a gabled roof, and a dinky gable above the concrete stoop at the front door. (In time there was a picture window at the front, lighted at night by a large table lamp.)

Because of the location there were only twenty subscribers to Mar Vista, and the other 32 houses were sold to the public; this brought in the banks with their prejudice against modern design and irregular setbacks. A number of loans were turned down. It is the richest of Ain's developments, and appreciation of it is shown by the maintenance and the low turnover. But it was a severe financial loss to the developer.

"He carried out the plan without changes, he planted every tree and shrub Eckbo called for in the landscaping," Ain said. The development brought Ain no profit. The houses, which have weathered well and sit beneath fine trees, are in demand today. One was advertised in 1979 as "Ain-designed house for $130,000."

(I know nowhere except Los Angeles that houses are listed for sale by the name of the architect. An ad in the *Times* is more effective than real estate agents in finding a buyer who respects the architecture. This has happened since the late fifties. When a Schindler house is sold, the new owners are observed by other Schindler owners so they are careful about the changes they make. The fragile heritage of the early modern houses in Southern California has an unofficial Architectural Watch and Ward Society.)

Mar Vista Housing today. Photo: Marvin Rand.

The floor planning which developed out of the Guggenheim Fellowship came together in an easternized version in 1950 for an exhibition house for the garden of the Museum of Modern Art in New York (a joint project with the *Woman's Home Companion*). The estimated cost for the eastern model was $15,000-$20,000, but there were 400 more square feet. One change in the plan was the bathroom split into three parts; one bath had all the fixtures, the adjoining children's bath had only a basin and toilet, and in the parents' dressing room lined with wardrobe closets was a basin. The split bath (aimed at reducing the runs of plumbing pipes) was considered a breakthrough in the late forties. *Life* magazine showed a long boxcar type dividing the two bedrooms, with doors opening from both rooms to shared bath and shower, and basins and toilets with one access. The amount of talent concentrated on shortening the plumbing runs, and the ganging up of kitchen and baths, often played havoc with the plan. Then it occurred to someone that this was silly when the money saved was leaking out all over the rest of the house. So the split bath became as obsolete as the drying yard. The quick acceptance of the washer and dryer was underestimated by Ralph Rapson in an innovative plan in 1945 for an *Arts & Architecture* Case Study house project (a roofed garden runs down the center of the plan and all rooms face it). Rapson's rendering of the house showed a helicopter hovering over the flat roof, as if the owner was coming home to the suburbs from his day at the office. His wife is waving to him. Where is she? Hanging out diapers in the drying yard. Rapson's money was on the wrong machine.

Ain's sliding wall has also departed from architecture. It seems to belong to that postwar period when dual and triple use of space was considered a sign of sincerity; a single-purpose room showed a lack of ingenuity. (But this multi-use preoccupation was not new, it runs deep in the American spirit—you can see in the Bettman Archives such double-function pieces as the combined piano-spare bed.)

The art in the museum house included a Rene Magritte oil and prints and drawings by Braque, Hopper, Miró, etc., ranging in value (the museum noted) from $100 to $900. Ain was for some reason annoyed that such "expensive" art appeared in a low-cost house; but owners of a modern house were more likely to buy a Magritte or a Braque drawing than a Corot reproduction. During the McCarthy period the FBI is reputed to have instructed its agents that subversives preferred "genuine" oil paintings to reproductions; and having an architect at all for a small house was as good a clue to a "red" as a copy of *Consumer Reports* on the bookshelf.

The exhibition house marked the end of a period. It had started with what Ain called in November 1945 "the long-awaited era of the postwar house." He predicted then that "millions with hopes based on widely publicized visions of the house of tomorrow will be disappointed."

Ain was a realist and held out no false hope. "It is no advantage whatever to the prospective homebuilder that modern materials, techniques, and regional planning are theoretically capable of providing for better and cheaper dwelling units than accepted standards."

But he was an idealist who gave the better part of ten years to fighting against prevailing industrial, economic, and real estate practices which had kept the house of tomorrow the house of yesterday.

He was ready to forego the feast. It was the crumbs he fought for—and for the most part lost. There was little to show for his work in simplifying the house: the twelve-foot plan module which made one rafter size do for an entire subdivision; longitudinal roof framing which eliminated the need for beams over window openings, allowing them to extend to the ceiling; the single plumbing assembly. Most of this simply faded away, as lost as the old laundry tray. What remains is the spirit that shaped the rooms and the light that entered them. When you opened a front door he told you forthrightly what was there—conversation space, work space, play space, quiet space—but he didn't tell you how much of his spirit was there.

His mission in social housing failed, as did Job Harriman's mission at Llano del Rio. But the cooperative farm, like Park

Museum of Modern Art exhibition house, New York, 1950. Ain, Johnson and Day. Photo: Ezra Stoller.

Planned Homes and Avenel Veterans Homes and Mar Vista, kept alive the humane standards one generation passes on to the next.

Two small bare-bones office buildings and a project designed in 1947-48 were affected by the cooperative housing then on the boards, and they led ultimately to a simplification of Ain's large postwar houses.

His approach was never regional. Most of California's regionalism started outside the major cities, and Ain, a product of the city, rarely left it except for his year at the Llano del Rio colony. The area in which he had grown up in East Los Angeles was something of a colony of first generation Americans, with no stored-up memories

of California usages to pass along. As Ain's major influences in architecture were two transplanted Viennese, it was not surprising that he was relatively free of the California traditions that moved Harwell Harris. Ain's tradition was closer to the European. By 1940 at age 32, he was impervious to influences not moving in his own direction.

He had taken the principles of uniformity of Neutra's window walls and bent them to include setbacks and expression of wall, playing off solid against pierced planes. After working his way through Schindler's three-dimensional explorations Ain returned to wall and surface.

The war had imposed strictness, and the low-cost housing imposed severe economy. There was strictness from

another direction. Joseph Johnson was at Harvard Graduate School of Design in 1937, the first year Walter Gropius arrived, and he knew Gropius's work in Germany and England. Alfred Day, a graduate of Cornell, was also aware of developments in Europe. Ain, Johnson and Day's commercial buildings are reminiscent of Gropius and Fry's classroom wing at Impington College. It was easier for Ain to digest Gropius than vernacular California.

The 1948 Hollywood Guilds and Unions Building on Cahuenga Boulevard (now destroyed) was a one-story **T** plan with flat roof, patios extending from sliding glass. The building would have worked as well as a kindergarten, for windows

Miller house, Beverly Hills, 1948. Ain, Johnson and Day. The servants' rooms are over the garage. Photo: Julius Shulman.

started at desk height and patios would have served for outdoor instruction. (But not during the seventies when vandalism was so frequent that schools were based more on the fortress than the greenhouse.)

The bony structure of exposed posts, fascia, mullions, and transoms is sharply delineated in white, contrasting with the dark colors of the stucco walls. It recalls the white scored bays of Norman Shaw, or the white mullioned facade of a Mackintosh tea room. The heavied white line was then rare in modern architecture in Southern California; the thin steel line was the sophisticated line. In Ain's hands it was like crisp white ribbons tying an odd-shaped box together—rarely the Harvard Graduate School box.

A 1947 study for an office for three attorneys was a rectangle hollowed out at one side by a large court, into which first and second floor offices emptied. The exposed structure of four-by-four posts ex-

tended two stories, the space between filled in with glass. Attorneys' offices, library, and lounge were turned toward the court. As in the Guilds and Unions offices, the rhythm of window wall was not interrupted, the white lines of transoms and clerestory crossing white posts. When the drawings were published in *Arts & Architecture* (May 1947), no facade was shown—Ain's way of emphasizing the interior environment, the important point of the design.

The offices of Ain, Johnson and Day, another building with revealed structure, grew out of James Garrott's suggestion that Ain buy the narrow lot adjoining his on Hyperion Avenue and design two offices. When completed Ain often walked across the court to talk to Garrott. "He was very stimulating," Garrott said. "The Westchester Municipal Building and library was my job but Ain started throwing out so many ideas that I added his name to the

plans. On his own work he was slow to make up his mind. When we had an office together before the war I saw how he suffered over a plan. He threw away a dozen for his own house before he was satisfied. In the late fifties I pulled a plan away from him before he was ready to let it go and he ripped out part of the construction to make a major change. He could do three different plans to cut the cost $1000 and charge for only one. He was touchy when he was brooding over a plan—he would take it home at night and wall himself off from his family."

Josef van der Kar, a colleague and close friend called it, "Greg's uneasy perfectionism."

Other work in the Ain, Johnson and Day office beside the office buildings, the early Community Homes, and Mar Vista, were the Briehl Clinic and numerous houses, the best being for Miller, Shairer, Wilfong, and Hurschler.

The lath house off the Miller dining room. Photo: Julius Shulman.

The Miller living room with the sliding door to the bedroom open. Photo: Julius Shulman.

In the almost opulent Miller house of 1948, the walls are stucco and striated plywood panels; with the joints of the panels suppressed the material is more akin to plaster than wood. The simple large shapes, never interlocked, are played against each other. Between the two roofs is a small countermovement, a clerestory lighting the kitchen, a grace note between two heavy chords. One of the fascias which bind it all together is the end member of a trellis shading a combined service yard and potting shed. Backed up against the yard is a lath house, a rather elegant structure that connects with the dining room. Horticulture was the hobby of one of the Millers, both doctors, and the lath house was resplendent with plants in bloom.

It is essentially a one-bedroom house, really a one-space house for the bedroom can be opened to the living room, and the living room turns a corner into the dining room. The space spills out everywhere into the garden.

Wilfong house,
Altadena, 1949. Ain,
Johnson and Day.
Photo: Julius
Shulman.

The deck off the
Wilfong living room.
Photo: Julius
Shulman.

The long rectangular Wilfong house in Altadena (1949) has much subtle weaving of darks and lights on different planes on the view side. Rising above the surface play is a tight composition of forms—second story and chimney mass, and low clerestory windows resembling dormers.

To catch the summer breeze the living room wall slides open to a raised deck, making the two a single space. Parallel white lines of fascia and deck rail hang in space between the recessed living room glass, the deck floating beyond the foundation wall.

The Shairer house (1949) is a two-story house on a flat lot in West Los Angeles, with drive-through carport and glass lighting a stairwell. Ain's skill with

clerestories doesn't work in a two-story house. I came once from Davidson's Jokl house to the serene Shairer house and was surprised to find the interiors shadowy. Davidson's flat-roofed house has skylights in halls and baths, kitchen and living room; the 30 years' growth of trees now casts a deep shade on the Ain house and produces a curious mood. In the living room, occupied temporarily by three generations of Shairers, the activities of all were spread on desk and sofa, piano and tables. There was a sense of continuity as strong as in a morning room scene in a Chekov play. Women gathered, their lives unrolled in idle talk. For the first time I saw how an Ain house shaped lives. They were all so much at home in that room, which looked

out on what in another climate might have been a cherry orchard. They were as unconcerned about my presence as if I were the fictional character. "I must have the trees trimmed again," sighed Mrs. Shairer. Her vacationing daughter went back to her typewriter.

Upstairs there were bedrooms at the corners, as if balanced by a Palladio—except the glazed stairwell gave an imbalance to one corner.

The large Hurschler house of 1950 in Pasadena is closer in feeling to the Wilfong house. The approach is under a trellis supported by pipe columns, a detail used often in school architecture of the same period. (However, in Ain's 153rd Street School of 1957 in Gardena, the supports for the

Shairer house, West
Los Angeles, 1949.
Photo: Marvin Rand.

covered walks are redwood four by fours.)
In context with the 1950s, the light crisp
structure seems especially suited to the
client, a Swiss importer of textiles.

Next door to the Hurschler house is
Greene and Greene's Culbertson house,
whose heavy, beamed pergola structure
rises darkly and majestically above the
Hurschler house, the wide eaves of the
gabled house contrasting with the lightness
of color and structure of the Ain. The
Culbertson house was built for the semiarid climate of 1911, for a land with few
native trees except the sycamore and fan
palm; subsequently the heavy watering of
planting alien to the climate brought the
water to the surface and in time changed
the climate. The cooling of the climate

throughout Southern California has made
the sleeping porch obsolete. The Spanish
Colonial revival style with thick walls (false)
and small openings is better for keeping
heat out than in. The misty air of Santa
Monica makes Neutra's Lewin house, with
its bank of windows on the south, more
comfortable than John Byers's splendid
Spanish Colonial houses of the 1920s.
Pasadena, once a favorite wintering place
for easterners because of the dry, warm
air, determined the plan of Greene and
Greene's Gamble house of 1908 — no social
room except the dining room is oriented
to the south; the living room on the northeast is shaded by a wide porch.

Eckbo landscaped most of Ain's
buildings, and although his favorite plant

materials — echium, New Zealand flax,
ajuga — have disappeared, the Eckbo circle
and equilateral triangle are still there in
the redwood rounds, tree wells, and
triangular beds in the entrance garden.

The two houses for Leo Mesner on
Valley Vista Boulevard in Encino are on
a steep hillside above a canyon, the shelf
of land so narrow that the garage consumed
most of it. In the first one (1950), the house
seems to cling to the narrow street by dead-
man's hands, a technique used for anchor-
ing a house by cables to a block buried
under the street paving, a favorite of young
engineers from the war plants who after
the war could afford nothing but an "unbuildable" lot. They built some engineer-

ing stunts in the Hollywood Hills and in the canyons; those on decomposed granite are still there, some on oily shale have slipped down the hills.

The first Mesner house, all on one level, swings out over the slope, and a large deck hanging in space is level with the tops of eucalyptus trees in the canyon. It was planned as a single space open to the view, but since open planning is less appreciated today than three decades ago, the space has been reorganized into rooms by the use of high storage cabinets. The drive-through garage is now a glass-roofed garden room facing the conversation area around the fireplace. The young graphic designer who made the changes cherishes Thoreau, but not to the extent of adopting Thoreau's scheme for a small open-plan house with one corner for writing, one for eating, one for sleeping, and one for talking to a friend—Thoreau used the singular.

The second Mesner house (1953) is several hundred yards away, but slower descent of the slope made possible a garage and two-story house, even a swimming pool on the downslope. Decorative tiles on the fireplace wall and in a grid pattern on the exterior stucco wall on the canyon side are as close as Ain ever came to a decorative flourish.

Departing from Ain, Johnson and Day emphasis on revealed structure, Ain returned to a style more typical of early work when the partnership was dissolved. Mass rather than structure was emphasized in the United Lodge of Theosophists, Laguna, which he did alone.

The best of the buildings on which Garrott collaborated was the house for the labor attorney, Ben Margolis, mentioned earlier. A late one, a house for Dr. Leon Kaye in Tarzana (1963) is almost unique in Ain work because of the repeated use of the hexagon. (The closest thing to it is the hexagonal trellis Ain used to cover a court when making additions to the Dr. David Elterman house in 1962.)

Josef van der Kar who did working drawings and oversaw construction of the Kaye house for Ain said, "Greg had lots of fun when he designed it. It was out of Frank Lloyd Wright, of course. There were also Wrightian touches in Ain's fireplaces. But Ain was too serious to use his sense

of play in architecture very often."

Ain's rigor was illustrated in a story of van der Kar's about Paris. "When we went to the Union Internationale des Architectes meeting there in 1955 Ain was put up in elegant quarters, but he was envious when he saw my simple room on the Left Bank, and immediately moved across the river into an uncomfortable room."

Of Ain's conduct in the classroom he said, "When he was a design critic at USC, he was never laissez faire. He wanted students to work."

One of his students, Ena Dubnoff, said of Ain: "He asked us first what the problem was, then we had to retrace the steps we took to arrive at the solution. In that way we saw the flaws in our solution. It was a lesson in logic."

"He never mentioned his own work, he didn't try to shape us, he was teaching

us to think," said Bernard Judge, another Ain student. "He was one of my two mentors. The other was Buckminster Fuller. It was all post-and-beam at that time at USC, except for Greg, and everyone discouraged me from doing a dome. But Greg supported students who wanted to experiment. He said, 'Try it.' All he asked from us was conceptual clarity. His interest in art and literature and philosophy provided a rich intellectual environment."

Students who wanted to get into design fast didn't like him, said Alson Clark, architecture librarian at USC. Dubnoff agreed. "He was considered an intellectual who talked over our heads. But some of us caught the hang of listening to him and spread the word. By the time I graduated he was the most popular critic in architecture."

Ain arrived for class an hour early to walk on campus. Soon the students began

Margolis house, Los Angeles, 1951. On an upslope, the front door is off the motor court, and social rooms above are level with the terrace. Photo: Marvin Rand.

Kaye house, Tarzana, 1963. The hexagons are one of Ain's few tributes to Wright.

following him on his walks. He was a distinguished Pied Piper with his mane of white hair, his tanned, animated face, the quizzical expression in his light brown eyes, his bursts of speech followed by a long, thoughtful pause, then broken with another barrage of words. Walking made his mind work in leaps; it loosened fragmentary brilliant ideas, expressed usually in the form of questions, often whimsical. The ideas and the delivery were curiously at odds with his straight almost military carriage.

He drove to campus in one of his classic cars—a Pierce Arrow, a Cadillac ("The only well-designed Cadillac"), or a 1938 Packard, all in mint condition. He had a light American or European sports car as well, and according to Richard Tufeld (the television announcer for whom he designed a house in 1959), "Greg never left a car the way it came from the factory. We both

spent as much time redesigning them as went in in the first place." The automobile was the only thing in which Ain could tolerate show. In his renderings of buildings there was often a long sleek sports car in the drive.

Ain was asked in 1963 to become Dean of the School of Architecture at Pennsylvania State University. He recruited van der Kar, who during the 1940s had been technical director for the General Panel production center in Burbank where components of the Wachsmann-Gropius houses were manufactured; before that he had worked on the Dymaxion house for Buckminster Fuller. Ain also engaged Ena Dubnoff as an assistant professor.

From the time Ain began teaching in 1953 until he went to Pennsylvania in 1963 his commissions were few. One house which was on the boards when he went to USC was for Dr. Fred Feldman, in the

hills above Beverly Hills. The house, below the street level, has a glass wall facing a soft downslope, heavily wooded. Mrs. Feldman said, "It was the first time Greg had ever done so large a kitchen. I insisted on the kitchen facing the same view as the living room. The official entrance is on the opposite side but everyone walks past the kitchen to the living room."

Ain's completed work from 1953 to 1963 was six houses, two schools, the Theosophists' Building, Westchester work, Dominguez Park Directors' Building, and five additions to existing houses. Even the additions were thoughtful and exquisitely planned. The addition for the Ben Berg beach house at Malibu was a second story with a wide deck on two sides, one for morning sun and afternoon shade, the other facing the sea view toward Palos Verdes. A shade garden on the leeside connected with a first floor study. Ain had designed a house for the Bergs in 1940, never built; the difference that had occurred in his design in two decades was startling. The first house was more articulated, the chimney stack a sculptural event, the fenestration restless; the second a straightforward plaster envelope whose subtleties came from the pressure of plan.

There were disappointments. He said of the two schools, one in 1957, one in 1960: "It's impossible to introduce anything new to the board of education. They are still back in the day of the double loaded corridor, artificially lighted. They always delete clerestory lighting."

At Penn State, Ain spoke for the first time from a position of authority. In the revision of the curriculum he stressed team work and an interdisciplinary faculty. In those years of student revolt when demands were presented defiantly, Ain considered first the merit of the student proposals rather than their manners. It was the high period of the interdisciplinary faculty; few architectural schools were without social scientists, economists, psychologists, urbanists, traffic engineers, etc. on the faculty. Architecture, the oldest of the professions, was the least confident of survival. Certainly it never occurred to the social sciences to put an architect on the faculty.

Team work in the 1950s and 1960s had

replaced the cry of the 1940s for social participation. Ain's one-man office with a collaborator or the three man and two draftsmen office of Ain, Johnson and Day, gave Ain little direct knowledge of team work, but as the small office offered no opportunity for success, architectural schools assumed the student would enter a large or middle-sized office. The one-person office was considered extinct in the 1950s.

"All professionals are going to have to develop the capacity to derive personal satisfaction out of contributing to a team effort," Ain wrote during his years at Penn State. It appeared to be a warning to his own generation to learn to like a bitter pill.

Administrative chores were alien to Ain. He spent more time with faculty than students, except for a project for a real house he designed with students. But talented teachers rarely make good administrators. As the work became more and more frustrating he isolated himself in his office. After four years of increasing pressure he had a breakdown and, in 1967, resigned.

He spent some weeks in a hospital then returned to Los Angeles. He was 60 years old and without a practice; his energies were too low to face opening an office. He was invited back to USC to teach but his old rapport with students was missing. Old friends employed him to do the preliminary designs for several buildings, but the indecisiveness that was at the base of his drive for perfection had accelerated.

His last commission was for a cooperative colony for a study group to which he and his wife belonged. The site was the floor of a canyon, crossed by a stream, a beautiful site which Ain talked about excitedly. He was designing the community center first and the houses were to follow.

He was very enthusiastic about the job. Each time we talked his descriptions of the project varied, and as I questioned him I discovered that a new solution had replaced the old. This went on until a multitude of solutions had piled up on his drafting table. His ability at making a choice under pressure, abandoning all others, was gone. Architecture was infinite in the number of solutions it offered; the richer it became in possibility the more unattainable the right solution—even the single

one. Academia had somehow played him false.

His eyesight began to fail; first he could not drive at night, then he was not permitted to drive at all. He closed his office in 1968 at age 62 and got a divorce. He bought a bicycle. He haunted bookstores. He lived in the Bubeshko apartment houses designed by Schindler on Griffith Park Boulevard. Later he moved to a Unitarian retirement home. After a month there he spoke to no one, ate his meals in silence, and took long walks.

Ruth March Ain (by 1980 she was Ruth March French and had retired from teaching drama in a Pasadena school) said of Ain: "He could never argue a point. He withdrew into silence. Even with his carpenters. When they did something wrong he would put a tool kit in his car at night and drive to the job and tear it out. He rebuilt it the way he wanted it.

"He was wonderful when I was pregnant with both of the children but he had little interest in their care. He was more comfortable with one of his classic cars or with students. He implanted an idealism in the students and a devotion to high standards that has gone with them into middle age. He took charge of his children's minds as his father had his. Emily and Christopher were hurt by his impatience. In the best of his relationships there was always the danger of saying something that would suddenly make him remote. His silence was reproof, and that led to my frustration and anger." This marriage, the longest of his four, lasted less than ten years.

Ain came to stay with me for a week in 1979 when we started the long talks about his life and work. At first he dismissed outright what he had accomplished; the endless questions about a building wearied him. But we continued each day to work through from nine to one or two when we would drive up the coast or go to a restaurant with a garden for a long lunch. He would express scorn for the largeness of the portions served, boasting that he cooked a quart of soy beans which lasted him for days. But after he had drunk a glass of wine and eaten all of his big lunch he became more outgoing. He was cheered immensely when Ena Dubnoff came to the house for supper.

In the following two months the three of us went of Sundays to see his houses. The appreciation of clients who had lived so long in one of his houses stirred him. When we went to the second A.O. Beckman house (1950) in Sherman Oaks (owned by a screenwriter and actress) they were removing the paint from the ash plywood of the cabinetwork. He talked about the plan of the house. The entrance flanks the two-car carport, and a handsomely detailed stair is lighted at the landing by a tall window. The living quarters are all on the upper level, the road and garage having been cut into the slope. The living room bank of windows faces a long valley, and on the opposite side is a sliding glass to a deck—a bridge from the deck leads to a garden cut into the soft rise of the hill. The materials are plaster and redwood stained a deep gray blue.

The first Beckman house was unmistakably the work of an architect with new forms to express; the second subordinated form to siting, orientation, and plan. A reminder of Flaubert's approach to style—if you see a beautiful phrase, cut it out. There was no beautiful or quotable passage in the second Beckman house.

When we visited the Richard Tufeld house Ain was embraced by the owner. (Tufeld had contracted his own house and another designed by Ain.) The Tufeld plan was shaped by the growing family; starting as a minimal house with a large living room and one bedroom, three other bedrooms were added which broke up the space with jogs and built-ins. The flat Tufeld lot did not engage Ain's ingenuity; there were too few problems for Ain, the pilgrim, to wrestle with.

Ain's favorite work was his Dunsmuir Flats because it had tested all his skills and had given him the assurance that he was not an architect just by chance.

But the thornier the path, the more Ain was at home. Like John Bunyan's pilgrim he preferred "the side of the hill called Difficulty." His secret favorite would surely have been the project that only the angels could build.

Raphael Soriano,
1907- .

Raphael Soriano

Now at 76, Raphael Soriano believes that his contemporaries who contributed most to architecture were Fuller, Nervi Maillart, Mies, Candela, and Frei Otto. He despairs of his profession because it has missed its great opportunity to take full advantage of the new technology the twentieth century offered.

Soriano finds reason for hope that his framing system of aluminum will be revived and he will have 100 houses to build. At times, talking of the many commissions that have fallen through, he can say, "My talents have been wasted," then laughs. "There is still time. My grandfather lived to be 120."

On his office walls are three National AIA awards and seven from local chapters; awards from *Progressive Architecture, Architectural Record, House & Home, Arts & Architecture, Sunset,* and from the city of Los Angeles for his Adolph Office Building and Laboratory, "one of 36 significant buildings in the city between 1947 and 1967."

He spent twenty years perfecting his system of steel framing for housing and office buildings and then when he had developed it to the point that costs were below wood framing he began investigating lighter metals.

Soriano is a romantic technologist, the true missionary of Southern California—the only one in town until Konrad Wachsmann arrived in 1963, ten years after Soriano had moved to Northern California, a steel man in a wood country.

His architecture comes out of reason rather than intuition. This is often discounted because he was blessed with a hearty appetite, a sound stomach, and a life-affirming nature. Even his seriousness as an architect and his pioneering work in steel framing is questioned because he created no monument like the Eames house. Most of Soriano's works have been razed or mutilated.

He has lived modestly all his life; like the poet and the peasant he cuts away what is not essential to his needs, and his architecture is never self indulgent. A consummate moralist, he damns freely what he sees as extraneous to twentieth-century technology. But he would have perished long ago if he indulged in the self pity his neglect gives him the right to feel. He lives contented with himself and his life on a houseboat on Tiburon's Main Street Wharf. The greatest of his needs is music. It is more than food to him, it is breath. He breathed it as a child, and at age 23 he discovered the similarities between the mathematics of a Bach fugue and the poetry of a cross-section of, say, the Simplon Dam. Music and architecture are one to him.

Konrad Wachsmann said, "The real creative act will come through science and technology." Soriano has said, "Architecture determines; technology commands."

Raphael Soriano was born in 1907 on the Greek Island of Rhodes. His ancestors were driven out of Spain during the Inquisition, and found their way to the Jewish quarter in the old fortress area of the capital city. His grandfather was born on the French side of the Pyrenees, in Bayonne, and being an expert linguist and natural teacher he instructed Raphael in French, Latin, and modern and classical Greek. The Codrons, his mother's people had come originally from Austria; being one

"His buildings may seem on paper as hard as nails, but in reality they are as romantic as the ancient buildings of Soriano's native island of Rhodes," said Peter Blake. The entrance to the **1950 Curtis house** on Stone Canyon Rd., Los Angeles. Photo: Julius Shulman.

of thirteen daughters at a time when education was thought to be wasted on women, his mother learned to read only after her marriage. The household spoke Spanish, an archaic Spanish, Raphael learned when he was first invited to lecture in Madrid. "Some of the terms you use have not been heard since the days of Cervantes," a Spanish attorney told him. As Felix Candela listened to him at the VIII Pan-American Congress in Mexico City he recalled his native Spain, and sent Soriano a book about his shell constructions, inscribed "with affection and admiration" for his lecture in the "delicious language with the flavor of old romance, impassioned but friendly and cordial."

He grew up as an agnostic. His father told him that religion was being honest and kind. Raphael thought of this as he looked at the symbols of faith around him, the heavy fortress walls, the large sandstone blocks of the Crusader's Palace. His ambition was to build something or to be a composer.

Raphael's father taught him to play the violin, and he rapped his son's knuckles with the bow when he made a mistake. Raphael liked his gentle grandfather better, and it was to him the boy went for help in his studies in school. Nevertheless, with the first money he earned in America he bought a violin.

His father owned a dry goods store and from an early age Raphael's skill with figures earned him the privileges of keeping the books. His father sold the store and dreamed of retiring to his own plot of land. Raphael dreamed of running off to Sterns Drive in Hollywood where his three aunts had immigrated in 1919.

In the College St. Jean Baptiste in Rhodes, Soriano was pronounced a *bon point* student, memorizing and reciting a page of poetry each day—often a page from a Racine or Corneille play; by the end of three years he knew them all by heart, and when the scholarly examiners quoted any line he could continue. To his father, Raphael at fifteen was still a child, and he tied his son's legs together and beat him for small misdeeds. Raphael began to plot ways to get to Sterns Drive. Through his aunts he got an affidavit to enter the United States, and when his father went

to visit his sister in Cairo, Raphael borrowed money from his grandfather for his passage to America.

He was held up at Naples for six months waiting for his name to appear on the quota. He earned meals by washing dishes, translating letters, and writing replies in French. By the time his name came up his ribs were sticking out. He arrived in New York September 24, 1924, so weak that he was hospitalized. His sickness was mainly terror that he would never be able to repay his grandfather. At home they had tea and bread for breakfast, but at Ellis Island where Raphael was held, he ate scrambled eggs and toast and milk. After a week he had gained enough weight to be allowed to proceed.

In Hollywood, he spoke no English so he got a job with a Rhodesian cleaning vegetables and packing them into crates. The crates of tomatoes and artichokes took all his strength to lift. He attended the Los Angeles Coaching School, and when he learned enough English he got a job at Grand Central Market. "I arranged the beautiful displays of vegetables on the Hill Street side of the market," he remembered. Less rewarding was his task of unloading damaged tomatoes selling for ten pounds for a dime. He began at once repaying his grandfather and saving a little each week to buy a violin. In time he moved from Grand Central Market to a fruit stand across from the Clark Hotel where many musicians stayed. He bought a copy of a seventeenth-century Maggini violin, a sturdy instrument with a powerful tone, and began going to concerts. When the musicians from the Clark bought fruit from him he would tell them, "I heard you at the Philharmonic last night" or "I heard you at the Bowl." At age nineteen he still had not decided whether he wanted to be a great composer or an architect. But how could he go to school when he had to work?

One day a man stopped at his stand who was speaking French with a companion. Raphael answered them in French. One man watched him thoughtfully, then said, "Your French is very good but your accent—I can't place your accent." He was Rene Bellé, a professor of French literature at USC. They talked several times after that, and Professor Bellé urged him to con-

tinue his education. Aside from mathematics and languages his education had many gaps. Nevertheless, a teacher at the Coaching School helped him enroll at USC in architecture. He could stay as long as he maintained a B average.

The School of Architecture was in a one-story wooden building on 35th Place, now occupied by the cinema arts department, already ramshackle in 1929 but remembered as fondly by the students as was the old redwood architecture building by John Galen Howard at Berkeley.

Having no scholarship, Soriano worked from 5 P.M. to 1 A.M. at the fruit stand, and after a few hours sleep went to 8 o'clock classes. He carried a full sixteen units each semester during his five years at USC. He didn't do too well his first semester; then Professor Bellé urged him to take a French course to bring up his grade average.

As in most Beaux Arts schools, the students spent the first year learning the tools and grounding themselves in the classics; they studied the Greek and Roman orders, proportion, light and shade, the grand plans of the eighteenth and nineteenth centuries. The *projets* were usually monumental public or private buildings, railway stations, post offices, and such industrial buildings as cement or steel plants. Residential work was only peripheral, but occasionally there would be a grand villa to design. When Soriano was instructed in the second semester to design a villa in any style he chose—which meant nothing later than the Victorian era—he asked, "Style? What does style mean?"

Robert Boyle, a fellow student, remembered him as coming to class dressed for the market in corduroys and looking like an Italian peasant. Sometimes his brief case was stuffed with avocados. It was a time when students wore pressed gabardines, tweed, and cashmere sweaters; it was also a time when avocados were rare and cost a dollar each. Soriano sold them to the students for a dime. "He had a lot of charm and was popular with students and faculty. He didn't play around, he was very serious—he was better at engineering than most of us."

The students were exposed through the magazines to Frank Lloyd Wright and to the Europeans. "Raphael preferred the Europeans," Boyle recalled. "He brushed aside our arguments that the Bauhaus was too simplistic. He was never a conformer."

During the summer of 1932 he worked without pay in the Neutra office on the theoretical project Rush City. This was a greater influence than USC; however, the discipline of the Beaux Arts system was valuable even if he never applied his knowledge of historic styles.

After five years of study the students were graduated into a world brought to its knees by the Great Depression. One classmate, Albert Nozaki, gave up the search for a job and went on to graduate school in the east; then, armed with a master's degree, scoured the eastern cities for jobs, winding up in New York. Finding nothing, he wrote letters to the architects of the most prestigious buildings in New York and each one granted him an interview. In their splendid offices they talked at length of their past exploits. But in their silent drafting rooms were sometimes as many as a hundred unused boards draped with oilcloth. Nozaki went home and got a job as a set designer with a Hollywood studio where Robert Boyle was also working.

In 1946 Nozaki bought one of Soriano's early houses (the 1938 Ross house) which he and his family still occupy. He said of it, "Raphael used all the principles of planning we were taught at USC."

Soriano fared better—perhaps because he was burdened with few middle-class notions about the status of the architect. After graduation, he worked for a few months in Schindler's office, but soon gave up the 50 cents an hour to return to Neutra who paid nothing. Neutra was then in his new house on Silver Lake Boulevard. "I didn't understand Schindler's drawings," Soriano said. (Schindler was then designing the McAlmon house; his full-time draftsman was Ed Lind who understood Schindler's shorthand for his complicated plans, often no more than memos to himself to take to the site while supervising construction.)

Soriano was still paying off bills for his final year at USC when his father wrote him, "Dear Son, I forgive you. Please send $400." He got a loan from the Morris Plan and went to work on WPA projects in the

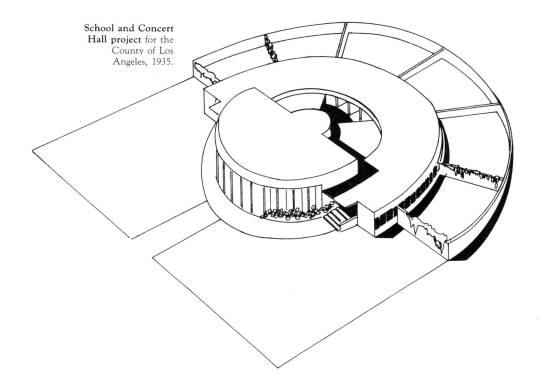

School and Concert Hall project for the County of Los Angeles, 1935.

county engineer's office. Some of his jobs there during 1935 and the spring of 1936 were the design of a minimal house of concrete for families on relief, a dormitory for 50 unemployed men, and a combined school and concert hall.

In the office he met Cassatt Griffin, who gave him a thorough training in low-cost construction. "He clarified many things for me as I followed him around, asking why he did this or why he didn't do that. People naturally assumed that my interest in steel came from Neutra, but he was framing mainly in wood while I was in the office. What I learned from Neutra was how to handle four by fours."

True, he did take over Neutra's framing, even painted the exposed posts a steel color to match the sash. He also used Neutra's ribbon windows, his smooth stucco skin and flat roofs, his continuous fascia, the built-in furniture—always in-line, not Schindler's staggered volumes; he took over the low horizon line of the rooms, and the indirect lighting—even some of Neutra's awkward entrances which required some side stepping when two guests and the host met at the front door.

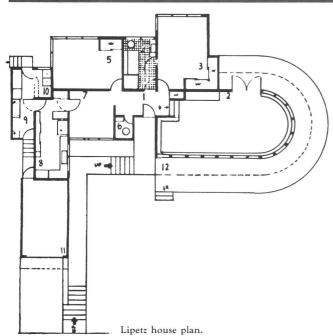

Lipetz house, Los Angeles, 1936. Music room. Photo: Julius Shulman.

Lipetz house plan.

His first commission came out of a kindness to a stranger. He went to see a French film at the John Reed Club and translated the jokes to a woman sitting behind him. Learning of his interest in music she invited him to a concert at which her cousin, Helene Lipetz, was playing the piano. It turned out that Helene and Manuel Lipetz wanted a house with a living room large enough to seat twenty people comfortably while listening to music, a room, moreover, with splendid acoustics. They were impressed by Soriano's knowledge of music and entrusted him with the job.

The site was high above Silver Lake with a wide view of the almost untouched hills. The two-bedroom house was designed entirely around the music room, which occupied over a third of the total area. The floor level was stepped down so the ceiling of the 15-by-31-foot music room was 10 feet high; the north end where the musicians sat was semicircular, and the sides and curved end were continuous windows and a pair of French doors to the terrace. Built-in seating was along one end and one side, with mahogany paneling above and below the windows. The many feet of shelves for a record collection under the windows favored the acoustics, and the

Spencer Austrian house, Los Angeles, 1938. Photo: Julius Shulman.

continuous light trough of wood acted as a baffle to eliminate reverberation.

The delicacy was in the proportions of the room and the exquisite acoustics; the circulation for the house took the hindmost. The circulation was by way of a double-loaded corridor, a central hall stretching from the music room at the north to the kitchen door at the south, all rooms emptying into the hall.

By the time the house was finished in early 1937 there were commissions for two very low-cost ones. The Priver house (1937) of 500 square feet was built of redwood siding for $2000. It was essentially one space, the large studio/dining room opening into the bedroom by a folding wall. The bedroom on the street side had a continuous bank of high windows, and two sides of the living/dining room were typical Neutra windows facing a canyon view and a sundeck. Outside the twelve-foot-long pullman kitchen was a deck with stairs down to a terrace cut into the slope of the hill.

In 1938 Soriano designed a two-story house for the young attorney Spencer Austrian on Landa Street in Echo Park.[1] The main living quarters were on the second level, and below was a studio apartment and a two-car garage. The 800 square feet of living space, and two-car garage cost $6 per square foot. The rhythm of four-by-four posts with casement windows and fixed glass between, capped with an overhanging flat roof, was in Neutra's International style.

1. Spencer Austrian was one of the young attorneys who volunteered time to write briefs for labor cases handled by John Beardsley of the ACLU at Second and Broadway, or Leo Gallagher at the International Labor Defense up the street in the old Mason Theater Building.

Ross house, Los
Angeles, 1938. Photo:
Julius Shulman.

Two other houses, the 1938 Ross house in the Echo Park area and 1939 Dr. Gogol house, near Griffith Park, were on steep slopes with a game room and utility room cut into downslope, and two stories on the street side. In the Ross house the two bedrooms on the top level opened to a view terrace on the flat roof.

The 1938 Polito house was unique among Soriano's early work. The three-story sheer wall of the front facade appears to be the back of a small office building, with double garage and uninflected front door right on the street. The side view, less strict, had recessed balconies on the two top floors.

The 50-foot rise of the lot left little usable outdoor space, so the architect incorporated into the house a large patio off the third floor bedrooms; a bridge led to the upper hillside.

The Polito house brought to five the number completed in the two years since Soriano had left his job with the county. All were wood framed, ceilings were standard eight feet except the Lipetz music room, and doors were standard—later he would hold to the eight-foot ceiling height while using eight-foot doors, reasoning that the cost of the custom-made doors was offset by the cost of plastering above the standard size one. His module was based on the three-foot-six standard steel sash. There were many refined touches like the troughs for indirect lighting, the hardwood paneling, and built-in sofas, desks, and chests of drawers. His color palette was off-shades of brick, rose, and orange for carpeting and linoleum in kitchens, bathrooms, and on countertops. He showed no inventiveness in floor planning, continuing to use in the lowest cost house full walls in the kitchen and separation between kitchen and service; dining rooms were nearly always separate from living. Had Soriano become lost in a large office in 1938 he would only be remembered as a promising Neutra follower.

But late in 1936 Soriano met Fritz Ruppell, who had perfected a system for steel framing called Lattisteel; it was a light weave of steel angles welded together and strengthened with plumber's steel straps. Ruppell was using it as reinforcement in concrete for lift-slabs. Soriano persuaded

Polito house, Hollywood Hills, 1938. The garage and entrance are located on street level of the steeply sloping lot. Photo: Julius Shulman.

Model of the the Jewish Community Center, East Los Angeles, 1939. Photo: Julius Shulman.

The main entrance to the Community Center is at the upper level. Photo: Julius Shulman.

Ruppell to let him design a prefabricated warehouse of the material, built for Lee and Cady in Ferndale, Michigan by Lattisteel. Although it was some years before Soriano would use it in a house, steel became his goal and Ruppell his mentor.

Soriano was one who learned best by doing. He may have been excellent at engineering at USC, but there was little exposure to actual construction. Cassatt Griffin had been important in his development because he taught him what was not in books—process. Soriano badgered Ruppell as he had Griffin—not about the bearing loads of steel, or the aesthetic of steel; on aesthetics he could trust his eye, which always told him that the detail that was best was the one that tended to disappear, and that, finally, was a matter of great care. He was out to learn process. The three men who lingered most affectionately in Soriano's mind were Griffin, Ruppell, and the engineer on all his steel work in Southern California, William Porush, professor at California Institute of Technology.

Late in 1938 he received his first large commission, the George and Ida Latz Memorial Jewish Community Center in Boyle Heights, a two-story building of 5000 square feet on a site adjoining a smaller outmoded one. Soriano worked out with Ruppell the framing members of round steel columns and open web joists. The lower floor, somewhat below grade, contained a large activities room, dark room, and committee rooms; as the site sloped up, the main floor, with large assembly hall and classrooms, was level with the playground at the back. A wide overhang on the street side (south) shaded the panels of fixed glass and ventilating awning glass in the assembly hall, while the committee rooms below were lighted by a ribbon of awning glass.

The building department, which had no previous experience with two-story pipe columns, insisted that they be filled with concrete—lally columns—but Soriano could easily prove with his calculations that the columns, on a twelve-foot-square grid, were adequate without the concrete. This led to a change in the building code.

Late one day in November 1938 as Soriano finished a tour of inspection of the steel framing and was leaving, he turned in the street to call out to the welder, "Get those rivets absolutely plumb." As his attention was fixed on the riveter he was struck by a speeding car. His legs and a hip were fractured, his jaw and nose broken. He was in traction in the hospital for six months, his jaw wired together, then in a body cast for months. There were two operations on the hip, hours of dental work, and when an infection developed in the nose, bone was removed from his breast bone to rebuild the nose. During this time, locks and hardware for the Community Center were brought to the hospital for his approval.

"The only architect who visited me was Neutra. It cheered me so much that I had a lap board brought to my room and began designing the Kimpson house in Long Beach." After six weeks in the hospital, tended by nurses sent in by Fritz Ruppell, his sunny, ever-hopeful nature, and his bantering made his room the favorite meeting place of the interns. When the Community Center opened in 1939 he was taken by wheelchair to the inauguration ceremonies. Sitting between Mrs. Latz, donor of the building, and Dore Schary, he joked about being struck down while lost in admiration of the building.

When the Kimpson house was going up he went on crutches by the old Red Car to Long Beach to oversee construction. His energy was boundless, and he set out to make up his lost year.

Beside the 1940 Kimpson house, there came in rapid succession the Koosis house (1940) in the Hollywood Hills, with a **U**-shaped plan around a paved terrace, and the most innovative in those prewar months, the combined house/studio for the USC ceramics professor Glen Lukens. (1940) He began using brick fireplaces, which he had felt were anachronistic in houses with central heating, but clients clamored for them; and he began designing his own chairs and tables, usually of the same hardwood plywood as his paneling, and he tried out obscure glass screens as separation between rooms. His color palette expanded to include blue-gray, bottle green, and canary yellow.

The first story of the Jewish Community Center is partially below grade. Photo: Julius Shulman.

Steel framing of the Jewish Community Center is composed of pipe columns and open web trusses. Photo: Julius Shulman.

Lukens house, Los Angeles, 1940. Photo: Julius Shulman.

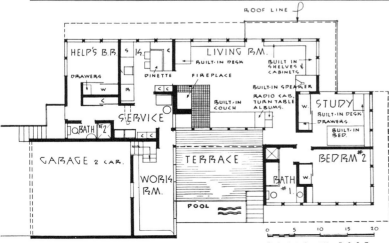

ROOF LINE

HELP'S B.R.   LIVING RM.
DRAWERS   BUILT-IN DESK   BUILT-IN SHELVES & CABINETS
W   DINETTE
B   FIREPLACE   BUILT-IN SPEAKER
SERVICE   BUILT-IN COUCH   RADIO CAB. TURN TABLE ALBUMS.   STUDY
BATH #2   BUILT-IN DESK DRAWERS
BUILT-IN BED.
GARAGE 2 CAR.   TERRACE   BEDRM #2
WORK RM.   BATH #1
POOL

SCALE IN FEET
0 5 10 15 20

Lukens house plan.

The living room of the Lukens house. Photo: Julius Shulman.

Furniture and a lamp in the Lukens house designed by Soriano. Photo: Julius Shulman.

The Lukens site, near USC, was a sliver off an old estate with mature trees. The recessed deck on the south was the key to the circulation between living and work quarters. An obscure glass wall hid the activities in the workroom from the deck, also opened by glass doors to the living room. The workroom has a direct passage across the roofed end of the deck to the study and bath, with owner's bedroom next to the bath. The entrance on the north leads to the living room, with corner fireplace of brick, built-in sofa, and music center; around the walls were cases and shelves for the display of ceramic pieces. Beyond the kitchen, where dining was in a comfortable corner, was the bedroom and bath for the student helper.

Rarely had Soriano the opportunity to design a house on a lot with so few problems—it was wide enough to stretch the house out, and had only a few feet variation in grade, handled nicely by putting the entrance level with the street and a deck on the garden side. The excellent circulation and the good scale are the result.

Ibert house, West Hollywood, 1942. Photo: Julius Shulman.

Strauss house, Los Angeles, 1941. Photo: Julius Shulman.

Curiously, the 1941 Strauss house used the wood skin in much the same way the Lukens house used plaster, taking no advantage of the greater flexibility of the material. The roof was flat, and the narrow wood siding continued much as a plaster cornice over an open porch. He solved well the problem of a corner lot requiring a deep front setback, which threw the house to the high, narrowing end of the lot close to the side street. Nevertheless, he faced the living room and patio toward the side street, separating it from the traffic below by a translucent fence; the house was high enough above the street to have the best view of the golf course 50 yards away.

The Ibert house, also of wood, was built in the West Hollywood hills in 1942; materials were bought and stockpiled in the early months of the war: steel windows, sliding doors, copper screens, plumbing fixtures, heating, ventilating systems, electrical wiring. A large house—the living/dining room of 700 square feet was larger than some of his small houses—had three bedrooms and a view deck on the second story.

In the meantime Soriano had been preparing for change. In 1940, he was commissioned to build the Hallawell Nursery and Garden Center in San Francisco. It was delayed a year because the site, a eucalyptus grove at the corner of two boulevards in a residential district, had to be rezoned. Two problems to be reckoned with were the filled ground which would not support great weight, and the excessive wind pressure from the Bay, both of which suggested lightweight steel.

Soriano argued at the rezoning hearing that his low steel sales building, surrounded by paved terraces connected with lath houses, would be residential in character and much of it obscured by a long wind screen of aqua glass. There would be none of the usual unsightly sheds. Because of the nature of the business and the delicacy of the design, the rezoning was granted for the sales office, lath houses, and greenhouse.

Hallawell Nursery, San Francisco, 1942. Sales Building. Photo: Julius Shulman.

The lath plant booths at the Hallawell Nursery. Photo: Julius Shulman.

When the bids came in, the cost was so high that the only hope of carrying out the plan was by returning to his friend Fritz Ruppell. He found that by contracting the construction himself, and working through subcontractors, he could cut the cost in half. So the structure was prefabricated in Pasadena and trucked some 400 miles to San Francisco. (This was before the freeway system was in, and both the ridge route and coast route to San Francisco had hazardous stretches for the heavy load to traverse.)

Soriano followed the truck with two welders. When the prefabricated walls of the 1200-square-foot sales office, the four-inch pipe columns, and the eight-inch open web joists of the 9000 square feet of lath houses were unloaded, the erection of the first steel nursery was started—and finished in less than a week. As the module was twelve feet, the subcontracted work went fairly fast.

When the rust coat was applied to the steel, Soriano liked the red color so much that he kept the final coat on the lath the same color. The long white fascia of the sales office, supported on slender pipe columns, the aqua glass walls, appeared residential indeed. The walk to the sales offices bordered with flowering plants of the season would have stopped the eye of even Walter Doty, then garden editor of *Sunset*. The only identification with com-

merce was the modest silhouetted name of the business at one end of the fascia. Extending out from the side of the sales office were the red lath canopies, a gauze of color seen through trees.

There is a wondrous neatness in all Soriano does. In the sales room, he instructed the clerks how to load the trays to reveal the label on each pack of seeds, the salesmen in the lath houses how to store the additional flats of the same plant material in the racks below, and how to load the staggered plant bars and store the surplus stock. This storage system was Soriano's substitute for sheds, where surplus stock was usually stored. His years of arranging fruit and vegetables had taught

The lightweight
Lattisteel framing of
the Katz house.
Photo: Julius
Shulman.

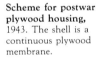

Scheme for postwar plywood housing, 1943. The shell is a continuous plywood membrane.

him to find shortcuts which created and preserved order.

Soriano had ordered the steel for the nursery before the shortages, so construction was not delayed. But by 1942 when it was finished such a building could not have been realized in steel. Exterior plywood was then available, however, and that same year Soriano did the first of two wartime housing projects using the material. Both of the houses of the resin-bonded plywood were on a five-foot module, and they employed many of the features of a mobile home. The first was a snap-in wall system with a central mechanical core. The roof trusses, canti-levered out from the core, could be folded back when the house was towed by truck from factory to site. At the site the house was slid into a ten-by-twelve-foot trench which contained plumbing and utility connections. The roof trusses when opened

up, anchored by cable, then roofed, covered a 60-foot paved square. The glass and sandwich panel walls of the 1800-square-foot house were snapped into place in channels. The rest of the roofed area was in carport, covered patios, and overhang. The radiant heating was in coils in the ceiling; the furniture was built in.

The following year a simplified proto-type was of a single membrane of molded plywood in 10-by-48-foot sections. The roof, which incorporated a corrugated plywood truss, curved down into the wall. An advantage over the earlier model was that the houses could be nested for transportation, and assembly was with stainless steel bolts and straps. Kitchens and baths were stamped out of stainless steel, a variation of Buckminster Fuller's Dymaxion house baths. The house was dropped onto a slab which was imbedded with radiant heating coils. The greatest advantage was that the houses could be

added to, as they came in 500-,750-, and 1000-square-foot sections—all adaptable to a 50-foot lot.

This scheme took third prize in *Arts & Architecure*'s 1943 competition for war-time housing.

During the war there was mainly remodel-ing of existing offices and shops—for an optometrist, a restaurant, a furniture store addition. The two most interesting jobs were 1948 interiors and facades for Ciro of London branch shops in San Francisco and Beverly Hills (in collaboration with Serge Chermayeff). Both shops were nar-row awkward spaces entered through deep-ly recessed doors, flanked by showcases. The interiors had the richness of small jewel boxes, with their leather and mirror-covered walls. Sales were at small tables, with the customer seated across from the salesperson.

His largest building to date, a five-story

Katz house, Van Nuys, 1947. Photo: Julius Shulman.

Krause house, Whittier, 1949. Photo: Julius Shulman.

office building for doctors in Beverly Hills was not built. The 40-foot street facade was half an open lobby, the rest an office with a 20-foot long panel of glass from floor to ceiling, separated from the street by lush planting. The upper floors were a composition of wide white stripes of balcony parapets and dark stripes of inset glass walls.

In 1947, Soriano had his first chance to try out Ruppell's Lattisteel as framing, in the Katz house in Van Nuys. Only the exterior plywood walls related to the wartime work. A photograph of the framing shows the Lattisteel extending above the open web joists, and the wood framing of an overhanging canopy above the entrance. The garden side was a sensitive arrangement of plaster walls, high glass, and floor-to-ceiling glass broken up into square panes. The Katz house received a 1948 award from *Progressive Architecture* in a competition for small houses.

When it was first published in *Arts & Architecture* (October 1947), the editors noted that steel framing was "still a relative rarity in residential construction. . . . There is no questioning the fact that for purposes of speed, efficiency, and flexibility it has a number of advantages over wood," adding that it was difficult "to conceive of space more logically allocated, or of a greater feeling of openness."

One last house in the 1940s was the large Krause house in Whittier. By 1949 he had abandoned the Neutra module (as had Neutra), and used glass in the largest available sheet the budget would bear. He had begun to use steel framing after the war as soon as the restrictions allowed, setting pipe columns at the edge of the overhang, which created a gallery around the house. By 1949 his work deviated from Neutra's in many ways; indeed, Soriano himself was becoming an influence on younger men—two were his erstwhile draftsmen Craig Ellwood and Pierre Koenig. Soriano had carried steel as far as his middle-class comfortable clients would allow, but he exposed only the pipe columns, and in one case the steel decking; all other steel was hidden behind plaster. In 1949 Eames had exposed the steel in his Case Study house, but he was his own client and could do what he liked;

what he liked was to use the same steel framing that Neutra had in the Lovell house, and to expose it. But one could not jump directly from Neutra to Eames and leave out the important work of Soriano between.

Of Soriano, Peter Blake once noted: "What sets Soriano apart from most of his fellow Technocrats is that he is also an exceedingly sensitive artist, with a first-rate understanding of color, of plant life, of all art. His buildings may seem on paper as hard as nails; but in reality they are as romantic as the ancient buildings of Soriano's native island of Rhodes. . . he is a poet as much as a Technocrat."

The first years of the 1950s were for Soriano ones of intensive search. There were four significant houses. The first was the 1950 Curtis house, on a site at the corner of Sunset Boulevard and Stone Can-

yon Road. It was his first house without bearing walls. The structural bays were 10 by 20 feet — two 20-foot bays wide and twelve 10-foot bays long. Within this columnar layout was the garage, the long covered walk from street to entrance, and two patios. Four steel columns along the entrance walk did double duty as support for trellis and the roof of a 10-by-40-foot guest house. The columns defined the perimeters of the 4000-square-foot roof.

The only thing in the house that was not factory built was the concrete slab. While less spectacular achievements have been widely recorded almost nothing is remembered today of the prefabricated Curtis house.

Architectural Forum described the process:

"The first thing architect Soriano did when he started on his experiment was to order a great many industrial parts from

a great many different factories. He ordered forty-nine 3½" lally columns, 8' long; thirty-two 6" I-beams, 20' long; some 4" channels and 45 sq.ft. of 1½"-deep, 18-gauge steel decking. He also ordered about $3500 worth of storage walls, about $1300 worth of glass, some sheets of corrugated plastic, of plywood, of gypsum board, and of ½"-thick insulating cork. These items, together with all the other odds and ends that go into a building, were scheduled to arrive on the site in a steady flow.

"The flow started the moment the column footings were in place. First to go up was the steel frame — columns, I-beams, and channels. Four men and one crane operator put it up in eight hours. Next came the steel decking; two welders had it in place in ten hours. It took exactly eighteen hours to put up a 4500-square-foot steel umbrella — and thus give the other trades a protected place to work.

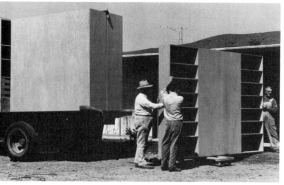

Factory fabricated storage walls were trucked to the Curtis site. All of Soriano's buildings from 1950 on used storage wall partitions. Photo: Elizabeth Soriano.

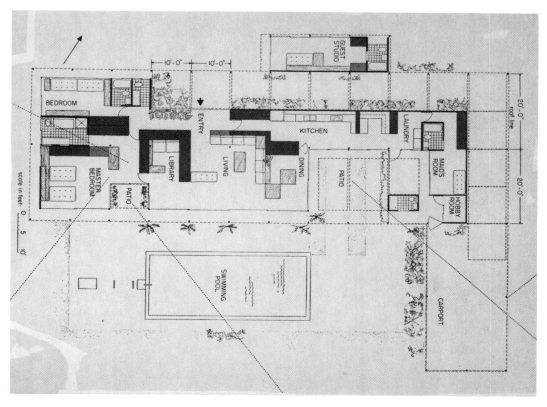

Curtis house plan.

"Fascia channels (which had to be welded in place with great precision to asure a trim building silhouette) took longest of all to put up: a total of seventy-six man/hours were spent to do a perfect job. But while the fascias were being welded in place, other men were busy pouring the floor slab with its electric conduits, glass fiber insulation, and electric radiant heating system; and when the slab had been topped off with a ¼" layer of cork and the ceilings finished in gypsum board, the stage was set for the next phase of the experiment."

This phase was to roll in the factory-built storage walls which partitioned all rooms. The partitions were composed of wardrobe closets, drawers, shelves, storage cabinets, counters—all the built-ins required for each room in the house; incorporated in them were lighting fixtures and switch panels, telephone connections and

doors. The thickness insured quietness for each room. After this operation the eight-by-ten-foot fixed and sliding glass and the sandwich panels for exterior walls were installed.

The war had taught the architects a great deal about factory-assembled elements, and although house building was still a field industry there were numerous instances of quickly built war housing in the early 1940s. One was William Wilson Wurster's Defense Housing at Mare Island Navy Yard; studs and other framing lumber were precut, wall panels marked off in modular units on a jig table, then the sheets glued and nailed to two-by-three studs, roof panels prebuilt. All the elements needed for three houses were trucked at one time to the site. They were minimal houses which could be demounted at the end of the war. Defense housing in Pennsylvania by Gropius and Breuer used stan-

dard details, but the operation added more to good site planning and floor planning (kitchen-dining-living was one space 10 by 30) than to process and scheduling.

The war had simply put to use Joseph Paxton's 1851 application of prefabricated elements, and Eli Whitney's principle of interchangeable parts.

Soriano's building materials were recognizable as coming out of any steel catalog; the method of joining them was easy to grasp. From that time on his work varied only by the different use and different site problems; the only major change was the longer spans used when the steel decking was introduced in larger sizes, and when he substituted aluminum for steel.

This might mark the end of his story. There was no longer any mystery in what he was up to. Yet each of his buildings was unique.

Case Study House, Pacific Palisades, 1950. Entrance walk, carport. Photo: James H. Reed.

The partially roofed outdoor dining room of the Case Study House. Photo: James H. Reed.

The Colby Apartments and the 1950 Case Study House for *Arts & Architecture* magazine were designed while the Curtis house was being finished; delays in starting construction on the apartments held up completion until 1952, but the Case Study was finished in December 1950. The Schrage house, another rigid steel frame building with factory-built partition walls was started in Los Angeles in 1952.

The Case Study site was above Sunset Boulevard in Pacific Palisades, a flat pad on top of a low hill. But it was high enough so the glass walls of the living room and two bedrooms faced the view on the west. The 40-by-75-foot roof covered 2800 square feet of living space, double garage, entrance walk, and part of the outdoor dining space. Two 10-by-20-foot bays were omitted from the outdoor dining roof.

After the house was entirely finished the factory-finished storage walls were installed. In the open plan, only bedrooms and baths were completely enclosed. There were wide openings between living room and family room/dining room and family room and outdoor dining bay.

A new material used here was industrial-weight corrugated glass; it separated the entrance walk from the bedroom and, lighted from behind, it illuminated the carport and entry. The material was customarily used for factory skylights. He also used for the second time (first in the Curtis house) an industrial cork of chocolate brown in a coarse texture, usually under outside covered walks. Although it was a beautiful texture and color, it flaked badly and was soon abandoned. Another material not commonly used for exteriors was masonite (rough side out) for outdoor storage cabinets. A less rich brown, it nevertheless had an appeal for Soriano.

The eight-foot-high ceiling and doors gave a horizontal emphasis to the small house, which played against the vertical rhythm of the round steel columns. Columns occur nearly always near or inside a storage wall, which minimizes their presence. The steel roof decking is covered by plaster board for ceiling. Only the columns, ten feet apart, outside the glass are an emphatic steel note.

Soriano wrote (*Arts & Architecture*, January 1950) in reference to the house:

"It is sometimes difficult to speak of the architect without thinking of music, especially from the point of view of Alain speaking of Bach: '*Qu'il n'y a de drame qu' entre les sons eux-memes; drames dont il est possible de meler quelques chose.*' It is not a question here of emotions or tumultuous passions—it is simply the drama of the sounds themselves, and not the drama of man insofar as man has confused his own realities."

The Korean War interrupted the flow of steel, so the Shulman house and Colby Apartments used steel only for primary structural members; the secondary ones were wood. The Shulman house, which was occupied before completion in March 1950, is extremely well preserved—perhaps because it has had one owner, the eminent architectural photographer, Julius Shulman, whose photographic studio is directly across a pleasant patio from the house.

The site was a flat pad up a steep road off Woodrow Wilson Drive, with a view of the canyons and the city. Behind the house was a slope of layered silt and basalt. The major difference between the Shulman and the two other houses of 1950 was the use of screened cages off the living room, kitchen/dining, and master bedroom. Shulman made a handsome vista of the walk along the south side of the house, with sliding screen panels open to reveal the continuous paved terrace under the eaves; the dark green plastic screening made the cages a shimmering transition between house and garden. Shulman takes credit for the cages, but Soriano has integrated them masterfully into the composition.

The large motor court off the studio led to steps to the front door (of corrugated aluminum); the difference in level of studio and house separated the two functions, reinforced by the planting separating the studio patio from the motor court.

Soriano often used a diagonal wall to funnel visitors from front door to the living room. In this case the built-in storage cabinets in the hall narrowed the entrance hall. The cabinets were below ceiling height which broke up the mass and brought south light into the hall. The chocolate brown sheet cork on the walls contrasted

Shulman house, Los Angeles, 1950. A view from the detached studio toward the patio and main house. At right are steps to the house entry. Photo: Julius Shulman.

Looking across the patio from the studio to the living terrace. Photo: Julius Shulman.

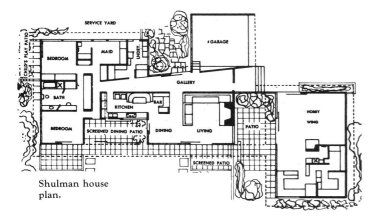

Shulman house plan.

The screened patios off the bedroom and living room in the Shulman house. Photo: Julius Shulman.

The living room of the Shulman house. Photo: Julius Shulman.

with the light elm color of the cabinets. North light is introduced into the hall by a planting court reached through sliding glass.

The living room, glazed on part of the east wall and all of the south wall, faced the view; on the hall side of the storage cabinet were closets for guest wraps, and on the living room side a long built-in sofa facing the view of the garden in the foreground and the canyons below. Flank-

ing the sofa was a fireplace of dark red Roman split bricks on the east wall, and built-in music center extended out from the other end of the sofa. Soriano had designed a large raised pad for seating near the glass—intended as a place to sprawl while listening to music or looking at the view (a forerunner of the next generation's piled-up cushions on the floor). Alas, the raised pad was so rarely used that it was eventually removed.

Otherwise, the room was essentially as planned, even to the gooseneck bullet lamps in brushed aluminum, so popular in the 1950s; they sprang from walls or built-ins or bed heads. The dining end of the living room led to a screened outdoor dining cage; another reminder of the 1950s was the pass-through kitchen and outdoor dining. Also typical of Soriano of the 1950s was the brick red color of the exterior stucco walls.

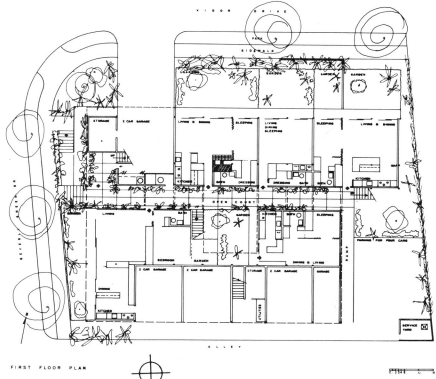

FIRST FLOOR PLAN

Colby Apartments
plan.

Colby Apartments,
Los Angeles, 1952.
Courtyard. Photo:
Julius Shulman.

**The owner's
penthouse** of the
Colby Apartments is
surrounded by decks.
Photo: Julius
Shulman.

The ten-unit Colby Apartments, which received a National AIA award, was a rectangular block on a sloping site, with two stories on the high side and three on the low. The penthouse balcony protected the entrances to the first floor apartments on the north, which were entered through private gardens separated by translucent fences. Access to other apartments was through a central court which split the block into two wings. Each apartment had a garden or a deck.

There was no uniformity in the layout of the single or double apartments, or the owner's penthouse, which opened the major rooms to a balcony or deck on three sides. The use of the movable storage walls as partitions gave a great flexibility to the interiors.

Elaine Sewell who lived in two of the apartments before her marriage to architect Quincy Jones recalls such refinements as a glimpse through the living room to a light well in the bedroom. "He wasted no space on corridors; there was a nice flow from room to room," she said.

Situated near Twentieth Century Fox Studios, the apartments were in demand by actors under contract to the studio. Recently a long-time tenant, fearing the building would be destroyed by a new owner, was investigating ways of saving it.

**Adolph's Office
Building,** Burbank,
1958. Street elevation.
Photo: Julius
Shulman.

An event which defined Soriano's direction was the Alcoa Aluminum conference in Boca Raton, Florida in 1950. Although he had long wanted to move on from steel to other metals—and aluminum was the natural first step—the discussions opened up many new possibilities.

The words Acropolis, Rheims, and the Spanish Steps have a magic for some architects but what stirred Soriano were the names of new alloys: titanium, beryllium, tantalum, molybdenum. "We are living in the most exciting period of the history of the world," he wrote of the metals available.

That was the rosy future. As for the present he began the serious study of aluminum as a substitute for steel.

He saw as the chief advantages of aluminum its malleability, ease in drilling, the lightness—the heaviest members usually weighed no more than 32 pounds—and parts could be assembled by unskilled labor. No welding or grinding was necessary. The material could be shipped in flat bundles that were easily handled by one or two men. But for the time being he still needed steel columns for strength.

Another change in his life came in 1950 with his marriage to Elizabeth Coberly, a photographer with three children.

Two large projects on which design started in the early 1950s were delayed for a number of years. One was the very fine Adolph's Office Building and Laboratory, initiated in 1953 but not completed until 1958. The site was a nondescript street in Burbank, a small city that is hot in summer. Soriano gave the building a built-in environment and climate control. Only about half the 25,000-square-foot site was covered space. A colored drawing of the plan shows green weaving through the pattern of offices so intricately that no office is without a share of the 3000 square feet of small and large garden courts. Along the front and side streets are wide planting strips which cooled the offices and screened them from the street. The parking areas and truck delivery were carved out of the northwest side in small bites so the offices and laboratory moved around them.

The 20-by-40-foot modular layout of the 8-inch steel **H** columns left considerable leeway in locating the offices, and the frequency of mechanical outlets (heat, cooling,

A view from the executives' bar and dining room across the patio to the conference room. Photo: Julius Shulman.

Adolph's laboratories. The plan, cut up by planted courts, turns all work spaces toward greenery. Photo: Julius Shulman.

air exhaust, telephone, loud speakers, etc.) along the floors made possible relocation of the storage wall partitions. The high-ceilinged space accommodated the open web beams and ducts while the office ceilings were lowered to control sound transmission; between the tops of the storage walls and the ceiling were sound-proof plexiglass transoms with hardware of nylon.

One third of the building was in executive offices and a conference room, which faced a large court and swimming pool; a second third along the front and one side was in employees' offices and courts, and the remaining third in laboratory and mechanical equipment.

Except for the steel columns the framing was of aluminum; even the screen enclosing the upper part of the building is of pierced aluminum.

Soriano's largest building in the south was a collaboration on the 131-bed San Pedro Community Hospital, finished in 1961. Most of the collaborators were design critics at USC, where Soriano was frequently invited to speak—"to clean out the students' ears." The group was made up of architects with small- or medium-sized offices who had pooled their resources to compete with architects with large organizations for big jobs. The group, which called itself Project Architects, was composed of Arthur Gallion, Dean of the School of Architecture at USC, Maynard Lyndon, Jones and Emmons, Honnold and Rex, and Soriano.

The hospital was very efficient but as with most hospitals few innovative ideas were introduced—none of Soriano's storage wall partitions and frequent runs of floor outlets for changing the layout; nor were there any of the ideas Quincy Jones developed in his report of the 1970s for the ideal hospital: interstital floors in which part of the space was retrievable, combined mechanical systems, and movable walls which allowed departments to be telescoped or expanded.

While the hospital was in design Soriano moved to the Bay Area, living with his family in Belvedere and opening his office in the houseboat in Tiburon. The wood tradition of the Bay Area, as already noted, made this a strange choice for a

**Steel-framed house
for mass production**
for Eichler, Palo Alto,
1955. The patio off
the living room.
Photo: Ernest Braun.

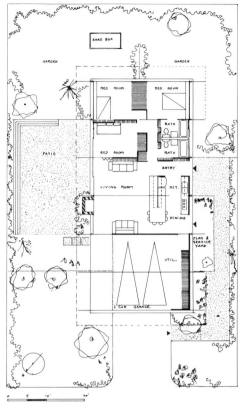

Prefabricated partitions used throughout the Eichler house. Photo: Ernest Braun.

Eichler floor plan.

steel man, moreover one who did not drive a car. A taxi driver who enjoyed Soriano's company provided him for a monthly fee with what amounted to private chauffeur service to business appointments in San Francisco. He commuted by plane to Burbank to oversee construction of the Adolph's Office Building in 1956.

The logical next step when working with industrial materials was mass production. All of his houses in the Bay Area seemed to be part of an open-ended tract, although in one case there was a single house, in another two. He never quite succeeded, however, in breaking into mass housing, a field overrun with unqualified practitioners.

He had a vast knowledge of his materials, of construction and costs, which he had accumulated from research, from contracting his own buildings, and even doing his own shop drawings had taught him much.

In financial affairs he was clear cut and

pragmatic, coming easily to agreements with developers or bankers. His bohemian style of dress and office in a houseboat was no cause for distrust in a city as urbane as San Francisco. His reputation as a fine architect, one whose work had received wide attention, was also a factor.

The stumbling block to his success as a major figure in mass-produced housing seemed to be that although he was open to new methods to improve construction procedures, they could not be at the sacrifice of aesthetic considerations.

"I don't want to build junk," he said.

While continuing his exploration of aluminum, he framed his houses in steel. A house in 1955 for the enlightened developer Joseph Eichler in Palo Alto was the smallest, wholly industrialized house in the United States. When it was featured with others in a *House & Home* story on steel framing (November 1955), the editors noted: "People have been using *some* steel in *some* places for a good, long time. But

they haven't been using it as a material in its own right. . . . Steel today is not a raw material to be fashioned on the site, but a vast catalog of reasonably well-coordinated components. And the truly astonishing fact is that you can now find a completely shop-fabricated steel part for almost any wood part that goes into today's house."

The Eichler house was composed of seven identical welded, light steel frames spaced ten feet apart; the steel cage was topped with the fluted steel decking and closed in with three types of wall paneling: floor-to-ceiling fixed or sliding glass, plywood in steel frames, or fiberglass panels. Interior partitions were shop-fabricated of ash plywood. The cost of the house with two bedrooms and den and two baths was $7 per square foot, which Eichler said compared favorably with the hundreds of wood-framed houses on neighboring tracts. Although the house received much critical attention, Eichler decided not to go ahead with a whole tract of steel-framed houses.

The McCauley houses had unroofed courts cut into the plan. Photo: Elizabeth Soriano.

The builders house for McCauley, Mill Valley, 1959, was designed for mass production. Photo: Elizabeth Soriano.

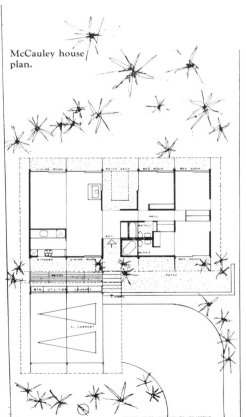

McCauley house plan.

RAPHAEL S. SORIANO, F.A.I.A., ARCHITECT

In 1959, Soriano interested a Beverly Hills developer (McCauley) in two small steel houses on a wooded hillside in Mill Valley. The plans were different but both had a plastic roofed deck off the living room, and one had a small glass-walled interior court off the living room and master bedroom to bring in the south light. The living room and bedroom, divided by accordion doors, faced a balcony overlooking the trees. Soriano used the setting to create his two most romantic houses.

In 1960, another possibility for a group of houses arose when Vera Mahoney interested Soriano and two other architects in developing a large piece of land at Strawberry Point on the San Francisco Peninsula. Soriano made plans for a house on the hilltop for the owner—a most unusual house for him because it was prestressed concrete and the living quarters were on top of a cylindrical shaft. In 1960, bomb shelters were often incorporated in houses, and the base of the Mahoney house

was designed as a refuge from attacks. Parking was reached by a drive curving up the circular base to the living level at the top, where all rooms gave onto an encircling balcony with a view of San Francisco Bay. The owner abandoned the project.

Another circular form appeared in 1960 in a project for a group of houses along the coast of the Gulf of California in Guaymas, Mexico. The houses were hung from tapered aluminum trusses which fanned out from a masonry hub at the center of the drive-through carport. Living quarters with wide balconies were in a semicircle facing the gulf. It was something of a kit house which could be built by unskilled labor, once the aluminum trusses and aluminum frame were in place. The scheme, said Soriano, was based on a Japanese fan to which additional ribs could be added or subtracted. Houses could be as small as ¼ of a semicircle, or with the addition of ribs could become ¾ of a circle. None was built.

Vera Mahoney house, Strawberry Point, Project, 1960. In the concrete shaft is a bomb shelter.

Scheme for a housing project, Baja California, 1960. The prefabricated aluminum frame can be erected in segments for a small or large house.

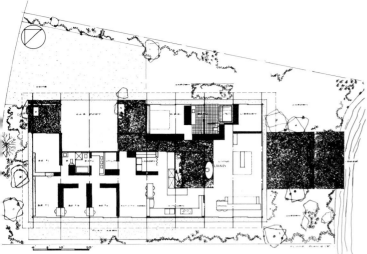

Cooke house plan.

Cooke house,
Belvedere, 1961.
Despite the romantic
setting, it returned to
the more pristine
design of the Case
Study house. Photo:
Elizabeth Soriano.

**A view from the
front door** of the
Cooke house toward
the water. Photo:
Elizabeth Soriano.

The Dr. Cooke house (1961) built for a neighbor in Belvedere was sensitively sited on a small piece of land, with terrace and boat dock on the lagoon. The prefabricated steel trusses, which spanned 41 feet, arrived at the site in bents, i.e., connected to steel column supports. Soriano cut courts and carports into a rectangular plan, and used Mexican polished pebbles as a surface in the concrete slab of the entry, courts, and hearth.

The Cooke house brought back some of the old pristine character of his Southern California work, which softened and dimmed in the design of prototypes for popular housing. The Soriano of Bach and Corneille had returned.

The opportunity to build a tract of all-aluminum houses came in 1965 when Soriano interested a Dallas developer in putting up eleven houses on land he owned on Maui in Hawaii. A corporation called Soria was set up to handle the business operations and shipment of the trusses and storage walls from San Francisco.

Soriano's structural system did not vary but as always he was generous in providing a selection of floor plans. There were detached minimal houses which could be expanded from a square to a rectangular plan by adding prefabricated segments; clusters of units in one or two stories in double rows; and (Series 10) a superior plan for three-bedroom houses; the entrance hall was a hyphen between the two segments, and courts were placed in front and back of it. The plans in which kitchenettes with accordion doors faced the entrance were congested, however. These are called housing for students, the elderly, and young couples.

The long-span aluminum frame with no bearing walls was designed to take hurricane-force winds. Six unskilled men assembled the frames of four 2600-square-foot houses in one day.

So says Soriano's brochure, for which he did the makeup and all the writing. But it was not effective in attracting customers for more than eleven houses, so the project stopped there. Soriano's marriage had broken up by this time so he took over the photography, with the result that only his own inadequate color slides document

All-aluminum houses, Maui, 1965. Eleven prefabricated houses were shipped by boat from San Francisco. Photo: Raphael Soriano.

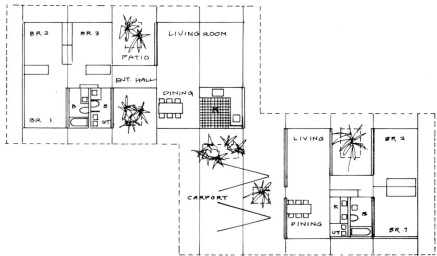

Plans for two- and three-bedroom houses, Maui.

the job. These he copied by Xerox for his brochures. Soriano's dear friend Allan Temko said that Soriano was troubled by his divorce and other litigation in the 1960s, and his office suffered, finally dropping to skeletal size.

But he snapped back in 1966 when Alcoa became interested in his project for an aluminum tower. It started with A. Cal Rossi, Jr.'s decision to demolish a 10,000-square-foot apartment hotel on Nob Hill and replace it with a tower; he had conferred with other architects, but when the city opposed a highrise for Nob Hill he dropped it. Then from Temko he heard of Soriano's 1000-foot-high tower in which Fritz Close of Alcoa was interested. Temko advised Rossi that "if the tower works as art your chances for getting permission from the city to build will improve."

Temko followed this with a letter to Rossi:

". . . three quarters of a century have passed since 1889, when Eiffel masterfully completed a tower as tall as the one you contemplate. In spite of the steady development of nonferrous metallurgy in the twentieth century no one has ever proposed, much less attempted to do as well as Eiffel, or better, in so revolutionary a material as aluminum. Thus, if this tower is built, it can stand as a symbol of our age in the same way that the Eiffel Tower is an incomparable masterpiece of an earlier age of iron and steel. Precisely because aluminum is revolutionary it demands an unprecedented expression. . . . Tubular construction is of course not new. In a sense it dates back to the first bridge of bamboo, which structurally is a tube; metal tubes on a grand scale were used a century ago in the Firth of Forth Bridge. Your tower would display as no other structure in history the full daring that is possible in tubular construction."

The polychrome aluminum structure 1000 to 1300 feet high narrowed at the midpoint as it rose, belling out at base and top. The tubular steel section was chosen because it had the greatest resistance to buckling and because it could be easily extruded or cast. In considering the round plan in the nature of the structural unit, he saw that spacing of the columns on the round reduced wind action and minimized

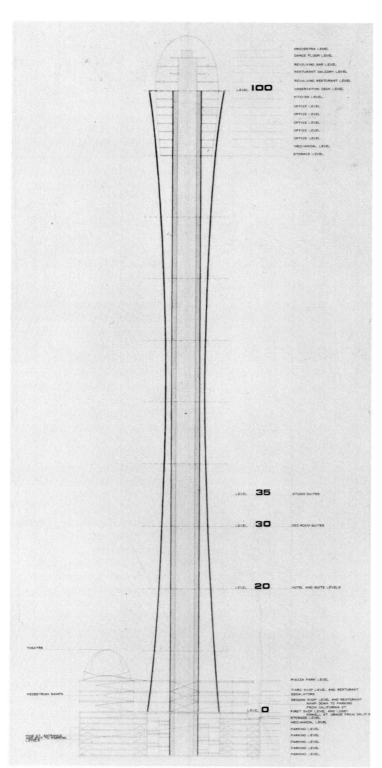

LEVEL **100**

ORCHESTRA LEVEL
DANCE FLOOR LEVEL
REVOLVING BAR LEVEL
RESTURANT BALCONY LEVEL
REVOLVING RESTURANT LEVEL
OBSERVATION DECK LEVEL
KITCHEN LEVEL
OFFICE LEVEL
OFFICE LEVEL
OFFICE LEVEL
OFFICE LEVEL
OFFICE LEVEL
MECHANICAL LEVEL
STORAGE LEVEL

LEVEL **35**   STUDIO SUITES

LEVEL **30**   BED ROOM SUITES

LEVEL **20**   HOTEL AND SUITE LEVELS

THEATRE

PEDESTRIAN RAMPS

PIAZZA PARK LEVEL
THIRD SHOP LEVEL AND RESTURANT
ESCALATORS
SECOND SHOP LEVEL AND RESTURANT
RAMP DOWN TO PARKING
FROM CALIFORNIA ST
FIRST SHOP LEVEL AND LOBBY
POWELL ST. GRADE FROM CALIF. S.
STORAGE LEVEL
MECHANICAL LEVEL
PARKING LEVEL
PARKING LEVEL
PARKING LEVEL
PARKING LEVEL
PARKING LEVEL

LEVEL **0**

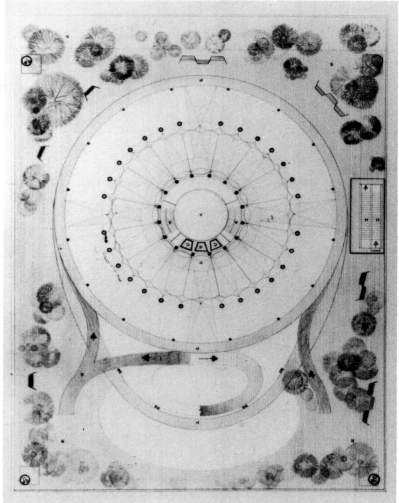

Ground level plan of
the mixed-use tower.

The cross-section of
the San Francisco
Tower. The
circulation and
mechanical equipment
are at the center of
the 1000-foot tower.
The structure
dwindles at midpoint
and expands at top to
reduce wind pressure.

173

vibration. To gain strength, the aluminum tubes were tapered downward to foundations and tapered up to increase the interior space, and narrowed at mid-height to reduce wind pressure. T.Y. Lin was the engineer on the project.

The Federal Aviation Administration was not happy about a tower on Nob Hill, and when they would not yield, the plan got stuck in City Planning. In the end the apartment house was remodeled and became one of the fanciest addresses on the hill.

In 1970, after the prison had been closed on Alcatraz Island and a new use was under consideration Soriano revised his tower plans for a symbol to peace on a proposed World Peace Island. He planned two smaller circular buildings as a World University and a Peace Museum with assembly hall. In the scheme the buildings occupied only twelve percent of the land, the north end all in park land. But Soriano's World Peace Island came up against stiff competition from joint ventures of developers and architects, one of which was favored by the mayor. In the end nothing was built, and the island is now occupied by Indians.

Most architects in their seventies retire and occasionally consult, build small projects, or remodel for former clients. Soriano, thinking in terms of large housing projects or towers, was not content to take this route. Instead, with grants from the Graham Foundation, he has been writing his autobiography. It is written in the form of *pensées*, each building or experience a springboard to polemical statements about the state of architecture today.

Every surface and cupboard in the one-room living space in the houseboat is now piled high with documents of his work, and his drawings are so buried that it is impossible to examine them. Along one wall is a couch for sleeping and sitting, and close to this is the one large piece of furniture, a combined drafting board/dining table/reading table/music center. Beyond the table is a kitchenette and bath with a shower.

We talked at the table, and he stopped at noon and six to cook our lunch and dinner — a pudding of eggs and vegetables, a steamed fish, washed down with a glass of chablis. As he uses few spices and no sauces, the flavors come from the ingredients. One evening it was a chicken cooked slowly in its own juices.

The door to the dock was always open during the day and people wandered in to ask for information about the ferry or other tenants. On Sunday afternoon friends who had not seen him for months greeted him with great bursts of affection.

Seeing him in this cramped room, remembering the openness of his houses, watching him put his hand into a pile of papers and come up with what I had asked for, I was struck with his ability to deal with whatever came his way — and always buoyantly. We worked sometimes as long as twelve hours, and in his company there was a tendency not to tire.

He seemed timeless. But as I was leaving I asked about his health, and he said without complaint that he had developed arthritis, which had settled in the area of the injuries from his accident 40 years ago. This was worse when days were damp or foggy. But he had no plan to move, unless rising rents drove him out, for where else could he live with the Bay his front yard, and the boardwalk to the ferry boat his stoop?

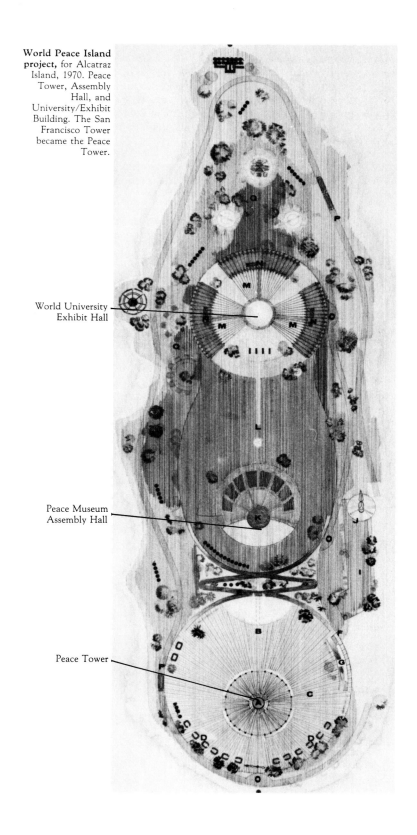

World Peace Island project, for Alcatraz Island, 1970. Peace Tower, Assembly Hall, and University/Exhibit Building. The San Francisco Tower became the Peace Tower.

World University Exhibit Hall

Peace Museum Assembly Hall

Peace Tower

J.R. Davidson

1922   Shops for Stiller Shoes, Berlin.

1923   Hupfeld Piano Showroom and Auditorium,
        Berlin.

1927-29 Shops and restaurant, 3900-4101 Wilshire
        Blvd., Los Angeles.

1932-35 Hotel Knickerbocker, Chicago. (alterations)
        Hotel Shoreland, Chicago. (alterations)
        Pearson Hotel, Chicago. (alterations)

1936   Sardi's Restaurant, 6313 Hollywood Blvd.
        at Vine, Los Angeles. (destroyed)

1937   Maitland house, 230 Strada Corta, Bel Air,
        Los Angeles.
        Stothart house, 2501 La Mesa Dr., Santa
        Monica. (now Phillips house)

1939   Berkson houses, 4619 Hayvenhurst Ave.,
        Encino.

1940   Gretna Green Apartments, 12201 Dunoon
        Ln., Los Angeles.
        Sabsay house, 2351 Silver Ridge, Silver
        Lake, Los Angeles.

1941   Thomas Mann house, 1550 San Remo Dr.,
        Pacific Palisades.
        Vigeveno house, 145 Besant, Ojai.

1942   Medical building, 6222 Wilshire Blvd., Los
        Angeles.

1945   Cron house, 540 S. Barrington Ave., Los
        Angeles. (destroyed)

1946   Case Study House, 4756 Lasheart Dr., La
        Canada.
        Crosby house, 473 Denslow Ave.,
        Westwood, Los Angeles. (additions in 1954
        for Dr. Charles Furniss)

Kingsley houses, 1620 and 1630 Amalfi Dr., Pacific Palisades.

1947 Davidson house, 560 S. Barrington Ave., Los Angeles. (destroyed)

1948 McFadden house, 1052 Toluca Lake Ave., North Hollywood.
Goss house, 1771 Royal Oaks, Duarte.

1949 Osherenko house, 1005 N. Alpine Dr., Beverly Hills.

1950 Schapiro house, Waverly and Maxwell sts., Los Angeles.
Rachford Harris house, 379 Fordyce Rd., Encino.

1952 Dann house, 1369 Londonderry Pl., Los Angeles.

1957 Egeberg house, 6918 Oporto Dr., Los Angeles.
Fenichel house, Crestline and Tigertail Rd., Los Angeles.
Munk house, 290 Westgate Ave., Los Angeles.
Rabinowitz house, 2262 Stradella Rd., Los Angeles.

1958 Jokl house, 563 N. Bundy Dr., Los Angeles.

1966 Westgate Apartments, 955 Westgate at Darlington Ave., Brentwood, Los Angeles. (altered)

Harwell Hamilton Harris

1934 Lowe house, 596 E. Punahou Dr., Altadena. (collaborator: Carl Anderson)

1935 Laing house, 1642 Pleasant Wy., Pasadena.
Fellowship Park house, 2311 Fellowship Pkwy., Los Angeles.

1936 De Steiguer house and shop, 20 Glen Sumner Rd., Pasadena.
Gramer house, Santa Monica Canyon. (project)

1937 Kershner house, 3905 Brilliant Wy., Los Angeles.

Joël house, 1742 Silverwood Terr., Los Angeles.
Entenza house, 475 Mesa Rd., Santa Monica.
Clark house, Carmel-by-the-Sea.
Buick Sales and Service Building, 1246-58 Glendon Ave., Los Angeles.

1938 Bauer house, 2538 E. Glenoaks Ave. at Arcade, Glendale.
Granstedt house, 7922 Woodrow Wilson Dr., Los Angeles.

1939 Pumphrey house, 615 Kingman Ave., Santa Monica.
Blair house, 3763 Fredonia Ave., Los Angeles.
Harris house, 410 N. Ave. 64, Pasadena.
Power house, 5160 La Canada Blvd., La Canada.
Hawk house, 2421 Silver Ridge, Silver Lake, Los Angeles.

1940 Grandview Gardens Restaurant, 951 Mei Ling Wy., New Chinatown, Los Angeles. (altered)
"America at Home," South of the Golden Gate Room, New York World's Fair.
Motel for *Architectural Forum*. (project)
Schwenk house, 14329 Millbrook Dr., Van Nuys.
McHenry house, 624 Holmby Ave., Los Angeles.

1941 Havens house, 255 Panoramic Wy., Berkeley.
Naylor house, 3 Arden Rd., Berkeley.
Alexander house, 2265 Micheltorena St., Los Angeles.
Sox house, Ridgeview Dr., Menlo Park.
Treanor house I, 343 Greenacres Dr., Visalia.

1942 Birtcher house, 4234 Seaview Ln., Los Angeles.
Brown house for *Ladies Home Journal*, San Diego. (project)
Segmental House for Revere Copper and Brass Co. (project)
Lek house, 1600 Mecca Dr., La Jolla.
Libbey-Owens-Ford Solar House. (project)
Meier house, 2240 Lakeshore Ave., Los Angeles.

1943   Postwar House and Adobe House for *Sunset* magazine. (project)
North Country School, cottage for headmaster, Lake Placid, N.Y.

1944   Shumway house for *Woman's Home Companion*, Greenfield, Mass. (project)

1945   Pottenger Hospital, Monrovia. (project)
Harwell H. Harris office, 2311 Fellowship Pkwy., Los Angeles.
Pennington Tool and Tea House, Pasadena. (project)
Ingersoll Model House, Ingersoll Steel and Disc Div. of Borg Warner Corp., Kalamazoo, Mich.

1946   Palos Verdes College, site plan and schematics, Palos Verdes. (project)
Sobieski house, 1420 Sierra Madre Blvd., San Marino.
Treanor Equipment Co., U.S. 90, Delano.

1947   Calvin house, Sitka, Aka.

1948   Cruze studio, 2340 W. 3rd St., Los Angeles.
Johnson house, 10280 Chrysanthemum Ln., Los Angeles.

1949   Milvia Apartments, for Weston Havens, Milvia and Blake sts., Berkeley.
Mulvihill house, 580 N. Hermosa Ave., Sierra Madre.
Wyle house, 1064 Rancho Dr., Ojai.
Gerald Loeb pavilion, Tenaya East, Redding, Conn.

1950   Ray house, Burma Rd., Fallbrook.
English house, 1261 Lago Vista Dr., Beverly Hills.

1951   Hardy Cottage, Portugese Bend Club, Palos Verdes. (destroyed)
Chadwick School, 26800 S. Academy Dr., Rolling Hills. (administrative offices and faculty cottages, 1948; recreation room, 1949; senior boys dormitory, 1951; activities building, 1951)

1952   National Orange Show, Feature Exhibit Building, Plaza, and Entrance Mall, Mill and E sts., San Bernardino. (collaborator: Jerome E. Armstrong)

Cranfill house, 1901 Cliff Dr., Austin, Tex.
Harwell H. Harris house, Mission Rd., Fallbrook.
Lang house, 700 Alta St., San Antonio, Tex.

1953   Duhring house, #4 Greenwood Common, Berkeley.

1954   *House Beautiful* Pace Setter House 1955, built in Dallas for Texas State Fair of 1954. (moved to 13030 Stone Brook Cir., Dallas)

1955   Townsend house, 230 Simpson, Paris, Tex.
House for Frigidaire Div. of General Motors. (project)
Homestyle Center Exhibition House, Grand Rapids, Mich. (project)
Austin Corp., Balcones house I, 5002 Edgemont Rte.; house II, 3303 Laurel Cir., Austin, Tex.
Johnson house, 1200 Broad Ave., Fort Worth, Tex.
Antrim house, 6160 N. Van Ness, Fresno.

1956   Motel-on-the-Mountain, site plan and cottages, Suffern, N.Y.
St. Mary's Episcopal Church, Big Spring, Tex.

1957   Embassy office building and staff housing, Helsinki, Finland. (project)
Kirkpatrick house, 457 Harbor Rd., South Port, Conn.

1958   Eisenberg house, 9624 Rockbrook Ave., Dallas, Tex.
Talbot house, 1508 Dayton Rd., Big Spring, Tex.
Cranfill Apartments, 1911 Cliff St., Austin, Tex.
Security Bank and Trust Co., Owatonna, Minn. (remodelling of Louis Sullivan's Farmers Nat'l. Bank, 1908)
Trade Mart Court, Stemmons Expwy., Dallas, Tex.

1959   Greenwood Mausoleum, White Settlement Rd. and University Ave., Ft. Worth, Tex.
Treanor house II, 2617 Oldham Rd., Abilene, Tex.
Woodall house, 808 W. 14th St., Big Spring, Tex.

1960   Wright house, 3504 Lexington, Highland Park, Dallas, Tex.
Havens Memorial Fountain and Plaza, Shattuck Ave. at Kittredge St., Berkeley.

1963   First Unitarian Church, 4015 Normandy Ave., Dallas, Tex.
Paschal house, 1527 Pinecrest, Durham, N.C.

1964   Lindahl house, 305 Clayton Rd., Chapel Hill, N.C.
Security Bank and Trust Co., motor-bank, Owatonna, Minn.

1966   Sweetzer house, Laurel Park, Hendersonville, N.C.
Van Alstyne house, 1702 Woodburn, Durham, N.C.

1967   Sugioka house, 1 Bayberry Dr., Chapel Hill, N.C.

1968   Harwell H. Harris office, 122 Cox Ave., Raleigh, N.C.

1969   St. Giles Presbyterian Church, Fellowship Hall, classrooms, and office building, 5101 Oak Park Dr., Raleigh, N.C. (sanctuary, 1983)

1973   Kinabalu, tourist hotel and resort, Kota Kinabalu, Sabah, Malaysia. (project)

1976   Cullowhee Presbyterian Church, Cullowhee, N.C.

1977   North Raleigh United Methodist Church, 8501 Honeycutt, Raleigh, N.C. (project)

Gregory Ain

1929   Archie Lamm Five Foot Module House, Los Angeles. (project)

1935   General Electric Competition House. (project)
Archie Lamm Five Foot Module House, Study Two. (project)
Galka Scheyer addition, 1880 Blue Heights Dr., Hollywood Hills, Los Angeles.

1936   Edwards house, 5642 Holly Oak Dr., Hollywood Hills, Los Angeles.

1937   Byler house, 914 Ave. 37, Los Angeles.
Dunsmuir Flats, 1281 Dunsmuir St., Los Angeles.
Ernst house, 5670 Holly Oak Dr., Los Angeles.

1938   Beckman house I, 357 N. Citrus Ave., Los Angeles. (collaborator: Visscher Boyd)
Eisenstadt house, 3428 Blair Dr., Los Angeles.
Goldberg house, 4700 Noeline Ave., Encino.
Vorkapich studio, 2100 Benedict Canyon, Beverly Hills. (collaborator: Visscher Boyd)
Plywood Panel System. (collaborator: Visscher Boyd, project)
Becker house, 1828 San Jacinto St., Silver Lake, Los Angeles.

1939   Brownfield Medical Building, 2401 Manchester Blvd., Inglewood.
Daniel house, 1856 Micheltorena St., Silver Lake, Los Angeles. (collaborator: George Agron)
Eaton addition, 26915 Old Trace Rd., Los Altos.
Hay house, 3132 Oakcrest Dr., North Hollywood.
Hoffman house, 5732 Buffalo Ave., Studio City.
Minimum House. (collaborator: Allen Joseph Stein, project)
Homasote Panel System. (project)
Scharlin house, 2363 Silver Ridge Ave., Silver Lake, Los Angeles.
Tierman house, 2323 Micheltorena St., Los Angeles. (collaborator: Visscher Boyd)

1940   Hural house, 6781 Vineway, Hollywood, Los Angeles.
Lowcost Housing Development, Southgate. (project)
U.S. Plywood Offices, interiors, 1934 E. 15th St., Los Angeles.
Berg, Salkin, and Goldman houses around a pool, North Hollywood. (project)

1941   Ruth March Ain house, 7694 Willow Glen Rd., Laurel Canyon, Los Angeles.

Orans house, 2404 Micheltorena St., Silver Lake, Los Angeles.

1942 Domela house, 19100 block of Casa Dr., Tarzana.
Gateway to Music, 3505 Wilshire Blvd., Los Angeles. (remodel)

1945 Community Homes Cooperative, 280 houses, Victory Blvd., Reseda. (Ain, Johnson and Day, project)
Clay house, 12924 Sarah St., North Hollywood.
Leshing 16-Unit Townhouses. (project)

1946 Cole house, 3642 Lowry Rd., Los Angeles.
Lucile Street Veterans Homes, 1311-23 Lucile Ave., Los Angeles. (project)
Park Planned Homes, 26 houses, 2700 S. Highview Ave., Altadena.

1947 Lena Horne house, 2136 Nichols Canyon Rd., Los Angeles. (remodel)
Ain, Johnson and Day Office, 2305 Hyperion Ave., Los Angeles. (Ain, Johnson and Day)
Avenel Cooperative Housing, 10 attached houses, 2839-2847 Avenel St., Los Angeles. (Ain, Johnson and Day)

1948 Mar Vista Housing, 52 houses between Beethoven, Moore, and Meyer sts. and Marco Pl., Mar Vista, Los Angeles. (Ain, Johnson and Day)
Hacienda Village Housing Extension. (collaborator: Burnett C. Turner, project)
Hollywood Guilds and Unions Building, 2760 N. Cahuenga Blvd., Universal City. (Ain, Johnson and Day)
Kenny and Morris attorney's offices, Hill and Temple sts., Los Angeles. (building moved to 1557 Beverly Blvd., Los Angeles, Ain, Johnson and Day)
Miller house, 1634 Gilcrest Dr., Beverly Hills. (Ain, Johnson and Day)
Salkin house, 2230 Griffith Park Blvd., Los Angeles. (Ain, Johnson and Day)
Tartar house, 24011 St. George St., Los Angeles. (Ain, Johnson and Day)

1949 Shairer house, 11750 Chenault, Brentwood, Los Angeles. (Ain, Johnson and Day)

Wilfong house, 3250 Mesaloa Ln., Altadena. (Ain, Johnson and Day)

1950 Beckman house II, 15662 Meadowgate Rd., Sherman Oaks.
Dahlstrom house, 780 Laguna Rd., Pasadena.
Hurschler house, 1200 Hillcrest Ave., Pasadena. (Ain, Johnson and Day)
Museum of Modern Art Exhibition House, 4 W. 54th St., New York. (Ain, Johnson and Day)
Ralphs house, 1350 Linda Ridge Rd., Pasadena. (Ain, Johnson and Day)

1951 Briehl Psychiatric Clinic, 157 S. Doheny Dr., Beverly Hills. (Ain, Johnson and Day, destroyed)
Margolis house, 5786 Valley Oak Dr., Los Angeles. (collaborator: James Garrott)

1952 Mesner house I, 13957 Valley Vista Blvd., Encino. (Ain, Johnson and Day)

1953 Mesner house II, 14571 Valley Vista Blvd., Encino.
Feldman house, 1181 Angelo Dr., Los Angeles.

1955 Oliver house, 2885 Edgewick Rd., Glendale.

1956 Aladdin Records Building, 5352 W. Pico Blvd., Los Angeles.
United Lodge of Theosophists, 1175 South Coast Blvd., Laguna.

1957 Asher house, 263 Loring Ave., Los Angeles. (remodel)
153rd Street School, 1605 W. 153 St., Gardena.

1959 Tufeld house, 11020 Wrightwood Pl., North Hollywood.
Westchester Municipal Building, 7166 W. Manchester Ave., Westchester. (collaborator: James Garrott)

1960 Gallas house, 5326 Sherbourne Dr., Los Angeles. (collaborator: James Garrott)
Capistrano School, 22120 Chase St., Canoga Park. (collaborator: John A. Martin)
Skolnik house, addition to R.M. Schindler 1953 house, 2567 Glendower Ave., Los Angeles.

Director's building, Dominguez Regional Park, 19101 S. Towne Ave., Dominguez. (collaborator: James Garrott)

1962   Berg addition, 24912 Malibu Rd., Malibu. Elterman addition, 15301 Kingswood Ln., Sherman Oaks.

1963   Kaye house, 4670 Vanalden Ave., Tarzana. (collaborator: James Garrott) Lewin house, 5310 Jessen Dr., La Canada.

1967   Ginoza house, State College, Pa.

1971   Tuna Canyon Road Cooperative, 2000 S. Tuna Canyon Rd., Los Angeles. (project)

Raphael Soriano

1935   School and concert hall, Los Angeles County Regional Planning Commission. (project) Dormitory for 50 unemployed men, Los Angeles County Regional Planning Commission. (project)

1936   One-family concrete model for indigent housing, Los Angeles County Regional Planning Commission. (project) Lipetz house, 1834 N. Dillon St., Los Angeles.

1937   Priver house, 1830 N. Dillon St., Los Angeles.

1938   Austrian house, Landa St., Echo Park, Los Angeles. Polito house, 1650 Queens Rd., Los Angeles. Ross house, 2123 Valentine Ave., Los Angeles. Lee and Cady warehouse, Ferndale, Mich. (collaborator: Fritz Ruppell)

1939   Gogol house, 2190 Talmadge St., Los Angeles. Jewish Community Center, 2317 Michigan Ave., Los Angeles.

1940   Kimpson house, 380 Orlena Ave., Naples, Long Beach.

Lukens house, 3425 W. 27th St., Los Angeles. Koosis house, 1941 Glencoe Wy., Los Angeles.

1941   Strauss house, 3131 Queensbury Dr., Los Angeles.

1942   Hallawell Nursery, sales office, San Francisco. (destroyed) Ibert house, West Hollywood Hills, Los Angeles. Plywood Defense Housing Project #1. (project)

1943   Plywood Defense Housing Project #2. (project)

1945   Doctors' office building, Beverly Hills. (project)

1947   Katz house, North Hollywood.

1948   Ciro of London, branch jewelry shop, San Francisco. (collaborator: Serge Chermayeff, destroyed) Ciro of London, jewelry shop, Beverly Hills. (collaborator: Serge Chermayeff, destroyed)

1949   Krause house, 8513 La Sierra Ave., Whittier.

1950   Curtis house, 111 Stone Canyon Rd., Bel Air, Los Angeles. *Arts & Architecture* Case Study House, 1080 Ravoli Dr., Pacific Palisades. Shulman house, 7875 Woodrow Wilson Dr., Los Angeles.

1952   Colby Apartments, 1312 Beverly Green Dr., Los Angeles. Schrage house, 2620 Commonwealth Ave., Los Angeles.

1955   Eichler Builders House (Saunders house), Palo Alto.

1958   Adolph's Office Building and Laboratory, 1800 Magnolia, Burbank.

1959   McCauley Builders Houses, 20 and 24 Longfellow Rd., Mill Valley.

1960   Vera Mahoney Concrete House,
Strawberry Point, Peninsula. (project)
Guaymas houses. (projects)

1961   San Pedro Community Hospital, 1300 W.
7th St., San Pedro. (Projects Architects)
Cooke house, 150 San Rafael, Belvedere.
(altered)

1965   Eleven All-Aluminum Houses, Hawaii.
(altered)

1966   Alcoa Aluminum Office Tower. (project)

1970   Peace Island Tower. (revised version of
Alcoa Aluminum Office Tower, project)

General Bibliography

Andrews, Wayne. *Architecture, Ambition and Americans.* New York: Harper, 1947.

Banham, Reyner. *Theory and Design in the First Machine Age.* New York: Praeger, 1960.

Creighton, Thomas. *Houses.* New York: Reinhold, 1947.

Eckbo, Garrett. *Landscape for Living.* New York: Dodge, 1958.

Faber, Colin. *Candela: The Shell Builder.* New York: Reinhold, 1963.

Fitch, James Marston. *American Building: The Forces That Shape It.* Boston: Houghton Mifflin, 1947.

Ford, J. and Ford, K.M. *The Modern House in America.* New York: Architectural Book Publishing Co., 1940.

Gebhard, D. and Von Breton, H. *L.A. in the 30s.* Exhibition catalog. Salt Lake City: Peregrine Smith, 1975.

Gebhard, D.; Von Breton, H.; and Weiss, L. *Architecture of Gregory Ain.* Exhibition catalog. Santa Barbara: University of California, 1980.

Gebhard, D. and Winter, R. *Guide to Architecture in Los Angeles & Southern California.* Salt Lake City: Peregrine Smith, 1977.

Gillies, Mary Davis. *The Expandable House.* New York: Simon & Schuster, 1951.

Harris, F. and Boneberger, W. *A Guide to Contemporary Architecture in Southern California.* Los Angeles: Watling, 1951.

Hines, Thomas. *Richard Neutra and the Search for Modern Architecture.* New York: Oxford, 1982.

McCallum, Ian. *Architecture USA.* New York: Reinhold, 1959.

McCoy, Esther. *Case Study Houses.* New York: Reinhold, 1962; Los Angeles: Hennessey & Ingalls, 1977.

McCoy, Esther. *Five California Architects.* New York: Reinhold, 1960; Praeger, 1975.

McCoy, Esther. *Neutra.* New York: Braziller, 1960.

McCoy, Esther. *Vienna to Los Angeles: Two Journeys.* Santa Monica: Arts & Architecture Press, 1979.

McWilliams, Carey. *Southern California: An Island on the Land.* Salt Lake City: Peregrine Smith, 1983.

Mock, Elizabeth, ed. *Built in USA: 1932-1944.* New York: Museum of Modern Art, 1944.

Muthesius, Hermann. *Das englische Haus.* Germany, 1904.

Ortega y Gasset, José. *The Dehumanization of Art.* Collected essays. New York: Doubleday, 1956.

Peter, John. *Masters of Modern Architecture.* New York: Braziller, 1958.

Veronesi, Giulia. *Style and Design: 1909-1929.* New York: Braziller, 1966.

Wachsmann, Konrad. *The Turning Point of Building.* New York: Reinhold, 1961.

Periodical and Journal Writings about the Architects

Davidson

Architect and Engineer
Sept. 1935, p. 35
Dec. 1953, p. 38

Architectural Forum
May 1933, p. 381
Jan. 1940, p. 44
Aug. 1940, p. 116
Nov. 1943, p. 92
Sept. 1944, p. 115
July 1945, p. 122
Apr. 1948, p. 121
Mar. 1950, p. 126

Architectural Record
Oct. 1929, p. 335
Sept. 1930, p. 235
Aug. 1932, p. 88
Dec. 1937, p. 57
June 1939, p. 63
Nov. 1943, p. 75
Aug. 1948, p. 92
Sept. 1948, p. 114

Better Homes and Gardens
Aug. 1947, p. 42

The Californian
Mar. 1949, p. 48
Fall 1950, p. 5
Fall 1952, p. 34

House and Garden
Nov. 1939, p. 10
Aug. 1950, p. 45

Interiors
Nov. 1944, p. 66

Life
Oct. 22, 1945, p. 110

McCalls
Aug. 1949, p. 86

Progressive Architecture
Feb. 1954, p. 94
June 1956, p. 154

Vogue
June 15, 1931, p. 34

Harris

Architect & Engineer
Dec. 1935, pp. 42-45
Mar. 1939, pp. 38-39

Architectural Forum
June 1935, p. 42
Aug. 1935, pp. 316-17
Apr. 1937, pp. 278-81
Aug. 1937, pp. 47, 75-84
Oct. 1937, pp. 264, 318, 353-58
Aug. 1938, pp. 213-16
Nov. 1938, pp. 349-51
July 1939, pp. 16-18
Mar. 1940, pp. 171-86
Apr. 1940, pp. 13-19
Oct. 1940, pp. 248, 253
Feb. 1945, p. 112
Feb. 1946, pp. 94-96
Dec. 1947, pp. 100-103

Architectural Record
Feb. 1938, pp. 58-59
Oct. 1938, pp. 100-102
Apr. 1939, p. 67
Oct. 1939, p. 53
Jan. 1941, p. 95
Nov. 1946, pp. 84-85
Dec. 1946, pp. 159-60

Architectural Review
Dec. 1946, pp. 157-59

El Arquitecto, Buenos Aires
Aug. 1944

*Arts & Architecture/California Arts
  & Architecture*
Jan. 1935, pp. 20-21
May 1935, p. 27
Nov. 1935, pp. 20-21
July 1937, p. 33
Aug. 1937, p. 29
Nov. 1937, (Honor Awards)
Mar. 1938, pp. 27-29
May 1938, pp. 26-27
July 1938, p. 18
May 1939, pp. 16-17
Aug. 1939, pp. 19-21
Jan. 1940, pp. 28-29
Apr. 1940, pp. 13-19
Aug. 1940, pp. 22-23
Mar. 1942, (Exhibition) pp. 21-35

House & Home
Jan. 1953, pp. 126-31

House Beautiful
Oct. 1934, pp. 72-73
Mar. 1937, p. 46
Mar. 1940, pp. 90-93
Sept. 1946, pp. 110-13

Interiors
Sept. 1943, pp. 18-23
May 1948, pp. 83-84

Nuestra Arquitectura, B.A.
Jan. 1947, pp. 3-33

Pencil Points
July 1940, p. 438
Apr. 1941, p. 256
May 1941, pp. 324-27
May 1943, pp. 50-55
Sept. 1943, p. 27

Progressive Architecture
July 1948, p. 62
Dec. 1956, pp. 45-48

Ain

Architectural Forum
Apr. 1938, p. 332 (GE
  Competition)
Nov. 1940, p. 450
July 1941, p. 43
Apr. 1949, p. 126-28

Arts & Architecture/California Arts
  & Architecture
Aug. 1940, p. 24
Nov. 1940, pp. 20-21, 31, 38-39
Dec. 1940, pp. 26-27
Feb. 1941, pp. 22-23
Mar. 1941, pp. 24-25, 42
Apr. 1941, pp. 26-27
June 1941, pp. 32-33
Aug. 1941, pp. 32, 34
Jan. 1942, pp. 24-25
Apr. 1942, pp. 24-25
May 1942, pp. 23-34
Mar. 1943, pp. 36-39
Apr. 1943, pp. 36-37
Aug. 1943, pp. 24-27
Feb. 1945, pp. 29-30
Nov. 1945, pp. 32-35
Mar. 1946, pp. 40-42
May 1947, pp. 26-27
Aug. 1947, pp. 30-31
May 1948, pp. 38-41
Aug. 1948, pp. 30-31
Oct. 1948, pp. 36-38
Dec. 1948, pp. 26-27
Feb. 1949, pp. 25-27
Sept. 1949, pp. 40-41
Feb. 1950, pp. 26-27, 45
Apr. 1950, pp. 22-23
July 1950, pp. 40-41, 50
Apr. 1956, pp. 20-21
Jan. 1957, p. 16
Jan. 1966, pp. 14-15

Pencil Points
Apr. 1940, pp. 244-46
May 1940, pp. 322-23

Progressive Architecture
July 1947, pp. 14, 16, 66-69
June 1950, pp. 77-79
Feb. 1951, pp. 62-63
Dec. 1952, pp. 88-91

Soriano

American Institute of Architects
  Journal
April 1960, p. 87

Architect and Engineer
May 1956, pp. 14-21

Architectural Forum
Oct. 1939, pp. 252-53, 332
Apr. 1940, pp. 262-63
Feb. 1941, pp. 133-34
Dec. 1941, p. 401
Sept. 1942, pp. 146-47
Aug. 1943, pp. 92-98
Sept. 1943, p. 91
May 1945, p. 122
Nov. 1945, pp. 86, 157, 166
Dec. 1945, p. 84
May 1946, pp. 81-84
Oct. 1947, pp. 108-10
May 1948, pp. 60, 128, 136-37
Nov. 1951, pp. 214-19

Architectural Record
Nov. 1942, pp. 48-91
Feb. 1946, pp. 96-97
Mid-May 1956, pp. 202-203

Architectural Review
Sept. 1948, pp. 111-13
May 1957, pp. 356-57

Arts & Architecture/California Arts
  & Architecture
May 1940, p. 29
June 1940, p. 31
Aug. 1940, pp. 20-21
Jan. 1941, p. 28
Apr. 1941, p. 34
Aug. 1941, pp. 30-31
Dec. 1941, pp. 32-33
June 1942, pp. 32-33
Nov. 1942, pp. 28-29
May 1943, pp. 28-31
Aug. 1943, pp. 35-37
Oct. 1944, p. 32
Oct. 1945, pp. 44-45
June 1946, pp. 30-31
Feb. 1947, pp. 22-23
Dec. 1947, pp. 32-33
Apr. 1948, pp. 38-39
July 1948, pp. 41-42, 43
Nov. 1948, pp. 38-39
June 1949, pp. 36-37
Dec. 1949, p. 22

Jan. 1950, p. 26
Feb. 1950, p. 24
Apr. 1950, pp. 36-37
Aug. 1950, pp. 20-22, 37-38
Sept. 1950, pp. 36-37
Oct. 1950, pp. 28-29
Nov. 1950, pp. 30-33
Dec. 1950, pp. 28-35, 45-49
Jan. 1956, pp. 22-23
Nov. 1957, pp. 32-33
Aug. 1960, pp. 24-25

House & Home
Oct. 1957, pp. 104-107

Industrial Design
July 1960, p. 48

Interiors
Aug. 1949, p. 107

Magazine of Building
Feb. 1952, pp. 67-73

Pencil Points
June 1942, pp. 95-98
Mar. 1944, pp. 71-73

Progressive Architecture
Apr. 1948, p. 91
June 1948, p. 63
July 1949, pp. 46-48
June 1956, pp. 106-11

Index

T

Tartar house (Ain), 117
Task #4, 114
Taylor house (Davidson), 27
Temko, Allan, 172
Texas State Fair house (Harris), 53, 69
Tierman house (Ain), 98, 106, 110
Tierney, John, 10
Tischler house (Schindler), 28
Townsend house (Harris), 73
Treanor house (Harris), 74
Tufeld house (Ain), 139, 141

U

U.S. Embassy, Helsinki, Finland (Harris), 58
U.S. Plywood Corp., 118
USC-Pasadena school, 28
Unitarian Church, Dallas (Harris), 76
United Lodge of Theosophists (Ain), 138

V

Valeska, Lette, 91
Van Alstyne house (Harris), 81
Van der Kar, Josef, 134, 138, 139
Van der Rohe, Mies, 112, 142
Veronesi, Giulia, 7, 10
Vigeveno house (Davidson), 18, 19, 25
Von Sternberg house (Neutra), 88
Vorkapich house (Ain), 115
Voysey, C.F.A., 5

W

WPA projects (Soriano), 145
Wachsmann, Konrad, 82, 142
Walter, Bruno, 2
War Production Board, 60
Wartime housing projects (Soriano), 156
Wasmuth, Ernst, 8, 9
Wayfarer's Chapel (Lloyd Wright), 28, 67
Webb, Philip, 90
Weber, Kem, 2n., 10, 11, 12
Weese, Harry, 118
Wertheimer store (Messel), 2
Westchester Municipal Building and Library (Ain), 134
Wichner, Milton, house (Davidson), 91
Wiley, Charles D., 118
Wilfong house (Ain), 136
William Andrews Clark Memorial Library stacks (Davidson), 10
Wilshire Medical Building (Davidson), 21
Winter, Robert, 10
Wollstein, Greta (Davidson), 5, 6, 7, 9, 16, 25, 90, 91

Woman's Home Companion house (Harris), 60, 132
Woodall house (Harris), 73
World Peace Island project (Soriano), 174
Wright, Frank Lloyd, 8, 9, 36, 40, 44, 46, 58, 60, 76, 84, 87, 90, 98, 144
Wright, Lloyd, 40, 60, 67
Wright, S. Macdonald, 40
Wurster, William Wilson, 42, 49, 58, 62, 159
Wyle house (Harris), 56, 62, 63, 81